Not So Shii
So Happy People

How Bill Gothard, Church, and Family Taught Me Christianity Doesn't Work

by
Clint Heacock Ph.D.

Tim Sledge, Editor

INSIGHTING GROWTH
Publications Inc.

For my daughters, Bree and Alexa.

Clint Heacock, Author
https://www.facebook.com/DismantlingDoctrine

Tim Sledge, Editor

Cover Design Concept by Bree Heacock

First Printing: September 2024

Insighting Growth Publications
Houston, Texas

ISBN-13: 979-8-9912613-0-2 (Paperback)
ISBN-13: 979-8-9912613-1-9 (Kindle E-Book)

Table of Contents

Preface

The Terror of An Empty House

After school, my mom dropped me off at soccer practice. I said goodbye and raced off to the field while Mom arranged for the father of one of my teammates to take me home. After practice, I caught the ride my mom had arranged. When we reached my house, I thanked my friend's dad for taking me home, hopped out of the car, and ran to our front door. Like any twelve-year-old who's spent several hours on a soccer field, I was hungry, sweaty, and tired—in that order. All I wanted to do was join my family for dinner, jump in the shower, and go to bed, just like I always did after soccer practice.

Bursting through the door—never locked because we lived in a safe, rural area—I shouted, "Hi! I'm back from practice! What's for dinner?" Without waiting for a reply, I clattered down the stairs in our split-level house, heading for the dining room. My dad insisted that we eat our evening meals together as a family, and with six kids in the house, that was a big undertaking. Mom had a regular chore list that my sisters and I shared each night. Some of us helped prepare the meal, someone else had to set the table, and the rest were left to clear the table, do the dishes, and clean the kitchen after dinner. Although I was the youngest—and the only boy with five older sisters—that didn't exempt me from doing my share of chores. That day, I expected that despite being tired from soccer practice, I'd still be assigned to some aspect of

1

cleaning up after the meal. But I wasn't really concerned about after-dinner chores. I was starving! All I wanted to do was eat!

As I shot into the dining room, I was stunned to see no one there. The table was set. The chairs were arranged as usual in preparation for a meal, but no family members. I went into the kitchen, expecting to find my mom and some of my sisters busily cooking dinner, but—like the dining room—the kitchen was empty. No food had been prepared.

This was all extremely odd. It was well past the time when we usually ate. I was starting to feel weird, and my sense of apprehension grew as I searched from room to room downstairs. I rushed from the living room to the rec room, calling out, "Hey! Where is everybody? I'm home. Are we going to eat soon?" No reply.

All the downstairs rooms were empty. I was struck by a surge of panic as a terrifying thought raced through my brain. *"I wonder if Jesus has returned to Earth to take all true believers to heaven. Maybe the Rapture has occurred, and I've been left behind."* As quickly as this disconcerting thought hit me, I shoved it aside. "No. There's got to be a logical explanation." I noticed that my heart was pounding.

"Maybe they're all upstairs," I thought as I bounded up the steps to check the bedrooms. There was no logical reason why everyone would be upstairs before eating dinner, but the empty downstairs wasn't logical either. My apprehension shifted to fear as I searched from room to room, calling out for my sisters and parents. No response. Just silence. The last room I checked was my parents' room. It too was empty.

As I sat down on my parents' bed, I was breathing heavily and could feel a tightness in my chest. My fear and confusion had turned to terror. I had no idea what to do next. "Think," I told myself.

Grasping for a logical explanation while fighting the awful possibility that the Rapture had occurred, I started thinking of some simple, rational possibilities as to what had happened. "Maybe they've gone out to eat, or maybe they're running an errand," I babbled to myself as I battled my escalating sense of panic.

"I know! Check outside. See if one of their cars is gone." I rushed downstairs and out the back door, running over to the carport where my parents parked their cars. Both vehicles were sitting in the carport.

Where in the world *is* everybody? With my heart pounding even faster now, I leaned on my dad's car and tried to figure out what to do next. Then it hit me. "I know! They must have left a note. Maybe I missed it when I came through the front door. Check and see. They've probably just gone somewhere, and I didn't see the note they left." Hurrying back inside the house, I flew up the steps and frantically searched for a note. I found nothing.

This frightening event occurred before smartphones and the Internet. If you went out somewhere, the best you could do to alert someone was leave a note, put it somewhere it was likely to be noticed, and hope the message would be seen and read. On this day, there was no note—nothing! What in the world was going on? I checked the hallway by the back door, but again, no note.

My heart felt like it was going to jump out of my chest. I fought back tears. I was sobbing and breathing in ragged bursts. My head was spinning.

I returned to the stairs by the front door and sat down, trying to think clearly. I had to accept that what I feared had happened. And with my acceptance of the unthinkable event that had surely taken place came the realization that I was in serious trouble.

The Rapture has occurred! My entire family has been taken up to heaven to be with Jesus. I'd been left behind to face the Seven-Year Tribulation. My seven years of tribulation on Earth will be followed by an eternity of torment in the flames of hell.

I knew this was all predicted in the Bible. It was what I had been taught at my church and at the Christian school I attended. This was the only explanation that made sense. It explained why my family was *gone,* and why I had been *left behind.*

Now what? What should I do? If the Rapture had taken place, it was too late for me. My family's departure from the Earth without me indicated that I was not a true believer. I was now utterly alone to face the horrors of the Seven-Year Tribulation.

For the preceding two years—since my baptism at the age of ten—I had fooled myself into thinking I was a true believer. But now, a harsh reality was staring me in the face. I had been deceiving myself. I had never been a *true* Christian. The fact that I'd been left behind was the undeniable confirmation of this dreadful fact.

As I desperately tried to think of a way to confirm whether this end-of-times event had happened, an idea popped into my head. *Check the news.* If the Rapture has taken place, the newscasters who have been left behind will be talking about nothing else.

I'd been taught that the Rapture was a worldwide event in which all true believers would be snatched up to heaven when Jesus suddenly returned like the proverbial "thief in the night." This would happen when nobody expected it. One movie shaped my understanding of the Rapture more than anything else. I had seen *A Thief in the Night* during a Sunday evening service in our church a few years earlier. Now, I was convinced that I was one of the unfortunate ones who had been *left behind.*

I raced back to the kitchen and turned on the radio that was mounted on the wall. My dad was a great believer in new technology, and when our house was built, he installed a radio/intercom system with speakers in multiple rooms. Since my parents were strict fundamentalist Christians, this was the only radio allowed in the house, and we were only permitted to listen to the local Christian radio station. I twisted the dial from its normal position, searching desperately for a news station. *"Come on!* What in the world is happening?"

After a few minutes of listening to several stations, I was even more confused. No one was reporting that countless people had disappeared. I expected to hear accounts of millions of Christians being suddenly pulled out of their cars, houses, or places of work— wherever they happened to be when Jesus returned to Earth. This would surely be the biggest news story in history, and every news outlet would be talking about nothing else!

Although I could not find one report of the Rapture anywhere on the radio dial, the indoctrination that had shaped my thinking did not let go easily. Maybe it had all happened too quickly. The radio stations simply hadn't caught up to the story. I switched off the radio and sat down at the kitchen table. I tried in vain to slow my breathing as I thought about what to do next. I wasn't sure exactly how, but I knew that, above all else, I had to confirm whether the Rapture had occurred.

Then it hit me. In those days, many cars had bumper stickers that read, "In case of the Rapture, this vehicle will be unmanned." If the Rapture *had* occurred, Christians would have been snatched out of their cars as they drove around. I raced out the back door. From our rear deck, I could see a major road that ran not far from the rear of our house which was located just outside of Seattle, Washington. I stood there watching the traffic for five or ten minutes, expecting to hear the wail of ambulances and police sirens. But all I could see was the normal flow of evening traffic. I could see no evidence that ambulances were racing to scenes of horrific crashes caused by driverless vehicles. I could see no evidence that *any* car accidents had taken place. Everything seemed normal, but I still wasn't convinced that the Rapture hadn't occurred that day.

I'd heard that if a plane had Christian pilots, the unlucky passengers who hadn't been taken were doomed to crash—since no one would be left in the cockpit to land safely. If the Rapture had occurred before I got home that day, all the pilotless planes would have already hit the ground, but I wasn't thinking logically. Standing on the deck, I scanned the skies, looking for airplanes that might be crashing to Earth. I saw a few planes flying overhead, all continuing along their flight paths as usual. I reckoned, though, that maybe those planes had at least one non-Christian pilot, so the fortunate passengers were safe—for the time being.

I went back inside and sat down, still trying to calm myself and figure out my next steps. "Maybe television stations would be quicker to report on the Rapture than radio channels," I thought. TV wasn't allowed in our house because of the potentially evil influence of the secular world that it delivered. But I knew someone who had a television—my cousins next door, Dan and Andy. They weren't Christians, so I knew that if the Rapture had taken place, they would still be here.

I zoomed out the back door, cut across my cousins' backyard, and raced over to their house. Through their French doors, I could see that they were watching a football game on television with my Uncle Rick. I pounded frantically on the door. Startled, my uncle motioned me to come in. I burst inside, nearly sobbing.

"Whoa, man, what's going on?" he asked, with a look of concern on his face. "Everything okay? You seem upset about something. What's up?" I tried hard to think of the best way to calm down and explain my fear that I had missed the Rapture. But there was no way I could make my non-believing relatives understand that a history-changing *supernatural* event had just occurred. I had no time to even explain the Rapture storyline—it was impossible either to unpack the theology behind this predicted event or to explain how important this event was to me. Although they didn't realize it—according to my worldview—it should have been important to them too. They were nonbelievers bound for an eternity in hell.

I could not have imagined that things could feel more awkward than just before I burst into their home, but now, that is precisely what was happening. I doubted that I could make sense with anything I might say to them, given my panicky emotional state and my sky-high levels of anxiety, dread, and fear.

"Look, I just got back from soccer practice, and nobody is home," I finally blurted out. "Do you mind switching the TV channel to see what the local news is saying? I...I'm concerned about my family, that's all."

"Okay, no problem," my uncle said, sitting back in his chair. He leaned over and picked up the remote. As he changed the channel to a local news network, I sat down on the couch, trying to slow my breathing and calm my pounding heart. "Now I'll find out what is happening," I thought. "The Rapture will surely be all over the news!" But after watching for fifteen or twenty minutes and even switching to another news station, there was no breaking story about millions of people inexplicably vanishing from the Earth.

My uncle finally turned to me and said, "Have you seen enough? We want to get back to watching the game if you don't mind. I'm pretty sure your folks and sisters are around somewhere. There's got to be a logical explanation. I'm sure nothing bad has happened. Tell you what, why don't you wait here until they get home? We'll fix you something to eat, and you can watch the game with us." As tempting as that offer was, and even though I had felt like I was starving for something to eat when I had walked through my front door, I knew that watching television was forbidden. At this point, all I wanted to do was to get back home and wait for my family to show up.

I thanked my uncle for the kind offer, said goodbye to my cousins, and returned home. With the absence of any Rapture story on television, I was pretty sure the big event had not taken place. But I was still deeply concerned about my family. Where were they?

As I walked down the steps of my uncle's house toward my own backyard, I heard voices. My parents and sisters were walking down our steep driveway toward the house. They were laughing and having a great time! Two emotions struck me at that moment. I felt a massive sense of relief knowing with complete certainty that the Rapture had not happened, and I was safe. But I also felt furious! How could my family carelessly walk out of the house and not leave me a note? I couldn't believe what they had put me through. They hadn't given the slightest thought about how their actions would affect me!

I ran up the driveway and hurled myself into Mom's arms, sobbing with relief and releasing my pent-up emotions. Gathering around me, everyone was surprised at how I was acting. They peppered me with questions. "What's going on? Why are you so upset? What's the matter, Clint?" Wiping back the tears, I finally managed to explain why I was an emotional wreck. I came home from soccer practice to an empty house. I searched the house for a note but couldn't find one anywhere. I decided that the Rapture had occurred. You guys had been taken up to heaven, but I had been left behind.

As I explained what had happened, I caught my parents exchanging a knowing glance, which puzzled me a bit. "Tell you what," my dad said, interrupting my storyline. "Let's go inside, and you can tell us all about it."

My mom and dad sat me down at the kitchen table, and I went through the whole event in detail. I explained what I'd been through and the conclusions I'd drawn when I came home to an empty house that would typically be full of people. When I finished, my mother told me what had happened. On the spur of the moment, they had gotten a call from my grandmother, who lived just up the street. She invited them to dinner, and in their haste to walk to her house for a hot meal, they had rushed out the door—and had forgotten to leave me a note. My parents apologized profusely, but it was cold comfort given what I had been through. While I'd been panicking about missing the Rapture and facing seven years of tribulation followed by an eternity in hell, they'd all been having a great time at Grandma's house.

Looking back on what happened, I realize that when I ran from my house and burst into the home of my cousins' next door, I had entered a home that—while imperfect like any human family—contained more sanity than my own house. My parents had not staged the event to teach me a lesson. It was simply the result of their forgetting to leave a note explaining where they were. But the religious teaching that led me to conclude the Rapture had occurred was insidious. Surely kids raised in a non-religious home would not have panicked like I did. I knew, for example, that my nonbelieving cousins next door wouldn't have freaked out.

Along with my church and Christian school, my parents had indoctrinated me into a worldview that set me up for a feeling of constant uneasiness. I always felt a sense of anxiety, guilt, shame, and dread. Was I as obedient to God as I should be? Why couldn't I live a life of supernatural victory over sin? Was I a true believer? If the Rapture occurred, would I be left behind? And it wasn't just me who seemed to be having problems making day-to-day Christian living work as advertised. Although my parents took their faith in Jesus with utter seriousness, my family could not seem to achieve the promised results of faith and obedience in our home.

This book is the first in a series that tells the story of my spiritual journey. I spent nearly my entire life trying to be a good and faithful Christian. As I moved into adulthood, I sought to serve and please the Lord in every aspect of my life with every fiber of my being. I worked in ministry for nearly twenty years as a pastor and Bible college teacher. But as the years went by, I began to question and deconstruct. Eventually, I stopped believing in the Bible, Jesus, and God. One thread that runs through my whole narrative is that my experiences with faith are vitally intertwined with family events. Faith and family are two intimate and inseparable pieces of my story.

Based on the promises of the Bible, our family should have been blessed mightily by God. We tried to do things right and by *The Book*. My parents subscribed to popular evangelical Christian influencers of the day like Dr James Dobson and Bill Gothard. They patterned their marriage and child-rearing after the teachings of these men. Dad and Mom were heavily involved in what then was called *The Institutes in Basic Youth Conflicts,* now titled *Institutes in Basic Life Principles* or *IBLP*. They didn't just attend Gothard's lectures at the Seattle Center each year, they became involved in its leadership. For years my parents served on the Host and Hostess Committee, and my dad was president several times. My parents joined with a group of volunteers who facilitated Bill Gothard's nationwide seminars and helped ensure their success. Gothard's patriarchal model shaped my dad and mom's marriage. Gothard taught that the man is the God-ordained head of the house—the spiritual head of the family—who is ultimately responsible for all decisions. The wife's role is to submit joyfully to her husband's headship, as unto the Lord, as the Apostle Paul taught in the New Testament.[1]

But it wasn't just that my parents followed the advice of men like Dobson and Gothard. My family members were faithful church attendees of a Church of Christ congregation in a rural setting about one hour south of Seattle. My dad was an elder[2] in our church for years. He played the piano at church and regularly led worship services. My mom taught Sunday School. Together, my parents led the youth group, which met at our house for several years.

All the pieces were in place. All the elements of the formula for successful Christian living were lined up and in practice. According to the promises that both Gothard and our church proclaimed from the Bible, our family should have been a rousing success— the epitome of blessings, love, and joy, all flowing from the hand of God.

But it wasn't that way at all. My sisters and I endured countless spankings, making our home life abusive and full of fear. The corporal punishments were part of my parents' obedience to "setting the wayward child straight" according to biblical teachings. The atmosphere around our house was far from loving and nurturing. There were positive moments, but the environment was largely dysfunctional and toxic.

Where was God in all of this? Where was the blessing that we were supposed to receive by following the clear teachings of the Bible on home, family, and marriage? By all rights, our family life would have been dramatically different if all the promises we were taught were true.

The Amazon Prime Video documentary *Shiny Happy People: Duggar Family Secrets*[3] dramatically reveals the pain and destruction that followed in the wake of families who lived by Bill Gothard's teachings. I can relate, and that's why this first book in my series is titled *Not So Shiny Not So Happy People.* As you journey through my story, you will see that things weren't so shiny in my family, and we weren't all that happy.

Clint Heacock

---

1   See Ephesians 5:22 and following.
2   According to one set of biblical guidelines, church leadership structure often follows a model made up of pastoral staff—often paid—as well as elders and deacons—most often volunteer lay leaders. Elders usually serve on a board that meets regularly, and depending on the denomination, might have greater or lesser responsibilities and authority to make policies and decisions.
3   Olivia Crist and Julia Willoughby Nason, *Shiny Happy People: Duggar Family Secrets*, Prime Video, 2023.

Chapter One

The Only Thing You Have to Fear is Hell

I was five years old when I learned about heaven and hell during a summer Vacation Bible School. Most Vacation Bible Schools took place in church buildings, but this one was held at a neighbor's house. My parents thought it would be good for my sisters and me to attend. We went each day, Monday through Friday.

The devout couple who provided their home for the Vacation Bible School also led it. They served cookies and punch and let us play in their backyard for rec time—my two favorite events each day. I did not, however, enjoy the long classroom sessions, sitting in their living room with eight or ten other kids, listening to Bible stories that seemed to go on forever. We learned about Adam and Eve, Noah, King David, and other important Bible characters.

I was impressed that this couple used a flannelgraph as a teaching aid. Unless you're as old as me, you've likely never heard of a flannelgraph. A flannelgraph consisted of an easel and pieces of felt that had been cut into shapes to represent people and things. I was used to seeing flannelgraphs at church, but these people had one at their house. I vividly recall one flannelgraph lesson at the end of the week. Cut-out figures of angels and demons were placed on the board, accompanied by a glowing cloud representing God in heaven, where he presided over the final judgment of all humans.

Chapter One

On Friday afternoon, the last day of VBS, the couple grew very serious as they talked about how important it was for each of us to believe in Jesus. They stressed that we needed to believe in the reality of heaven and hell. They warned us that everyone sitting in that room would end up in either heaven or hell and would remain there forever.

Setting the flannelgraph aside, with a stern look, the husband told us: "Kids, it's imperative that you accept Jesus as your savior and believe in his work on the cross on your behalf." I didn't understand what this grownup language meant then, but I could tell he was deadly serious. He went on solemnly warning us, "Gang, if you don't believe in Jesus and how he bore our sins on the cross, then the consequences are indeed dire. God will not allow you into his heaven after you die. Instead, he will consign you to spend an eternity in conscious torment, enduring the agonies of the flames of hell." Quite a message for a group of five and six-year-old kids—especially since he was talking to us kids using "big words" that only adults would understand!

Looking back on that Vacation Bible School, I now recognize that it was likely the first of many similar experiences that contributed to my Religious Trauma Syndrome.[1] An elementary school child like me, at five years old, doesn't have the critical or emotional faculties to process intensive messages like, "You will go to hell for eternity if you don't accept Jesus as your savior." This is especially true when the messages are recurring and delivered by influential authority figures. As an adult, I now believe that this type of terrifying religious indoctrination of children is a form of abuse. My parents didn't see it that way. They thought they were doing the right thing. They thought it was a fantastic idea for us to go to Vacation Bible School that week to hear "great truths from the Bible."

Extremely concerned after that final talk, I rushed home and told my mother what I'd learned about salvation, heaven, and hell. Suddenly, I was facing the reality that I might be punished forever for not accepting Jesus as my savior. This was a brand-new concept for me. Even though I'd grown up in the church and had faithfully attended Sunday School weekly, this was my first time hearing this believe-or-die message.

"Do you believe in Jesus?" my mother asked me. When I said yes, she responded, "Well, there you go. See? There's nothing to worry about." Looking back, I'm sure my mother felt it was good that I'd been "scared straight." The fundamentalist couple holding a Vacation Bible School in their home had told us *the truth from the Bible,* and that was all that mattered from my mom's point of view. Never mind that hearing this "truth" was a traumatizing experience for me.

Although I was now concerned about going to hell, I walked away from the conversation with my mom feeling like I wasn't in much danger of going there. I guess I did believe in Jesus in my simplistic five-year-old way, although I didn't know much about him or the differences between believing and not believing in him.

Our family rarely missed a weekly service at our small, family-oriented Church of Christ. This *turn-or-burn* message wasn't just delivered in Vacation Bible Schools. It was the foundational belief behind sermons and Sunday School lessons. I just hadn't noticed it before that summer in Vacation Bible School.

To the first-time visitor, our church was a friendly and welcoming bunch. We were big on community and prided ourselves on our loving family atmosphere. The congregation held potluck meals throughout the year and had picnics at a local park on Sunday afternoons during the summer. I always enjoyed those times, playing games with my friends and eating the great food everyone brought.

However, things were not always what they appeared to be, both for our congregation and for my family.

---

1   "Religious Trauma Syndrome is the condition experienced by people who are struggling with leaving an authoritarian, dogmatic religion and coping with the damage of indoctrination. They may be going through the shattering of a personally meaningful faith and/or breaking away and deconstructing from a controlling community and lifestyle. RTS is a function of both the chronic abuses of harmful religion and the impact of severing one's connection with one's faith. It can be compared to a combination of PTSD and Complex PTSD (C-PTSD)." Source Marlene Winell, "Religious Trauma Syndrome," JourneyFree.org, referenced July 29, 2024, https://www.journey-free.org/rts/.

Chapter Two

What's Love Got to Do with It?

A s far as all our churchgoing friends knew, we were a happy and loving Christian family. Viewed from the outside, my parents seemed to enjoy a wonderful, godly marriage, a union blessed mightily by the Lord. But things were far from idyllic in our house. Behind closed doors, our home life was dysfunctional, toxic, and sometimes abusive.

In the summer of 1975, when I was eight years old, my favorite sister, Valerie, became pregnant at the age of seventeen. The way my parents handled her pregnancy created a depth of turmoil in our home. Looking back on it now, as a father, I can't imagine treating my children the way my parents treated Valerie.

In the wake of the scandalous news of Valerie's pregnancy, my father—an elder in our church—resigned in disgrace. I clearly remember the Sunday morning he stood before the church and said he had a very important announcement. Citing biblical teachings, with a choking voice, he proclaimed to the congregation: "The Bible states that if an elder can't shepherd his family, he has no business leading the flock of God. As I'm sure you all know by now, my rebellious daughter Valerie is pregnant, so I need to do the right thing. I'm going to step down as an elder." The response from the congregation was stunned silence. For a few moments, you could have heard a pin drop.

Chapter Two

After receiving this shocking news, the church didn't turn their backs on my parents. There seemed to be no shortage of people lining up to hug them that day. Many congregants tearfully prayed that "the Lord would be with our family through this trying time." Everyone agreed that my father had done the honorable thing by resigning. The overwhelming response was, "What a shining, biblical example of an elder following the clear teaching of the Word of God!" Here was a church acting as the body of Christ, demonstrating genuine love and compassion for my father and mother, two of its hurting members.

At home, no hugs or supportive prayers were offered for Valerie, no support for the rebellious sinner who had dared to embarrass my parents in front of their church friends. Our "loving" congregation—the same people who had embraced my parents—turned their backs on Valerie. She had clearly rebelled against God and her parents. Ostracizing her was what the Apostle Paul had commanded churches to do when a member is caught in a heinous sin.

By violating our church's strict evangelical purity culture code and losing her virginity before marriage, Valerie had forever destroyed her once-promising future. Never mind that my parents, in their pursuit of fundamentalist purity for their children, had failed to offer her even the basics of sex education. She didn't even know she was pregnant. It was my mother who noticed the bulge in Valerie's stomach while we were on a family swimming outing and petite Valerie was wearing a bikini. From my parents' point of view adolescent sex education wasn't necessary: "Why bother to educate someone who understands the imperative of remaining pure until marriage?" As they saw it, Valerie would follow the teachings of the Bible and remain a virgin until her wedding night because that was the commitment she had made to God. But now that dream of perfect purity was forever shattered.

Upon discovering that Valerie was pregnant, Dad and Mom's first response was not to embrace or console her but to spank her. She was seventeen! One would surely have to question how spanking her could help in any way—and spanking a pregnant woman? I believe spanking was their way of lashing out in anger over what she had done. In her rebellion, she had humiliated them as godly parents.

For Valerie, there was no support like my parents received from their church community. In her own home, she endured hateful arguments, shouts of anger, hurled accusations, and bitter recriminations. I can vividly recall huge screaming matches between Valerie and my parents. Over and over, my sisters and I watched silently as the whole affair descended into utter chaos.

My parents referred to these scenes as "family meetings." Attendance was mandatory. My sisters and I were compelled to watch our family tear itself apart. My father and mother forced us to make an impossible choice. We had to choose sides between our parents and Valerie. We loved them both, so this was an unthinkable decision. The entire experience was traumatic and emotionally scarring for me and for my other sisters, not to mention how tough it must have been for Valerie. She was placed on the hot seat, accused of multiple crimes like a victim of the Spanish Inquisition. Worse yet, she was allowed no acceptable defense. Nothing she might say could change the situation. She couldn't "un-impregnate" herself. Getting an abortion was out of the question since that would add yet another offense to the sin of having sex outside of marriage. Based on my parents' logic—shaped by their interpretation of the Bible—God was already angry at Valerie for getting pregnant. It would be senseless, they believed, to add the grievous sin of abortion to the equation.

My parents—heavily invested in the teachings of Bill Gothard's *Institute in Basic Youth Conflicts Seminar*—received counsel from that ministry and from our church. The prevailing "wisdom" was that removing Valerie from high school was the best option. After doing so, they placed her into a foster home in a city more than an hour's drive away. Callously, my parents made Valerie take care of registering at the new school. Months into her pregnancy, she was cut off from the support of family and friends and thrust into a previously unknown environment. Her sentence of isolation continued throughout her pregnancy. Valerie has shared with me how challenging and traumatic the experience was. She was on her own. She had been *left behind.*

Valerie had to drop out of high school when she grew too large to fit into the student chair desks. She had to earn her GED in later years as an adult. Her foster home wasn't exactly warm and welcoming either. Although run by a "loving" Christian couple, Valerie was little more than a domestic servant, working hard at menial chores around the house despite being pregnant. My folks provided no funding to help ease Valerie's financial burdens, and the "loving" host couple required her to pay what little money she could spare for rent.

My parents manipulated Valerie to give her child up for adoption. This was facilitated by a Gothard-affiliated adoption ministry ironically called "Burden Bearers." I'm not sure whose burdens they were bearing. Certainly not Valerie's, or the rest of us siblings, who had little or no capacity to process our intense emotions.

It appeared that my parents' decision to move Valerie a long way from home was their way of keeping this embarrassing scandal "out of sight." If they didn't have to see or deal with her daily, it was easier to act like things were okay with our family.

My sister Beth and I were able to visit Valerie once for about thirty minutes, and this was only because my mom had to drop off some desperately needed clothes because Valerie had outgrown her old ones.

None of us were present when her daughter was born, not even my parents. Valerie had to endure the pain, fear, and uncertainty of childbirth alone. And then came the heart-wrenching experience of having to surrender her newborn daughter for adoption. Where were those Burden Bearers? After handling her baby's adoption, they certainly weren't bearing Valerie's many burdens. For that matter, where was God in all this? My parents continued to shun Valerie, so moving back home didn't look like a viable option for her. She was on her own now.

During the pregnancy, our church formed a prayer chain—a group of dedicated believers praying for the same request—to pray more effectively for our family. I should clarify that those in the prayer chain were praying for my parents but not for rebellious Valerie. If she was mentioned in the prayers, the request was that she see the error of her ways, repent, and return to God. Despite all the prayers offered on behalf of my folks, nothing changed for the better, as far as I could see.

Sadly, God did not seem to be listening to the prayers of our church's dedicated believers. Why, I wondered, wouldn't God want to help restore our broken family? We certainly weren't being good witnesses to the gospel. Any nonbeliever who'd been privy to our vicious "family meetings" would most likely determine that our Christian household wouldn't be a good place to live. They certainly would not have been drawn to believe in Jesus by our example.

Chapter Three

Horror Films at Church

When I was nine years old, our church showed a chilling movie titled *A Thief in the Night*. The Sunday evening program was advertised as an enjoyable movie night: "Bring soft drinks and popcorn to church on Sunday evening and see a free film! Good fun for the entire family!" If you Google "A Thief in the Night movie," you'll see it listed as a 1973 Horror/ Thriller movie. There's nothing like a terrifying horror movie on a school night for the kiddies, and in a church no less, a place that—in theory at least—is supposed to be a safe haven from encountering terror and trauma.

Sitting through this movie just once would have been bad enough. But I was destined for multiple viewings. Just a few days after the showing at church, at the regular Wednesday night Bible study at our house, my dad borrowed the church's movie projector. He showed the film again just in case anyone had been unfortunate enough to miss it on Sunday! Sitting in my living room—another place where I was supposed to feel safe—I was forced to watch this frightening flick a second time. Even though I'd seen the movie a few nights earlier and knew the primary plot line, watching it again only reinforced its powerful and terrifying message. But even this wasn't the last time I saw it.

Months later, *A Thief in the Night* was shown on Friday night at my Christian summer camp when I was ten. It seemed that no matter where I went, I was confronted by this damnable movie that scared me to death each time I suffered through it.

Decades later, doing research for a podcast devoted to deconstructing the film, I discovered that it had been specifically distributed to churches nationwide rather than being released directly to movie theaters. As a result, an entire generation of young people in my age group had a similar experience to mine. I wasn't the only young person who suffered from Rapture anxiety, which, in my case, led to experiencing Religious Trauma Syndrome. Three other films followed in the *Thief in the Night* series, after which in the 1990s and 2000s came the bestselling *Left Behind* books and movies. So, the generation after me was also traumatized by the series of books and five movies that accompanied them.

A Thief in the Night was a low-budget, B-grade flick, but I was too young to notice the poor cinematic work. After I'd seen the movie the third time, I was profoundly traumatized. Returning home from summer camp, I couldn't stop thinking about the film. Several haunting scenes constantly replayed in my mind. I had recurring nightmares. Some nights, after waking up in a cold sweat, I'd crawl out of bed and sneak down the hall as quietly as possible. I'd peek in one room at a time, verifying that all my sisters and parents were sleeping soundly in their beds. I had to reassure myself that the Rapture hadn't happened while I was asleep, leaving me behind. Only after making the rounds, could I get back to sleep.

A Thief in the Night conveyed the absolute terror of facing a stark reality: God suddenly called every one of his faithful followers to be with him in heaven. Without warning, the Rapture occurred, and most of the world missed out. Now, it was too late, and the unfortunate people left behind were doomed to face seven years of bitter events in what was called *The Great Tribulation*. And these most awful seven years in human history would be followed by an eternity in hell!

Contemplating the frightening message of the movie, I decided that despite my earlier experience in Vacation Bible School and the conversation with my mother five years earlier, I couldn't be entirely sure that I was a true believer. One overriding fear constantly tormented me: What if the Rapture happened, and I missed it? Despite my mother's earlier assurances that I was already saved since I believed in Jesus, I decided I couldn't risk such a high-stakes gamble. I knew that I didn't want to be left behind at the Rapture to face seven years of tribulation, followed by an eternity in hell.

A few weeks after returning home from summer camp, I made an appointment with Jerry, our senior pastor. I felt I had nowhere else to turn. If anyone could help me navigate through my crisis of faith, it would be our trusted spiritual leader.

When I dropped by his office to tell him I wanted to talk to him, I noticed his framed Bible college degree hanging on the wall. At that moment, I concluded that here was a qualified and godly man who could give me the spiritual guidance I so desperately needed. I felt a massive sense of relief that I was finally in the process of doing the right thing. Finally, here was my God-ordained chance to unburden myself of the crushing weight of anxieties and fears I'd been carrying for so long about my eternal destiny.

Later, when I showed up for my appointment, I tentatively began to share some of the fears and concerns I'd been carrying since seeing the movie. Pastor Jerry leaned back in his chair, nodding his head with a look of confident wisdom as he listened patiently. He steepled his fingers and wore a look of deep concern on his face as I continued to talk.

As we discussed my thoughts about the movie and the various conclusions I'd come to after watching it three times, I began to feel a sense of safety. I could trust this man. Relaxing somewhat, I shared more of my fears and concerns. I told Pastor Jerry that whatever happened, I didn't want to be left behind if the Rapture occurred. I admitted that despite my mother's assurances about my belief in Jesus, I had finally begun to face the possibility that I might not be saved. After disclosing my pressing anxieties, I waited for Pastor Jerry's response with bated breath, desperately hoping he had grasped what was troubling me. Could he help me?

His first statement caught me off guard. He confronted me with the classic revival preacher's query: "Clint, if you were to die tonight, can you say for sure that God would let you into his heaven?" I'd never thought of it quite like that. I sat back in my chair and contemplated his question. It took only a few moments for me to realize that I had no choice but to admit—to my shame—that, no, I didn't think God would let me into his heaven.

Pastor Jerry furrowed his brow, leaned back in his chair, and looked at me thoughtfully. He was silent for a few moments. I could feel my heart beating fast. My palms were sweating. I wondered what Pastor Jerry would say next. I was sure I was on the verge of a critical moment. After looking up at the ceiling for a few seconds while tapping his fingers on his chin as if searching the heavens for inspiration, he finally spoke. "Do you truly believe, deep down in your heart of hearts, that you are, in fact, *a true Christian?*" I hung my head and mumbled that I was certainly not a true believer. My simplistic belief in Jesus had proven to be sorely lacking.

At that moment, I had a flash of inspiration. The simple solution was staring me in the face: *I needed to become a Christian. I* tearfully asked Pastor Jerry if he could help me out. "Please, can you tell me what I should do? How can I get saved? I must make sure that I avoid being left behind in the Rapture. Whatever happens, I want to go to heaven, not hell!"

With a grave look on his face, my pastor leaned forward and placed both hands palms down on his desk. Looking me straight in the eyes, he said, "So let me get this straight. You want to become a Christian? Is that what I hear you saying?" Overcome with emotion and unable to speak, all I could do was nod my head. His following statement put all the pieces into place: "At this point, it's all quite simple. All you have to do is get baptized. That's all there is to it."

Could it be that simple? That was it? All I had to do, after expressing my desire to become a Christian, was be baptized? A sense of relief washed over me, and I blurted out, "Yes! That's what I want to do! I need to get baptized." Pastor Jerry leaned back in his chair, his face lighting up with a beaming smile. "Great!" he exclaimed. "This is terrific news! Nothing is stopping you now from getting saved. As soon as we can, let's go ahead and get you baptized, son!"

Pastor Jerry promised that he would take care of all the arrangements, and right then and there, we scheduled my baptism for the upcoming Sunday evening service. Thanking him profusely, I shook his hand and left his office on cloud nine. I was so relieved. A huge weight had been taken off my shoulders, knowing that within mere days, all my troubles would be over because of the simple and straightforward act of baptism.

And that's precisely what happened. At the age of ten, in front of my church and my God, I was baptized.

In the Church of Christ, baptism is done by total immersion in a tank of water called a baptistry. The New Testament is written in

Greek, and the Greek word used for baptism in the Bible means "to dip or plunge." So, our church—along with Baptists and many other evangelical churches—firmly held to the belief that none of that sprinkling nonsense would do! You needed to be lowered all the way into the water!

I was disappointed when I learned Pastor Jerry would not be performing my baptism. Although my father had stepped down from the Elder Board because of Valerie's pregnancy, he was still an elder and that meant he could baptize me.

At Pastor Jerry's direction, my father was assigned to the task. Just before he lowered me under the water, my dad confidently stated a classic Christian formula: "I baptize you in the name of the Father, the Son, and the Holy Spirit." As I emerged from the water, spluttering and cold, I heard my father announce to the congregation, "Buried with Christ in baptism, raised to walk in newness of life!" Everyone clapped and cheered, and I could not wipe the smile of joy from my face as I scrambled up the steps and out of the baptismal tank.

Now, I was firmly convinced that I was saved. Being saved and knowing that I was saved was all that mattered. I was supremely happy that I'd been baptized and, therefore, safe to get into heaven when I died. A sincere belief in Jesus, combined with being baptized in the name of the Father, Son, and Holy Spirit, guaranteed my salvation. I walked out of that service feeling immensely joyful, knowing I was now wholly prepared and on secure ground should the Rapture occur.

Church members crowded around me in the foyer, hugging me, slapping me on the back, shaking my hand, and congratulating me on achieving this crucial spiritual milestone.

I had Pastor Jerry's word that I'd done everything right, so how could there be anything wrong or lacking in my new spiritual life with Jesus? I proudly told myself that as a born-again, baptized believer, undoubtedly on the road to heaven, things would change for the better.

I knew that the Father, Son, and the Holy Spirit—known in Christian theology as "the Trinity"—and in whose names I had been baptized, were now fully invested in helping me grow as a Christian. Not that I was a bad kid. I was, in most respects, a typical ten-year-old boy. But I expected that somehow, miraculously, with God's help, any bad stuff I was doing would stop. I thought I would be more kind and loving toward others. Being a Christian is about being like Jesus. Surely, God was vested in helping me improve my life.

Sadly, no one saw the need or took the time to explain how I should go about living my new Christian life. I didn't know what to expect, but I expected *something* to happen. I knew enough to believe that the all-knowing God of the universe had come into my life to "set up his throne in my heart." Now that I'd been baptized, I knew for sure that Jesus was my savior *and* Lord. My mother had told me that it was no good for Christians to accept Jesus as their savior but not to have him as their Lord. Such limited commitment was nothing more than *fire insurance*—becoming a Christian to avoid the flames of hell with no genuine interest in daily submitting to Christ's lordship. So, I figured I needed to start living my life in a way that reflected both of those realities. Jesus was my savior and Jesus was my lord.

I didn't know exactly what to expect, but I knew it was up to me to start making these things happen. And one thing I knew to do was to pray for my family.

My father baptized me about a year and a half after Valerie gave up her baby for adoption. I was still deeply traumatized after watching my family tear itself apart over Valerie's pregnancy. As a new Christian, I felt like I had an inside line to heaven, and I spent much time praying for my parents and sisters—but especially for Valerie. I begged God to intervene and do something—anything— to help ease our family's dysfunctional life of emotional pain. The Bible says a lot about forgiveness and restoration, so I hoped and prayed my parents could forgive Valerie and restore her back into the family like it was before she'd gotten pregnant.

Chapter Four

Trying to Love an Invisible Silent God

As the months unfolded after my baptism, I had to admit to myself that I was not living up to the high standards I had been taught were the norm for successful Christian living. Outwardly, my religious life looked pretty good. I rarely missed church, heartily sang worship songs, and won contests focusing on the content of the Bible. I earned gold stars for Bible verse memorization and Sunday School attendance.

But all these activities were going on before I was baptized. Now, my concern focused on private behaviors where—much to my chagrin—I had good reasons to wonder how much I had changed at my core since my conversion and baptism.

While many of my outward, public behaviors were modeled after what the dedicated kids at church were doing, there were not-so-public behaviors I shared with other friends from church that were anything but spiritual. We swore and smoked cigarettes stolen from Valerie. We tried to drink a little beer, but I couldn't stand the taste. I had my personal, private behaviors as well. I always had a few *Playboy* and *Penthouse* magazines stashed under my mattress.

I told myself I was in good standing with God since I regularly begged him to forgive me for my disobedient ways. But I couldn't stop sinning, and that felt like a severe problem. Why couldn't I get better at living the way God wanted me to? And didn't God want to help me improve my life? I knew I should be reading my Bible much more than I was, and my prayer life left much to be desired.

One afternoon, a few months after my baptism, my mom took me aside and startled me by asking: "How's your walk with God?" Completely caught off-guard, I had no good answer. I knew I couldn't fool her with a lie about such an important topic.

I mumbled that I thought my walk with God was going okay, but I could see she wasn't convinced. "Well," she said, crossing her arms, with a mildly annoyed look on her face, "It seems pretty clear that you can't answer my question. The fact that you can't give a straight answer tells me everything I need to know." Caught in her spiritual trap, I had no response to her statement. I looked up at her, tongue-tied and unsure what to say next. She had uncovered a severe lack of progress in my young Christian life.

She let me off the hook with a simple prescription. "Let me help you out. Now that you're a Christian, this is what you need to do: Read your Bible regularly and spend time in prayer every day. Trust me. Your walk with God will greatly improve if you are faithful in doing those two things."

When she told me what I should be doing, I felt a quick pang of remorse. I knew I was supposed to be prioritizing these two spiritual disciplines. I knew I was failing God, and I suspected I was a severe disappointment to him. Feeling deeply convicted, I admitted that I was ashamed of my lack of Bible study and prayer. And I had no excuse for my unacceptable behavior. A song I had enthusiastically sung alongside my church buddies for years admonished: "Read your Bible and pray every day, and you'll grow, grow, grow!" I had memorized these words but had not taken them to heart.

I asked my mom *why* I needed to read my Bible and pray to God daily. Matter-of-factly, she replied, "That's what all obedient Christians do. They do it so that they can learn more about God and *come to love him more.* Though it will take a lifetime, the Lord promises us that we'll grow to be like Jesus over time." I knew prayer and Bible study were important, but the part about *loving God* surprised me since nobody had explained this to me. Why hadn't Pastor Jerry mentioned this when I'd been baptized?

Later, as I reflected on the conversation with my mom, I admitted to myself that I already understood the serving and obeying part of my relationship with God. I knew that Jesus was my savior. I knew he was the king seated on the throne of my heart. I knew that every good citizen of heaven must obey their king. This all made sense, but up to that point, I hadn't realized *I needed to love God.*

Since my baptism, I had reassured myself with the certainty that I was now safely on my way to heaven, and that was pretty much all that mattered. Now, I had been confronted with the fact that I needed to develop my love for God. Reflecting on this, I realized part of my problem was struggling to manufacture feelings of love for God. No matter how hard I willed myself to feel love for God, I felt nothing. How was I supposed to love an invisible being I'd never seen, met, or spoken with personally? You don't converse with God like two people do over coffee at Starbucks. In all the times I had prayed to God, I had never heard him answer me audibly. It's hard to love an invisible, silent God. But I knew I had to try.

Over the next few months, I began to focus on learning to appreciate what Jesus had done for me on the cross. If God so loved me enough to send his only Son to die for my sins on the cross, then there might be a way that I could learn to love him back. I decided my love for God should be based on Jesus's selfless sacrifice on the cross for me. Since he had suffered for me, a worthless sinner bound for hell, the least I could do was to love him back out of sheer gratitude for rescuing me.

As I wrestled with learning how to love God, I listened to records by Mike Warnke, then a famous Christian comedian. I even got to see him perform a sold-out show at Calvary Fellowship Church in Seattle. So many people were attending that we ended up sitting in an overflow room, watching his performance on a movie screen as it was simulcast from the packed main auditorium.

With his graphic and sometimes lurid accounts of satanic ritual abuse and devil-worshiping Black Masses held in secret, underground covens nationwide, Warnke helped to fuel the "Satanic Panic" in the 1980s and 1990s. As a comedian, Warnke was genuinely funny and had an unbelievable conversion story. But in 1992, Cornerstone Magazine exposed Warnke as a serial liar in regard to critical parts of his testimony as a former drug-addled Satanist high priest. This revelation effectively ended Warnke's Christian celebrity status. To my knowledge, he has never admitted that he lied about his backstory. But I knew nothing of this when I listened to his records and attended his sold-out performance. Everyone believed his astonishing stories about being a heroin addict and a former high priest of a satanic coven.

The fact that Warnke was a Christian comedian meant I could listen to his records without fear of reprisal from my parents. This was despite Warnke's often disturbingly graphic descriptions of satanic ritual murder, sexual abuse, black masses, and other unspeakable occult crimes supposedly being committed across the country.

Sometime after my talk with my mother, listening to one of Warnke's records, *A Jester in the King's Court*, provided me with a significant insight in my quest to learn how to love God. After his comedy bit on the record, Warnke adopted a serious tone and related the story of Jesus's final hours leading up to his crucifixion. His suffering had begun the night before in the Garden of Gethsemane as he sweated real drops of blood while agonizing over the fate that awaited him. Warnke explained how it was scientifically possible for a person under immense stress to actually sweat blood. This was no metaphor that some liberal preacher could explain away as Jesus just sweating profusely!

Warnke then went into painstaking detail depicting every aspect of the cruel whipping Jesus endured and the merciless brutality of a Roman crucifixion. As he eloquently described the hideous scene, you could feel the intense pain of the lash on your own back. You could imagine eight-inch spikes driven through your hands into the wood of the cross. Warnke portrayed exactly how Jesus suffered in excruciating misery for hours, enduring maddening thirst in the hot sun and struggling in unspeakable agony merely to catch a breath. And because Jesus was God and man, he had known ahead of time what torture and pain lay in store for him, but that did not stop him from going to the cross to fulfill his destiny.

When it was all over, Jesus finally gave up his spirit by declaring, "It is finished!" And with that, Jesus died. But what exactly had Jesus finished? With that emphatic utterance, Jesus's perfect and sinless sacrifice completely satisfied God's righteous anger. What exactly was God angry about? Warnke declared that God was angry because of humanity's countless transgressions against him.

Jesus endured all that horrific pain and torture, Warnke concluded, because of your sins and mine—even though he didn't have to suffer and die. Jesus willingly gave his life for us. In a moment of weakness, the night before in the Garden, Jesus begged his heavenly Father to get him out of it. Ultimately, however, Jesus accepted that there was no other way to atone for the sins of humanity. "Not my will, but yours be done,"[1] he finally stated.

Resigning himself to his fate, he willingly faced his destiny on the cross. It was the only way humanity could be saved from sin. And since Jesus was the sinless God-man, he was the perfect sacrifice. He was the only one qualified for this incredible act.

Warnke declared that Jesus suffered and gave his life out of love for us poor, spiritually blind sinners. He stated that in our sinful condition, we all hated God and were rightfully bound for an eternity in hell. In the words of the Christian song, "It wasn't the nails that kept Christ on the cross; It was love. Pure love."[2]

Could I find it in my heart to develop a love for God upon hearing such a stirring narrative? How could I not at least love Jesus, considering the inconceivable agony he had endured on my behalf? But the truth was that even after listening to Warnke's incredibly moving story, I still struggled to manufacture genuine feelings of love for Jesus. I could imagine what enduring a hideously painful crucifixion must have felt like and could appreciate the intense anguish Jesus suffered on my behalf. However, even with such a dramatic portrayal of Jesus's suffering on the cross, it was still too abstract for me. It felt like ancient history.

I knew that I had to develop a love for God, but I couldn't make it happen. I was haunted by guilt for not being able to manufacture a way to feel love for God. But I couldn't figure out how to do it. I loved my sisters, parents, and friends, but they were real people with whom I had face-to-face relationships. I could have a chat with them while sitting across a table. We could have meaningful discussions. But how exactly was I supposed to love an invisible deity with whom I could not have an actual conversation? I prayed to him countless times, but I never heard anything back. My mom once told me that prayer with God was just like conversing with another person, but I felt that prayer was simply another name for talking to myself or thinking in my head.

For the next year or so after the talk with my mother, I tried extremely hard to live up to the standard of Christian behavior she told me was so important—praying, reading my Bible, and developing a love for God. I was determined to read my Bible daily in my quest to learn how to love and please God through my actions.

I decided I would read the Bible from cover to cover. Fired by righteous zeal, I started at the beginning and made a firm commitment that I wouldn't stop until I hit the end of Revelation, the last book in the Bible. Decades later, as a Bible college student, one of my professors stated that the worst mistake a new Christian can make is to start reading their Bible at Genesis. But that is precisely where I started reading. It made perfect sense to me. Everyone knows that's how you begin any new book—on the first page, not in the middle or at the end.

Genesis wasn't a terrible place to start since most of it was an exciting narrative beginning with the story of God's creation. From years of Sunday School lessons and creation science classes at my Christian school, I already knew that God had effortlessly created the heavens and the Earth from nothing in just six days. Each day was twenty-four hours long because that's all the time God needed! I also knew that God had completed the work of creation some six to ten thousand years ago, rather than the billions of years the secular, godless evolutionists claimed to be the actual age of the cosmos.

Once I made it past the creation story, I breezed forward, already familiar with the stories about Adam and Eve, Noah's Ark, and the adventures of the patriarchs—Abraham, Isaac, and Jacob. After finishing Genesis, I began reading Exodus. I liked the exciting story of Moses and the Israelites fleeing the cruel bondage they experienced in Egypt. I wondered what it would be like if rivers turned to blood, and we were deluged with flies and frogs everywhere. My vivid imagination served me well in this part of the Bible, and my reading through God's holy book was going smoothly. But everything came to a screeching halt when I ran into all the seemingly endless lists of covenant laws and arcane legal codes, beginning in Exodus chapters nineteen and twenty.

Although I struggled gamely through the rest of Exodus, by the time I made it as far as Leviticus, I gave up out of sheer boredom. I put my Bible back on the shelf where I'd picked it up months earlier. I felt like I had put forth a herculean effort, but I couldn't see the point of it all. I could only wonder how any of those bizarre Old Testament laws related to my life as a Christian boy living in twentieth-century America. But I felt guilty, too. I knew that reading the Word of God was extremely important for me. But if it is truly his Word, then why didn't he make it more readable, relevant, and applicable to life in any age? Maybe I should have started with the Gospel of Matthew. Unfortunately, by then it was too late, and the bad habit of ignoring my Bible—already present for some time earlier in my life—resumed.

Pastor Jerry had preached a sermon about Christians ignoring their Bibles and how important it was for us to read Scripture regularly. He stated that most Christians have nothing but dust on their Bibles from months and years of inattention.

I did the same thing as those phony Christians with dusty Bibles Pastor Jerry spoke about. Every Sunday morning as we left for church, I picked up my Bible from its shelf where it had lain ignored all week. I figured I'd at least earn a gold star for bringing my Bible to class, along with the added benefit of looking spiritual. But upon returning home, my Bible returned to the same spot where it had been before church, and the cycle would repeat the following week.

I felt embarrassed and ashamed whenever I was reminded of this spiritual discipline. I always vowed to try harder. I knew I was supposed to be developing an appreciation for God's Word, if not a growing appetite. But inevitably, I fell short.

I had been taught in church that God inspired the Bible in a way that made it completely true and totally reliable. I knew it was inerrant—without error in everything it taught—since the Holy Spirit had inspired the human authors to write everything exactly as God intended, yet without violating their personalities. Pastor Jerry informed us that because it was without error, the Bible was the infallible and authoritative guide for all aspects of life, faith, and practice for the Christian.

I knew reading the Bible regularly was extremely important, and I had a profound and nagging sense of guilt for consistently failing to do so. Just as I couldn't seem to drum up a feeling of love for God, I also struggled to manufacture an appropriate appreciation for the Bible. Deep down, I wasn't motivated to read a book I could barely understand. I was supposed to apply the Bible to every aspect of my life, but I had no idea how to do that. All I knew was that I was letting God down because I was surely displeasing him in a significant way.

My struggle with daily Bible reading wasn't the only part of my Christian life that wasn't developing. I felt like I was going through the motions in multiple areas of my Christian walk. And it seemed I was getting nowhere, just spinning my wheels spiritually.

Whatever assistance I hoped God would provide for me wasn't coming through when I needed it most. This was strange to me because I reasoned that surely God was in the business of helping his children grow spiritually and lead more successful lives. But I wasn't experiencing any of that, despite agonizing prayers begging God, Jesus, and the Holy Spirit for help. It seemed that not one member of the Trinity was there for me at a time when I needed them most.

Chapter Four

I was supposed to be getting "sanctified" as a Christian. In other words, I was supposed to be in a daily, lifelong process of becoming more and more like Jesus. This meant I would become more and more set apart, more and more holy, as time went on. But no divine help seemed to be forthcoming. Much of the time, I was wracked with guilt, anxiety, and shame, knowing God was undoubtedly disappointed in me for being such a screw-up. I didn't know what to do or where to turn. I was filled with a sense of depression and a constant sense that I was a failure, deserving of God's displeasure and wrath.

But none of this stopped me from "wearing the mask" when I was in church or around other believers. This double life only reinforced the deep sense that I was nothing more than a phony Christian. I was trying to live a victorious, supernaturally transformed Christian life, but I was failing miserably. I had no idea what I could or should do to find the discipline and strength, or whatever it might take, that would make a difference.

I had grown up in church and sat through hundreds of sermons and Sunday School lessons. But most of what I had learned didn't make much sense to me, and it certainly didn't seem all that relevant to my life. I didn't know what to do.

---

1   Luke 22:42, multiple versions.
2   Ron Hall, "It Wasn't the Nails" Ron Hall Music, 2022.

Chapter Five

Walking on Hot Coals

A year after my baptism an evening at summer camp made a deep impression on me. Our Pastor, Jerry, was the speaker that week. On Friday night, before we would all head home the next day, Pastor Jerry gave the classic campfire talk as we sat on logs around a blazing fire deep in the woods.

We listened intently as Pastor Jerry spoke of the dangers of falling away from Christian fellowship. This was the first time I'd heard that a seemingly faithful believer could "fall away," and I was shocked. But the momentary pang of anxiety I felt when I heard my pastor say these words was quickly quelled by the assurance I had from being baptized just a year before. I told myself that I was sitting pretty. I had nothing to worry about. I was good with God.

Pastor Jerry picked up a stick and scooped a few glowing coals out of the fire. As we all watched the coals slowly die out, Pastor Jerry warned that those fading embers could be any one of us. He cautioned that if we stopped attending church, stopped praying, quit reading our Bibles, and stopped fellowshipping with other Christians, we would spiritually "die out," just like the coals we saw dwindling away into darkness. "There's no such thing as a Lone Ranger Christian," he declared. Poking the blackened coals with his stick, he sternly warned us, Don't let this happen to you!"

Despite my initial success at quelling my feelings of concern, I began to feel uneasy about the possibility that my faith could somehow fade away. That couldn't happen to me, could it? Once again, I reassured myself that my salvation was secure. Hadn't I just gotten baptized? Wasn't I safely wrapped in the love and care of God? Surely, this falling away would never happen to me! But I still felt worried.

Pastor Jerry's next statement came as a huge relief. "As bad as things might look right now," he said, "I've got some good news for everyone." Just as the formerly burning coals were fading into the dark night, he pushed them back into the heart of the fire with his stick. Within moments, they were burning brightly again. Sitting back down on his log seat, Pastor Jerry declared with authority that this display was an example of how important it was for us to attend church faithfully, keep reading our Bibles, and continue praying to the Lord every single day. If we didn't stray too far, our fellowship with God could be reignited even when it appeared to be gone.

It was extremely important, he went on to say, that we stay involved in Christian fellowship. Wagging his finger at us, he gravely warned us to "Keep your feet firmly planted on the path of righteousness!" I didn't know what that meant, but it sounded serious. "Jesus teaches us in the Gospels that the road to heaven is exceedingly narrow. Very few people find it," he declared. "Unfortunately, the way to hell is wide, easy, and well-traveled. Sadly, most of the people in this world are on that road." He stated, "Spiritually blind to the truth, those outside of Christian faith are blissfully unaware of the horrific, agonizing torment awaiting them beyond the grave for all eternity." I wondered why God made it so difficult for humanity to get into heaven, and so easy for the masses to walk the wide road to hell. But Jesus said it, and Pastor Jerry's grave warning hit home.

Frightened by the power of his campfire demonstration, I took Pastor Jerry's talk to heart. I didn't want to fall away from my faith. I didn't want to die out as a Christian because I skipped church too many times, quit praying, stopped reading my Bible, or stopped associating with my fellow believers. But I felt that if anyone was on safe ground, it was me. I'd been baptized just a year before, was in church two or three times a week, had a Christian family, and attended a Christian school. I barely even knew any nonbelievers. Virtually all my friends and family members were Christians. I felt simultaneously afraid and safe.

That night around the campfire, Pastor Jerry gave us dire warnings of the dangers of getting away from church and Christian influences, but he said there was hope if you returned to Jesus after drifting into disobedience. If I didn't stray too far from God, I could come back. I could resume attending church, reading my Bible, praying, and fellowshipping with other believers. If I did all those things, it *sounded like* I would be safe. I would be one of the coals that returned to the fire and resumed burning.

But Pastor Jerry failed to address another possibility: C*ould a Christian lose their salvation*? As I thought about his message later, I wondered: When a believer strays and lives in disobedience, is there a point of no coming back? As an eleven-year-old boy, could I lose my salvation and end up in hell after being a true believer earlier in my life? What if Pastor Jerry hadn't put those coals back in the fire? Was that the end for them? I needed to know.

Some Christians believe "once saved, always saved," and speak of an "assurance of salvation." But that's not what I was hearing from my own pastor. What he did make clear was this: Stay in church, remain in Christian fellowship, and don't contemplate what dire things might happen if you started moving away from the fire. I wasn't sure if it was possible to stray past a point of no return, but in one sense, it didn't matter. Why would anyone even take the chance?

As I view it now, the warning issued by my pastor and by other Christian leaders in my life was an example of classic cult psychological tactics. The BITE Model™ of authoritarian control, developed by cult expert Dr Steven Hassan, is an acronym for "Behavior, Information, Thought, and Emotional control."[1] Cults and cult leaders exercise undue influence over their followers by making use of each element of this model. *One of the most effective ways to control adherents is by convincing them that there is never a good reason to leave the group.* If you *do* walk away, they say, you'll be doomed since *only we* possess the way to salvation.

The clear message to all the followers in these types of groups is: *Stay safely inside our bubble.* Don't risk your eternal destiny by leaving the security of the fold. And that described me. I was fully immersed within my safe Christian context. Between church on the weekends and midweek, Christian school five days a week, and summer camp, I was all in. There was little danger of my faith fading out and dying like the coals in Pastor Jerry's object lesson. But if I ever did begin to stray, the message from my religious community was: *The worst thing you could ever do is leave us.*

---

1 Freedom of Mind Resource Center, "BITE Model™ of Authoritarian Control," https://freedomofmind.com/cult-mind-control/bite-model-pdf-download/.

Chapter Six

Appearances Can Be Deceiving

D espite my superficial self-assurances that I was safe and secure in my walk with God, I had good reasons to be worried by Pastor Jerry's dying coals metaphor. A year after my baptism, there was no evidence that any type of supernatural, life-changing event had occurred in my life.

The church offered me virtually nothing in the way of post-baptism support: no special classes, no discipleship training, just the typical Sunday School lessons I had heard for years. I'd grown up in this church and had been attending since immediately after my birth. Thanks to years of Sunday School indoctrination, I had a lot of biblical teachings down pat. I could rattle 'em off with the best of them. I played the part with gusto.

But anyone who saw me with my church friends in our unguarded moments would have been shocked that a group of "Christian" boys could misbehave as we did. In addition to our swearing, our cigarettes, and attempts at drinking beer, we bragged about kissing girls—which none of us had done—and wondered aloud about the mysteries of sex. We traded a few *Playboy* magazines and lusted over images of beautiful, naked women.

Reading the graphic descriptions of freewheeling sex in the *Penthouse* "Forum" was stimulating, but it deepened the shame and guilt I felt as I was becoming hooked by the firm grip of pornography addiction. I knew this was a terrible sin because I'd heard about how God had killed Onan, according to the narrative in Genesis chapter 38. This was after God had already slain Onan's older brother Er for being "wicked in his sight." According to biblical Levirate law, Er's untimely death meant that Onan was forced to marry Tamar, his deceased brother's wife. Foolishly committing *coitus interruptus*, Onan had unwisely "spilled his seed on the ground" rather than impregnating his new bride as he was supposed to do. As punishment for shirking his husbandly duties, God put him to death, just as he had done with his brother Er.

In church tradition, over the millennia, that story had been conflated with masturbation, and it was clear that God deeply disapproved of "the sin of onanism." I was always worried about the consequences of indulging in this sin, considering what God had done to Onan. But I wasn't concerned enough to stop—I was a regular boy, and my feelings were normal human feelings. But my Christian faith generated shame and silence. I kept my sexual thoughts and actions secret.

In front of *other* Christians, I was as good as gold and thoroughly acted the part of a sincere and obedient believer. What I didn't realize at the time was that I was experiencing what psychologist and cult expert Dr. Robert Jay Lifton calls "doubling," which is the act of creating a parallel religious self alongside one's authentic self.[1]

By all appearances, I was as virtuous a Christian as any of my contemporaries. My classmates and I sang all the classic Sunday School songs with gusto. And I can vividly recall most of the words. "I'm in the Lord's army...YES, SIR!" we'd shout out as loudly as we could as we marched in time with the song and gleefully acted out all its various parts.

I vividly remember winning many *sword drill* competitions in Sunday School. A sword drill is a contest to find a Bible verse the fastest. To begin, all the students must hold their Bibles upright on their desks, clasping the cover with both hands. The spine of the book must rest firmly on each learner's desk. When everyone is ready and patiently waiting, the teacher calls out a Scripture verse reference and shouts, "Go!" The more obscure and harder to find the verse, the better. Old Testament minor prophets are among the favorite verses for this competition because hardly anybody ever reads them, and they're challenging to locate.

The point of the exercise is to be the first one to find the verse and read it aloud. I won many sword drills because I had earned a gold star in Sunday School for memorizing the names of all sixty-six books of the Bible in their correct order. This helped me find verses faster than anyone else. I knew exactly where all the books were, both in the Old and New Testaments. I added many gold stars next to my name on the board on the wall that listed the sword drill champions. Our Sunday School teachers said that according to Paul in Ephesians 6, the "Sword of the Spirit" is the Word of God. As Christians, we needed to know how to use all of it—including the minor prophets.

In addition to the books of the Bible, I earned many gold stars for memorizing multiple Scripture verses and received a few more for not missing a single Sunday School class for an entire year.

I once earned the princely sum of one dollar, paid by my dad, for memorizing all the verses of the 13th chapter of 1 Corinthians, the so-called "Love Chapter." After spending weeks working on it, one night, I proudly recited it to him without making a single mistake. I suppose this was his way of motivating me. David says in Psalm 119, "I have hidden your word in my heart that I might not sin against you."[2] By that logic, I should have been an absolute saint with all the Bible verses I had "hidden in my heart" over the years. But I was far from it!

---

1   Robert Jay Lifton, "Cult Formation," *The Harvard Mental Health Letter* Volume 7, Number 8 (February 1981).

2   Psalm 119:11, NIV.

Chapter Seven

Not Even the Muppet Show Was Safe

C hildren tend to adopt the same religion as their parents. One's religious preference also greatly depends on the part of the world where one is born and the dominant religious practices in that part of the world.

If I had come from India, I most likely would have been a Hindu or a Sikh. If I were from the Middle East, I probably would have been a Muslim. I likely would have been a Buddhist if I'd been born in China or Nepal. But since I was born in America to a Christian family and raised within an evangelical context, I became a Christian. Where I was born and the family I was born into meant that I lived in a Christian bubble. And like other young children, I didn't have the critical thinking skills or the context to doubt or question what I was taught.

My Christian bubble surrounded my church, my school, summer camp, and my home. If I had questioned whether this was a good or bad thing, my fellow believers would have explained that constantly being around other saved folks was all to the good. Why? Because of the positive influences of Christian fellowship and our church community on my young Christian life. In this bubble, we were supposed to be sheltered from the evils of secular humanism and its corrupting effects. My parents diligently tried to protect us from the dangers of the world. For example, we grew up without a TV in our house. We were only allowed to listen to Christian or classical music—absolutely no rock n' roll or secular music of any kind could be played in the house or car.

My dad had an extensive collection of vinyl LPs, and we could listen to them anytime without fear of getting into trouble. Of course, they were all pre-approved. They were either Christian music, family comedy records like Stan Freberg or Spike Jones, classical music, or my dad's preferred genre—country gospel. I recall being embarrassed by him every year as he forced us to attend concerts of the country gospel group The Crossroads Quartet, one of his all-time favorite acts. He'd bring his prized Bell and Howell cassette tape recorder with a little microphone and record the entire show. That way, he could listen to it repeatedly in the car while commuting to and from work.

Dire punishments awaited us if we broke the rules about listening to secular music. If my parents caught us listening to any radio stations other than the local Christian one, we'd get an immediate spanking. I vividly recall that when we were finally old enough, my mom would leave my sister Beth and me home alone while she ran errands. It was one of the first tastes of independence my sister and I experienced. Of course, we abused our newfound freedom to engage in "sinful" activities. The second Mom drove away, and we knew we were in the clear, we'd blast a rock n' roll station on the radio. Uninhibited, we'd dance all over the house, reveling in our all-too-brief moments of madness and rebellion. Since our hi-tech intercom radio had speakers upstairs, we could run all over the house and not miss a second of whatever "illicit" song we were listening to.

But we had to be extremely careful. It was essential not to get caught up in the moment and forget how long Mom had been gone. One of us would start keeping watch around the time we expected her back. Whoever was watching would frantically shout out a warning that Mom's car had been spotted rolling down our steep driveway. Knowing we had seconds to spare, in a blind panic, we would race to the radio, put it back on the Christian station, and switch it off. All this was done with seconds to spare. We would then dive onto the couch, pick up the nearest book or Bible, and act like we'd been innocently perusing pre-approved reading materials the entire time she'd been gone.

We knew there might be a price to pay if we hadn't been careful enough. As her first task upon entering the house, Mom always checked the radio dial. If the station wasn't quite right—a little too much static—or even if she suspected we'd been messing with the dial, we would get an immediate spanking. No matter what we said in our defense, it didn't matter as long as she even suspected we'd been listening to evil rock n' roll.

One summer, when I was ten, and Beth was eleven, we stayed with my grandparents on my dad's side for a week. To keep us busy while they were packing for an upcoming move, my grandmother gave each of us a little battery-powered transistor radio to listen to during the week. We were pleasantly surprised when, at the end of our visit, she said we could keep them as presents. Overjoyed with delight at receiving these prohibited gifts, we didn't even think to hide them from our parents. That was a huge mistake.

The second we arrived home, our mother rifled through our bags and confiscated the transistor radios. How did she know to check our bags? My grandmother may have slipped up and told my mom about giving us the radios. I have no idea what happened to them. We never saw them again. Afterward, we kicked ourselves that we hadn't thought far enough ahead to sneak them into the house. But even if we had managed to hide the radios, if we had been caught listening to them at any point, the inevitable outcome would have been a spanking, followed by the seizure of the "illegal" items. We would have been in even worse trouble.

It wasn't just music on the forbidden list of secular influences. Since we didn't have a TV in our house, the only television we were allowed to watch was *The Muppet Show* on Friday nights from 7:30-8:00 PM at our other grandmother's house just up the street. The second the show ended, we had to hotfoot it out the door because we would receive a spanking if we weren't home promptly by 8:05 PM.

There was always the exceptionally slim chance that my folks would let us stay a bit longer, but asking for an extension was risky. Beth called home on many a Friday at 8:00 PM to beg our parents to allow us to watch just one more show. But the answer was almost always a firm, "No, come home immediately." On rare occasions we were allowed to stay for another thirty minutes, and afterward, we had to double-time it down the street. If we weren't home promptly by 8:35, the result was an immediate spanking.

Our beloved TV-watching adventure ended after Alice Cooper appeared on *The Muppet Show* in October of 1978, performing *Welcome to My Nightmare*. He came out dressed as Dracula, accompanied by skeletons, skulls, and swirling ghosts. When he performed "School's Out," he appeared in a red jumpsuit with a devil's tail and cavorted around onstage with monsters. My parents later heard about his performance. They were outraged and immediately forbade us to watch the show ever again. Thus, even our sparse thirty minutes of weekly TV watching was forever denied since it appeared that *not even The Muppet Show was safe.*[1]

On rare occasions, we went to see a movie. But the only movies we were allowed to watch were G-rated Disney family films. No consideration was given to viewing a PG movie, much less an R-rated one. We enjoyed such classics as *Herbie the Love Bug*, *The Jungle Book*, and *The Apple Dumpling Gang*. My parents considered these and others like them to be wholesome films for the entire family, so we were on safe ground watching them. As with all their parenting actions, my dad and mom believed they were doing what was necessary to protect us from the evil influences of the secular world.

What might happen if we foolishly allowed any of these corrosive worldly elements to infect our lives? Spanking, it seemed, was my parents' answer to everything. They firmly believed that corporal punishment would not only drive the bad influences from our hearts and minds but would also deter us from straying into future sins. Spanking was another way of protecting us from evil.

But all those spankings didn't work as intended. From the ages of around eight to twelve, my sister Beth and I were typically spanked two to three times a day, and sometimes more. This high dosage of spankings did nothing to stop us from acting out and being naughty. Even my parents admitted this. But I saw no evidence that they ever questioned the efficacy of what is now, in my view, tantamount to both physical and emotional abuse.

No one in our church knew how things truly were at our house. In the same way I played the "doubling" game with my two identities, my family also had a private and a public face. Things were frequently well below the idealized Christian standards at home, but our family always looked great in front of the church. In the public eye, ours was a model Christian family, and my parents had a loving and godly marriage. My parents were pillars of the church. Dad played piano, led worship, and was an elder until he resigned when Valerie got pregnant. Mom taught Sunday School, and together they led the youth group for several years. Our family seldom missed a church service, and when we were on vacation, we always made the effort to attend a local church if we were away on a Sunday.

Although my parents believed they were protecting us from worldly influences, their actions fit the description of classic cult tactics and psychology. Earlier I mentioned Hassan's BITE Model™ of authoritarian control.[2] I consider what my parents did to be another clear case of how elements of this model were used on us. The effort to shelter us kids by our parents, church, and Christian school fit into the realms of behavior and information control. In addition to controlling what we wore, our hairstyles, and how we acted, we were "protected" from exposure to alternative points of view. Therefore, we were denied the experience of learning to think critically for ourselves. In this atmosphere, conforming to the expected outward appearances and adherence to the prescribed behaviors were equated with "being a good Christian."

The version of fundamentalist Christianity to which we were exposed was but one option from a wide variety of Christian traditions and the views and practices of other religions. But since ours was the only version we knew, it was therefore regarded as "the truth." Information about different points of view was denied to us. It's easy to understand how so many good Christian kids go off to college or university and end up questioning, deconstructing, and often leaving their faith when they discover, to their shock, that their narrow, sectarian worldview is far from the only viewpoint out there.

The notion that I was living in a controlled environment never occurred to me—not ever. The bubble was in place year-round, even in the summertime. My church buddies and I attended Christian summer camp each year. We responded to many speakers' calls to follow or recommit to God during the summer camp services. We dutifully pledged and re-pledged to serve, obey, and love God with all our hearts. Even though I'm not sure now that I knew exactly what it meant, I made many firm and renewed commitments at camp to "Make Jesus the Savior and Lord of my life." The camp preachers confidently proclaimed that constantly reaffirming these commitments would ensure that "Jesus was truly seated on the throne of our hearts."

Looking back on it all as an adult, I am struck by how desperately I wanted to make sure I got everything about my commitment to Jesus exactly right. I wanted Jesus to be seated on the throne of my heart, even though I wasn't sure what that abstraction meant as a young boy, later, as a teenager, and even as an adult.

In my religious bubble, getting everything right included staying separate from the evils of the secular world. And when even The Muppet Show isn't safe to watch, you can never be too careful!

---

1   Ironically, decades later, I played drums in a heavy rock and metal cover band where I live in North Wales in the United Kingdom. One of our signature tunes was "School's Out," and I always got a small malevolent feeling of pleasure every time we performed that Alice Cooper classic. Take that, Mom and Dad!

2   Freedom of Mind Resource Center, "BITE Model™ of Authoritarian Control."

Chapter Eight

Rapture Anxiety Is Hard to Beat

C oming home to an empty house when I was twelve and fearing the Rapture had occurred didn't come out of nowhere. Watching the end-times movie *A Thief in the Night* three times had terrified me and lit a fire under me to officially give my life to Jesus and get baptized when I was ten. I didn't want to be left on Earth when the Rapture took place.

But the fear of being left behind eventually returned. Constantly lurking in the back of my mind was the fear that I wasn't a true Christian. What if I had just gone through the motions? What if I had failed to meet some requirement I was unaware of? I lived in a state of constant dread that I would be left behind if the Rapture occurred during my lifetime.

In everyday conversations, "rapture" refers to a feeling of intense pleasure or joy. "Elation," "bliss," and "euphoria" qualify as synonyms. But in the vocabulary of many evangelical Christians, it's "the Rapture" with a capital R. The Rapture is a promised future event when—without warning—true Christians will be snatched up into heaven. Believers who are alive at the time of the Rapture will skip death and go straight "up" to be with Jesus.

The storyline of the movie, *A Thief in the Night*, follows the horrifying fate of all the unfortunate people who are left behind after the Rapture. Christ returns to Earth when everyone least expects him and takes all true believers with him to heaven. There is no confusion about why the rest of humanity was left behind. They missed the Rapture *because they were not true believers.* The film's title track, written by legendary Christian rocker Larry Norman, was fittingly called *I Wish We'd All Been Ready.* It describes the chilling fate of those who were not ready when Jesus returned, and the words haunted me for years afterward. The song contains a description of what life would be like after the Rapture:

> A man and wife asleep in bed,
> She hears a noise and turns her head.
> He's gone.
> I wish we'd all been ready.

> Two men walking up a hill,
> One disappears, and one's left standing still.
> I wish we'd all been ready.

> There's no time to change your mind.
> The Son has come, and you've been left behind

> Life was filled with guns and war,
> And everyone got trampled on the floor.
> I wish we'd all been ready.[1]

The opening scene of the movie takes place at the exact moment of the Rapture, as non-believers are suddenly abandoned to face an awful existence without God. The main character, Patty, wakes up one morning to discover her devout Christian husband mysteriously absent. News of the Rapture is blaring on her radio. Her Christian friends and family have suddenly vanished, just as described in Norman's song.

The individuals left behind face the horror of seven years of worldwide tribulation. The world's leadership is in the hands of the sinister, pitiless forces of the Antichrist, together with the aid of the mysterious "Beast," although nobody, even theologians, seemed to know what the Beast was. The Antichrist was a puppet of Satan himself.

In the days when *A Thief in the Night* and the three equally terrifying films that followed in the series were being shown in churches, rumors and conspiracy theories swirled around the evangelical world. Many Christians firmly believed that the Antichrist was alive somewhere in the world. Word was that he was living in hiding, being trained for his leadership role by the Illuminati, a covert and shadowy society of powerful individuals who secretly controlled the world. The Antichrist was biding his time, waiting for his moment of triumph when he would take over the world and establish a "New World Order."[2]

Immediately following the Rapture, God would rain down increasingly harsh and devastating plagues upon a world filled with people who had rejected Jesus. This time of tribulation would continue for seven years and would culminate with the triumphant return of Jesus to a world in ruins. Christ's mighty angelic army would defeat Satan and his demonic hordes at the battle of Armageddon, which would take place at Megiddo in Israel. The inevitable final judgment of God would follow this victory as all humanity stood before his Great White Throne. All nonbelievers would be consigned to the flames of hell, where they would be tormented forever, screaming and suffering in unspeakable agony. The righteous would enter an eternity of bliss with God in heaven, walking on streets of gold and living in heavenly mansions.

Years later in Bible college, I learned that the movie's theology was based on "premillennial eschatology." *A Thief in the Night* and the other movies in the series described what theologians call a pre-tribulation, premillennial view of the return of Jesus. Other Christian groups espouse a mid-tribulation or a post-tribulation view of the Rapture—if they believe in the Rapture at all. I also learned that not all Christians agreed with the premillennial approach. Christians from different traditions held what could be radically different views of the end times. The premillennial position was one way to interpret end-times apocalyptic books like Revelation and Daniel in the Bible. The two other primary schools of thought on what theologians referred to as "eschatology"—the doctrine of the last things—were known as *amillennial* and *postmillennial eschatology*. Christians of different persuasions often argued their positions on the return of Jesus vehemently, firmly convinced that views other than their own were radical misinterpretations of the Bible, if not outright heretical teachings.

But I knew nothing of these theological distinctions when I saw *A Thief in the Night* as a boy. I was "safe" in my Christian bubble. I had neither the intellectual capacity nor the necessary theological, historical, or biblical information to question any aspect of what I was being taught. Living in this Christian "parallel universe," I was vaguely aware that there were other believers who held differing views. Years later in Bible college, I was shocked to learn that there were *credible* arguments, based on Scripture, for views radically different from what I had been taught. I felt angry that so much information had been withheld from me by people I trusted.

A Thief in the Night made it clear that if you repented and became a Christian just 1 *minute after* the Rapture, you were still doomed to experience the terrors of the tribulation. Those who became Christians after the Rapture would be ruthlessly hunted down by the all-powerful forces of the Antichrist. If caught, they would face prison, torture, and—if they refused to recant their faith—beheading by a guillotine in a public square. I wasn't sure whether those who became Christians after the Rapture would make it to heaven, probably because the movie didn't make that clear.

The only thing that made sense was to choose *now* while there was still time. I remember listening to a fiery fundamentalist preacher speak in a revival service. At the conclusion of his sermon, he shouted to the audience that our only two options in life were to "*turn or burn!*" I took his message to heart because I didn't want to burn in hell for eternity.

One of the most problematic images that haunted me from the film was the portrayal of a liberal preacher. Before the Rapture, in front of a packed church, he was peddling a watered-down, feel-good, "everyone-will-go-to-heaven" universalist gospel. But the liberal pastor was shocked that he was not taken up to heaven when the Rapture occurred. According to the theology of the movie, *liberal Christians were not true believers and would be left behind when the Rapture took place.* Seeing the error of his ways following the Rapture, this minister deeply regretted pushing his wishy-washy gospel. After the Rapture, he repented and started preaching some good old fundamentalist hellfire-and-brimstone sermons. But now, his fiery sermons echoed pointlessly inside an empty church building. It was exactly like the Beatles song "Eleanor Rigby" describing Father McKenzie, writing the words to a sermon no one would hear.[3]

One of my Sunday School teachers taught us that the Holy Spirit would leave the Earth immediately after the Rapture. The Bible clearly teaches that the Spirit is instrumental in a person's coming to faith in Jesus, so it was hard to see how anyone could be saved after the Rapture. For the preacher portrayed in the movie, abandoning a liberal gospel and adopting what seemed to be an accurate, Bible-based approach was of questionable value when it came to his eternal destiny. One thing was certain. Even if he did have some thin hope of making it to heaven, he still had to endure seven years of hardship, tribulation, and misery on Earth. Since the masses of real Christians had been swept up to heaven in the Rapture, he had no faithful congregation to come and hear his sermons. As a result, the forces of the Antichrist deemed him harmless and left him alone to preach to his empty church. Their main objective was to hunt down those rebellious people who—though not professing belief in Jesus—had refused to receive the Mark of the Beast.

Although the minions of the Antichrist decided to ignore the liberal preacher, for others who became Christians after the Rapture—or refused the Mark of the Beast—one's fate would be horrific if captured by these satanic forces. In the movie, most of the world's population chose to follow the herd mentality and passively received the Mark of the Beast.

According to the book of Revelation, during the end times, you couldn't buy or sell anything unless you had this mark. The movie portrayed the mark as a tattoo on the hand or forehead, but that was just a guess. Nobody knew exactly what the Mark of the Beast was, but wild speculation combined with conspiratorial thinking provided a wealth of answers. Many believed it had something to do with the "cashless society" supposedly prophesied in the Bible. As a result, debit cards were suspect when they first came out. According to Revelation, the Mark of the Beast had something to do with the number 666. For some reason, this led to the belief that bar codes—when they first appeared on products in stores—were a precursor to the apocalypse. If you received the mark in the New World Order set up by the Antichrist, no matter what you said or did afterward, you would never enter heaven.

Most premillennial end-times experts were convinced that "The Beast" was an incredibly powerful supercomputer. The technology was all in place, but the time wasn't right for it to come online just yet—that would happen during the New World Order. Since Brussels was the European Union capital, end-times junkies speculated that the Beast computer would be located there. During the end-times mania inspired by *A Thief in the Night* and, later, the *Left Behind* books and movies, many evangelicals held to this belief that the Beast supercomputer was in Brussels. This powerful computer would contain a database that would be used to track down and seize Christians from all over the world once the Antichrist began his reign. The Beast's ultra-powerful computing abilities would also assist the Antichrist in monitoring economic activity worldwide once humanity had accepted the Mark of the Beast. Over and over, evangelicals bought into all manner of apocalyptic conspiracy theories—hook, line, and sinker. This Christian paranoia was fueled by works such as Hal Lindsey's bestselling book, *The Late Great Planet Earth,*[4] end-times prophecy conferences, and dark rumors about the coming end of days that swirled around churches nationwide.

Why would anyone, I wondered, choose to be left behind when the Rapture occurred, especially when it would be so easy to believe in Jesus now? Why would anyone want to spend the seven years of tribulation wondering if repentance and faith still worked as a pathway to heaven, all the while enduring the hideous events predicted for the tribulation years—awful events to be followed by an eternity in hell?

A Thief in the Night promoted a very clear theology: To be taken to heaven when the Rapture took place, *you had to believe all the right things.* Like that foolish preacher, if you fell into the trap of liberal theology, you were gambling with not just your life on Earth. You were betting on a high-stakes wager with God, and your eternal destiny was on the line. Since the risks were so great, getting everything right while you still had the chance was of utmost importance. Missing the Rapture and facing the horror of the seven-year tribulation was too awful a fate to contemplate—not to mention the likelihood of hell after that. But how could you know for sure that you believed precisely the right things? What if you got it wrong?

For years after seeing *A Thief in the Night*—three times no less—even after being baptized, I was utterly terrified by the possibility that I might be left behind when the Rapture occurred. It seems strange to think that a *movie* could influence me to get baptized and that its message would haunt me for years afterward. Reflecting on it now, as I described in the Preface, I can see that I suffered from Rapture Anxiety. Rapture Anxiety is an element of Religious Trauma Syndrome. I felt like a soldier in a combat zone, anticipating death and destruction at any moment. I lived in a state of constant anxiety and terror. Jesus could return at any second, which made the stakes incredibly high. It's easy to see why RTS is a form of PTSD and can require therapy to recover from its effects.

In those early years after I was baptized, sometimes, I wondered if I was a true believer, but at other times—because of the contrast between my religious and private personas—I was confident that I was not a true Christian. I believed that God sees and knows everything, and that included my thoughts. As David says in the Psalms, "Where can I go from Your Spirit? Or where can I flee from Your presence?"[5] You know when I sit down and rise up and, moreover, "you understand my thoughts from afar."[6]

In Sunday School, I memorized Jeremiah 17:9: "The heart is deceitful above all things, and desperately wicked: who can know it?"[7] I understood that my heart was deceitful and desperately wicked, and I knew the futility of pretending. I'd also memorized the Proverb, "Trust in the Lord with all your heart and lean not on your own understanding."[8] I knew that I could trust neither my own emotions nor my sinful heart. I might be able to fool everybody around me and convince them that I was a true Christian, but God knew the truth.

I was hounded by the fear that if Jesus suddenly came back, all my family would be whisked away to be with Jesus in heaven forever—without me. Hopefully, you can now better understand the story I told in the Preface about coming home and thinking the Rapture had occurred. That event was far from the only time this oppressive fear stalked me like a hungry wolf.

Yes, I had been baptized, and yes, I had been reassured by Pastor Jerry that I was a true Christian. But I was still plagued with doubts. I wanted to be entirely sure I would not be left behind. I figured the best way to play it safe would be to cover my bases regularly. Weekly, if not daily, I would re-pray the "sinner's prayer." In a desperate effort to rededicate my life to him, I would repent and beg God to forgive me of my many sins. After such prayers, I always asked Jesus to come into my heart, thinking that in this way, I could ensure he was truly the "Lord of my life."

I wanted to be entirely sure that I was a Christian. By praying the sinner's prayer daily, I figured, if the Rapture did occur, I would be taken up to heaven. I wouldn't be left to the cruel fate of enduring the tribulation. I must have prayed that sinner's prayer thousands of times. To be one hundred percent certain I was saved, every time there was an altar call at summer camp, I went forward to "recommit my life to the Lord."

I had heard a preacher at summer camp give a "good news-bad news" type of sermon based on a passage in the third chapter of 1 Corinthians. He explained how the Apostle Paul paints a vivid picture of what happens to believers after they die and are waiting to get into heaven. Paul claims that a test of "purifying fire" would be applied to all those lined up to enter heaven. Those who had been good Christians all their lives and had diligently stored up good works during their lifetimes had nothing to worry about. "Gold, gems, and precious stones" would be theirs to cherish for eternity in their mansions in the clouds. The purifying fire wouldn't destroy these quality items. They would survive intact into eternity. This was the good news, claimed the preacher.

He went on to state that there would also be some bad news. Those who had been lackluster, lukewarm Christians would squeak into heaven by the skin of their teeth. They would have no rewards laid up to enjoy. All the "wood, hay, and straw" of their worthless deeds would be consumed by the purifying fire on Judgement Day, leaving them with virtually nothing going forward into eternity. I figured that if I made it into heaven, I was likely to fall into that second category—no enduring treasures for me! I wondered what an infinity in heaven would look like without any lasting rewards—not a fun way to spend eternity.

Was there such a thing as a homeless heavenly beggar wandering the streets of gold with a cup in hand, begging for a holy handout? That might just be me if I was lucky enough to sneak through the Pearly Gates. The preacher painted a stark contrast between the two types of saints by comparing the worthless Christians to those who had clearly been better believers while on Earth. These virtuous Christians spent their lives selflessly serving God, never considering temporal rewards. In this way, the preacher asserted, these right-minded believers had sent ahead a load of "precious gems" to enjoy forever in paradise.

The preacher concluded his sermon by stating that the bad news wasn't *completely* bad. He finished by proclaiming, "Even a street-sweeping toilet scrubber in heaven, living in a tarpaper shack instead of a beautiful mansion, will be far better off than those poor unfortunates enduring eternal agony in the flames of hell. At least you will be sweeping streets of gold, which will be a far better eternal fate than screaming in unspeakable pain forever!"

As I listened to that sermon, I was convinced that most of what I'd been doing as a Christian up to this point in my life fell into the wood, hay, and straw category. Even though I'd been baptized, I felt horrible about what a lukewarm, lackluster Christian I was. When the sermon ended and the preacher invited us all to rededicate our lives to Christ, I offered up a heartfelt prayer. I promised to mend my ways in an effort to try and do better for God. I pledged to read my Bible daily, to keep it dust-free through constant use, and vowed to spend more time in prayer.

But a sense of nagging doubt and fear always lingered in my mind. I could never be one hundred percent certain that I was really saved. I might have slipped off the bubble somehow. I feared I would get left behind when the Rapture took place and be destined to face the entire seven years of tribulation. This would be followed by an eternity of torment in the flames of hell.

In the best-case scenario, I hoped I might qualify as a toilet scrubber or street sweeper in paradise. I held on to the slim chance that I could sneak through the Pearly Gates. In the worst-case scenario, I wouldn't be allowed inside and instead would be sent to hell. There seemed to be no such thing as "saved by grace through faith." For me, it was all about how I lived my life. What I did was more important than what I believed.

My church didn't help with my constant fears. If you sinned too much or backslid a little bit too far, could you lose your salvation? I wasn't sure. Recalling that Christian summer camp talk by Pastor Jerry around the campfire, I certainly did not want to be one of those coals that had fallen out of the fire and died out.

Chapter Eight

I adopted the theology of *A Thief in the Night*, but that left one question unanswered. If you missed the Rapture because you were not a Christian, you might attempt to become a believer later, but the movie didn't make it clear whether believing after the Rapture would get you to heaven. The film was crystal clear that missing the Rapture meant seven years of living in a dreadful, horrific state under the nightmare reign of the Antichrist. Missing the Rapture meant you were lost. You had been... *left behind.*

And there was no way to know when Jesus would return. You had to be always ready because you never knew the exact day or hour when Jesus would burst through the clouds. *Talk about emotional scarring and psychological trauma!*

———————

1   Larry Norman, "I Wish We'd All Been Ready," *Upon This Rock*, Capitol Records, 1969, (punctuation added).
2   I remember listening intently to Hal Lindsey, author of *The Late Great Planet Earth*, as he spoke on end-times prophecies at Calvary Fellowship in the mid-1980s. He confidently informed us that this event had something to do with the "revived Roman Empire" spoken of in prophetic biblical books like Daniel and Revelation. A vast number of Christians were alarmed when the European Union was established in 1993, believing that this watershed moment in world history was the precursor to the end of the world.
3   John Lennon and Paul McCartney, "Eleanor Rigby," *Revolver*, Capitol Records, 1966.
4   Hal Lindsey and Carole C. Carlson, *The Late Great Planet Earth* (New York: Bantam Books, 1972).
5   Psalm 139:7, NASB.
6   Psalm 139:2, NABRE.
7   Jeremiah 17:9, The Holy Bible, King James Version (KJV). Cambridge Edition: 1769; King James Bible Online, 2024. www.kingjamesbibleonline.org.
8   Proverbs 3:5-6, NIV.

Chapter Nine

Watching a Minister Crash and Burn

O ur Elder Board, the group my dad resigned from when Valerie became pregnant, was confident that a God-driven season of growth was in store for our church. The church members joined the Elder Board in optimistic anticipation about what God had in store for us. When I was eleven, several months after I was baptized in our church's small log building, the congregation had purchased a new lot down the street.

Having outgrown our smaller place of worship, it was time to construct a larger sanctuary to hold all the new converts God was preparing to send our way. The belief that new church members were coming our way was not just the result of the elders hearing God speak. Large housing developments were being built in the area, and the church needed to be ready to respond to people who would be moving in. The idea was that a newer, larger, modern structure would help attract new members. If we didn't build a new building, other churches would surely snatch up all those potential new converts. There was no way we could let that happen.

The new site was a heavily wooded two-acres. To pay for the new property and building, the church would use funds from the sale of our existing property plus funds accumulated after years of sacrificial giving for a new building.

Chapter Nine

Many church members volunteered to help clear the heavily forested land where our new building would stand. I spent many a Saturday on the site clearing brush and helping my dad cut up fir trees that had been felled by a logger, another member of our church. Occasionally, my dad would let me run the chainsaw. I thought this was cool, and my friends were green with envy. I also assisted in building the new church, which I enjoyed because I learned some valuable carpentry skills. The Elder Board must have saved tens of thousands of dollars on labor costs by tapping church members to do much of the construction work. None of us complained about the long hours. We were happy to serve God and we looked forward to helping expand his kingdom in our anticipated season of growth.

During this time, our church hired a dynamic minister named Mark who would serve as our youth pastor while also assisting Pastor Jerry and the congregation with this critical transition to a new location. Having recently graduated from Bible college, this was Mark's first assignment as a member of a local church staff. We knew him already since he had served as a counselor and worship leader for the Christian summer camp we attended.

Within a year we had a new sanctuary that was more than double the size of our original one. Surely with our new building and our additional minister, the church would now grow numerically, since nonbelievers would be getting saved, and Christians moving into the community would be joining.

Pastor Jerry seemed to be all-in for the move and the new building, but it turned out that not everything was fine in his life. Just a few months after we moved into the new building, I heard a rumor from my mother that he'd asked the Elder Board to let him take a sabbatical. He told them he was burned out from all the relentless work involved in overseeing the church relocation and the building program. Of course, this was in addition to all his regular weekly duties, which hadn't let up in the slightest. No wonder he was feeling exhausted. Apparently, Pastor Mark had not been as helpful as expected. The Elder Board flatly rejected Jerry's request, arguing that at their full-time jobs, they couldn't just take six months off work and "get paid to do nothing all day."

Shortly after making the sabbatical request to the Elder Board and having it rejected, Pastor Jerry resigned.

Decades later, as a pastor, I felt a lot of sympathy for what I had witnessed in Jerry's life and ministry. I, too, had the unfortunate experience of having to deal with tone-deaf elders who didn't have even a minimal understanding of the levels of stress pastors endure daily. In the view of many laypersons, the ministry is a nice, comfortable job, so why would anyone need a break from it, much less a sabbatical? Being a pastor can be—in many ways—one of the most thankless, exhausting vocations one can pursue. It's little wonder that so many pastors burn out and quit the ministry altogether.[1]

Everyone was shocked when Pastor Jerry abruptly walked away from the church. What was more surprising was that he also quit serving as a full-time minister and went to work for Alaska Airlines. My mother felt the Elder Board had given him a raw deal. He had served the church selflessly as the head pastor for over twenty years. As she saw it, the elders were too miserly and shortsighted to grant their minister a short respite to recharge his batteries. They may have been worried about what would happen if a visitor came to check out our church and the preacher in the pulpit was Pastor Mark who had a tendency to preach long and not-so-great sermons. Or, what if it was some other ineffective substitute for the full-time senior minister? All the time and money invested in a vision for growth could go down the drain without an able preacher in the pulpit.

From the elders' point of view, Jerry should have been more than grateful for all they had done for him. He either needed to put up or shut up. His response was to reject both options and walk away. My mom surmised that Jerry was probably happier working a secular job. He had better pay, shorter hours, less drama, fewer responsibilities, and free flight benefits.

The Elder Board was tone deaf to their own insensitivity. A few weeks after he gave his notice, we held a brief thank-you ceremony for Pastor Jerry one Sunday. We gave him some farewell cards with personal notes scribbled inside, said our tearful goodbyes, and wished him well in his new endeavors. And just like that, Pastor Jerry, who'd led the church for over two decades, was gone.

The church quickly moved on. We couldn't worry about our former pastor's new life once he was out of the picture. We were installed in our lovely new building. God's kingdom was on the move, and we were determined to be a part of it. We needed a new leader for our church. Surely, a dynamic preacher, someone unlike laid-back Jerry, would attract new converts.

---

1   According to a 5-year study conducted by the Hartford Institute for Religion Research, they have noted the following trend: "The further we are from the onset of the COVID-19 pandemic, the more we observe larger percentages of clergy pondering alternatives to their present congregation, vocation, or both. In the Fall of 2023, over half of religious leaders (53%) have seriously considered leaving pastoral ministry at least once since 2020... This is nearly 20% more clergy than in 2021 when 37% reported having such thoughts since 2020. (These findings parallel those by Barna Research.) Similarly, in the Fall of 2023, close to half (44%) of religious leaders have seriously considered leaving their current congregation at least once since 2020. This has more than doubled as only 21% of leaders reported having this thought in 2021." (Source: "Exploring the Factors Contributing to Growing Clergy Discontentment," *The Hartford Institute for Religion Research*, https://www.covidreligionresearch.org/wp-content/uploads/2024/03/Clergy_Discontentment_Patterns_Report-compressed_2.pdf.

Chapter Ten

I Admired My Dad Until I Didn't

When I was twelve, my close relationship with my dad ended. We had been very connected before our falling out, and I loved spending time with him. But that all ended one fateful Saturday, timed virtually to the minute I stepped through our front door, returning home from a disastrous week at Christian summer camp.

After a long ride back from camp in the church van, I only wanted to get home and rest. I viewed our house as a haven, a place of refuge after having a difficult week at a camp that none of my church buddies attended. We had gone on vacation earlier that summer, causing me to miss the week I usually went to camp with my churchmates. This time around, I had no friends to pal around with. As a result, I spent an extremely lonely week as an outsider.

One camp counselor took pity on me and tried to include me in various activities, but for the most part, I wandered the campground alone, unable to break into any of the little cliques. There's nothing like a week of isolation, feeling like a stranger alone in the crowd, at the vulnerable age of twelve, to make a kid feel desperately miserable, hurt, and lonely.

Finally home after that painful week, I'd barely dropped my bags on the entryway floor when my dad came walking up from the downstairs porch of our split-level home. He took no notice of the downcast look on my face and how bedraggled I looked. The first words out of his mouth were: "Oh good, you're finally home. Now that you're here, you need to mow the backyard."

Incredulous and open-mouthed at what I could only see as a profoundly insensitive and utterly ridiculous command, I told my dad I was extremely tired and needed to rest before mowing the lawn. "Look, it's late afternoon now. Can't I mow the lawn tomorrow after I get a good night's sleep? Surely one day won't hurt," I pleaded. "Absolutely not. You need to get on it right now," he countered irritably. "This is one of your chores, and since you've been skylarking at camp all week, the lawn has gone untended. I don't care what you say. It's got to be done today!"

No matter what I said or how stubbornly I argued, Dad refused to listen to any point I made. Red-faced with anger, he finally ended the argument by pulling rank. Shoving his finger in my face, he shouted: "Now you listen to me. I'm sick and tired of your lame excuses. I'm your father. I'm the head of this house, and I'm ordering you to mow the lawn right now! If you keep arguing with me, you'll get a spanking. After that, you'll still have to mow the lawn. It's your decision. Do it with or without a spanking!"

Get a spanking and then mow the lawn afterwards with a sore backside. Or I could just mow the lawn now. The decision was a no-brainer. I had to obey his unreasonable command or risk getting a spanking. Either way, that lawn had to be mowed right then and there. I really had no choice in the matter. In a state of complete disbelief, I went to my room and changed into my work clothes, hurling my dirty camp clothes into the hamper as hard as I could while swearing under my breath.

I was bitterly angry, and I felt wholly powerless. Resigned to my fate, I went outside to get the lawnmower so I could start the arduous task. When I walked out the back door, I was shocked to see that the grass was over a foot tall. This would be an extra-long job because I would have to go over it twice. Our yard was huge. Typically, it took me two or three hours to mow and rake the lawn, but on this occasion, this job would take at least twice as long.

Slamming the back door shut, I stormed inside and angrily confronted my dad. "How come you didn't mow it during the week? You've been here the entire time while I've been at camp. Surely, you couldn't have failed to notice that it was getting so tall! Why didn't you do it? Now, you've left it to me, and it will take me hours!" Throwing up his hands, he responded, "Well, I wanted to mow it, but it rained several times during the week, so I couldn't do it because the grass was too wet. Plus, we had a lot going on at church. But the grass is dry now, and it's your job, so quit arguing with me and get to work."

I couldn't believe my ears. As I mowed, I was seething with resentment. I silently rehearsed all the arguments and counterarguments I should have spoken to my dad. How unfair it was! "Total bullshit!" was my bottom-line response.

After four hours of back-breaking work, I finally finished, got something to eat, took a shower, and fell into bed, completely exhausted.

Although neither of us knew it at the time, our disagreement on that fateful Saturday spelled the end of my relationship with my dad. Things were never the same again, and it was only years later that we could patch things up to some extent.

Looking back on what happened as an adult and a parent, the fact that we fell out so horribly was tragic and deeply ironic. I was the only boy and the youngest in a household with five older sisters. My parents always treated me differently because I was their firstborn son. My dad and I had been inseparable from day one. As a child, I was his little buddy, always glad to tag along with him on trips to the hardware or auto parts store or anywhere else he went. I didn't care what we did. It was just fun to hang out with him.

Dad was a computer engineer who worked as a software analyst at the Auburn Boeing plant. But he wasn't just a computer nerd with no practical skills. He was a good, all-around handyman, and I loved helping him with odd jobs around the house. Together with my Grandpa Joe, he and Mom built our house. From Dad, I learned to love building and making things with my hands. I've spent most of my adult life as a carpenter and builder, and those skills are directly tied to my dad's influence on my life all those years ago. He was also a decent mechanic and taught me a lot about repairing cars.

Why did this event lead to such a deep rift with my dad? It wasn't because he left, or I left. We both continued to live in the same house. He was a Christian, and I was too. We should have been able to work things out in love or at least forgive each other later, as the Bible commands believers in conflict to do.

Surely the whole thing could have been written off to a typical teenager with a piss-poor attitude and an overbearing, tone-deaf father. This sort of thing happens all the time in homes across the world. So why did our relationship irreparably break down over something seemingly so mundane as an argument over mowing a lawn?

Why could we never make full amends and be close again, like we were before?

Chapter Eleven

Incest Isn't Always About a Bed

T he truth was that the demise of my relationship with my father had been a long time coming. It was no accident. Several years before that Saturday afternoon lawn-mowing confrontation, when I was nine or ten, my mother had insidiously begun to poison my relationship with my dad. For years, she engaged in a form of emotional incest with me as she put my father down during my ongoing private conversations with her.

Frustrated, miserable, and unhappy in her marriage, she found in me a willing ear to unload her troubles. She confided that my father was—in her view—a complete and utter failure. As a husband, father, and spiritual head of the household, he'd fallen far short of the mark that the Lord intended for godly fathers and husbands, as both the Bible—and Bill Gothard—taught. She had nagged him to lead Bible studies with us kids for years, but he never did. He wouldn't even read a good Christian book and discuss it with her! As the submissive wife, she wasn't allowed to take up the mantle of leadership in the home. She just sat back and shook her head, embittered and angry at how disappointing he was.

These revelations came as shocking news to me. In my eyes, my dad was great. As his only son—indeed, as his little buddy—I loved him with all my heart and had no idea he even had flaws. But as the years passed, and my mom's steady drip of poisonous insider information went on, it started to distort my perspective regarding my father. Eventually, I, too, began to view him with contempt. How could he treat my mother, and for that matter my sisters, so poorly? Why was he such a failure? None of it made any sense. My mother's one-to-one put-downs of my dad, over time, did irreparable harm to my relationship with him.

Even before my mom started her emotionally incestuous talks, my relationship with my dad was on shaky ground after the whole Valerie debacle. I lost a lot of respect for him when I witnessed how he treated her so shamefully. Instead of compassion for her, it seemed to me he felt sorry for himself. He carried a lot of resentment against Valerie for forcing him to resign from his prestigious elder role at church.

Over time, it became clear to me that my mother was desperately unhappy, trapped in a loveless marriage. She chose to confide in me—her youngest child and the only other male in the family—rather than seeking marriage therapy or individual counseling. I am confident now that much of my mother's frustration with my father's ineffectual leadership, as well as her unhappy marriage, grew out of Bill Gothard's patriarchal teaching to which both my parents subscribed. They were in agreement on one thing: They tried to pattern their marriage and child-rearing according to Gothard's model.

According to Bill Gothard's interpretation of the Bible, the man is the head of both the home and the marriage. While he should listen to his wife's advice and counsel, the husband has the final say in all decisions. For her part, the wife has to submit joyfully to his spiritual leadership and headship—just as the church submits to Christ. This was all explained within the context of Gothard's "umbrella of authority" model. Gothard based his view on what he considered "God's design for the family" as laid out in places like

Incest Isn't Always About a Bed

Ephesians chapter 5 and elsewhere in Paul's writings.

The problem for my parents was that my mother was a very strong-willed person, whereas my dad was quite passive. Before adopting Gothard's patriarchal teachings, their marriage had apparently been stress-free, and each partner quite happily functioned in their respective roles according to their strengths and personalities. My sister Valerie recalls what life was like before they were sucked into the Gothard cult. From her viewpoint, they had what seemed like a reasonably contented marriage and a relatively peaceful home life.

But their roles were drastically altered once they began following Gothard's teachings. I suspect that deep down, neither of them wanted to embrace these new changes. But they were committed to living by the Bible's teachings, and Gothard was the authority, teaching his views as foundational, God-ordained principles. So, they had no choice but to shoulder their unwanted burdens and try day-by-day to fit into roles that fit neither of their personalities.

For her part, my mother unloaded her misery and frustration on me. And in some perverted sense, she must have been having some emotional need for a male listener met by her own son. That's why they call it emotional incest. For my part, I felt sorry for my mom as I came to realize that not only was she deeply unhappy but also that my dad was a profound failure as a husband, father, and spiritual head of the household. Perhaps this was why God didn't seem to bless our family as he should. Was it all my dad's fault?

No wonder my relationship with my dad collapsed. Under the malign influence of my mother's poisoning of our relationship, I'd already slowly started to pull away from him before the Saturday confrontation that became "the straw that breaks the camel's back."

Chapter Eleven

After we fell out, I stopped being his tag-along buddy. When he invited me to accompany him on an errand, I felt trapped. I desperately wanted to avoid spending time with him. I had no desire to engage in pointless small talk with him. I would try to devise some convincing reason why I couldn't go with him. After a year or so of this, he finally stopped asking me to go with him. I think losing his little buddy hurt him deeply.

Unfortunately, my father did not have the emotional capacity to sit down with me and talk things through or to ask me why I had grown so distant, both physically and emotionally. It just happened, and neither of us knew what to do about it. If we suspected that at least trying to talk might help, neither of us acted on it.

My father, my mother, and I formed a dysfunctional triangle set in motion by a revered Bible teacher named Bill Gothard.

Chapter Twelve

Subtract Two Friends Add One Bully

In the summer before I started the seventh grade, I was still struggling with my perceived failures at living the victorious Christian life. And it was that same summer when I experienced the breakdown of my relationship with my dad. But I focused on looking forward to the new school year.

My small Christian school had made some big changes. They were experimenting with mixed classes and different teachers, rather than having all students in the same grade sitting in a classroom with the same teacher all day. They were preparing us for the kind of schedule we would have in high school. I felt like I was growing up and was excited about learning different subjects from different teachers.

I started the school year on an emotional high. My best friends, brothers Mike and Carl, were just as enthusiastic about the upcoming year. I'd grown up with Mike and Carl from infancy at our church, and the three of us were inseparable. I'd frequently stay with them for a few days, or they'd come stay at my house. I went on vacation with them a few times in the summer, and we always had a blast playing together.

Mike and Carl's dad, Brian, was the caretaker at our Christian school. The school's campus had been an Army missile base in the Cold War era. All the buildings looked depressingly identical—one story tall, with cinderblock walls and flat roofs. Each room had the same metal-framed windows with wired safety glass. Mike and Carl's family lived on the school's campus in a small apartment that Brian had renovated, turning it into a cozy home.

I always looked forward to staying with my two best friends during the summer. We rode our bikes all around the empty campus and built increasingly dangerous jumps. Left to our devices all day, we did everything we weren't supposed to be doing. Clambering up with the aid of a ladder, we ran around on the flat roofs of the buildings. We explored the deserted side of the former base—off-limits behind a chain-link fence—which we were expressly forbidden to do. Typical kids, we had a great time doing all the things we weren't allowed to do during the school year. Helen, their mom, worked as the school secretary, and she tried to keep an eye on us during the day—but with little success.

As the three of us started the seventh grade together, we loved the new academic arrangements. Our new year was off to a great start!

Just like my family, viewed from the outside, Brian and Helen's relationship was a wonderful and godly marriage. Both active in church, Helen taught Sunday School, and Brian volunteered for many ministries. But it turned out that not everything was great in their marriage.

One day, just a few weeks into the start of seventh grade, Carl informed me—completely out of the blue—that he, Mike, and their mother were moving to Missoula, Montana. He dropped this bombshell news on a Wednesday, and by the following Saturday, just like that, they were gone. My best friends were suddenly ripped out of my life. After a tearful goodbye on Friday at school, that was it. *They moved, and I didn't see them until five years later.*

The strange thing was that the principal of our school—who everybody called "Mr. E"—had moved his family to Missoula earlier that summer. He'd taken a job there as principal of a Christian school. So why, of all places, would Helen move to Missoula just a few months later? Speculation and gossip at church went into overdrive. Had she been carrying on a secret affair with Mr. E.? People surmised that if the scandalous news broke, Mr. E. would lose everything. Perhaps he'd quickly left for Missoula to put some distance between himself and Helen. I never found out the truth, but the whole thing was certainly strange. Regardless of her reasoning, the snap decision tore her family apart, and devastated me too.

All that week, I begged God to intervene and do something to stop this shocking move from happening. Why, of all people, did *both* my friends have to go away? My parents even intervened, trying vainly to reason with Helen. Could Mike and Carl come to live with us until they could at least finish the school year? After that, if she still wanted to live in Missoula, they could join her in the summer. With some time to reflect and think about it, maybe she and Brian could get back together. That would be the right thing to do. They informed her that Scripture makes it clear that God hates divorce, and Jesus forbade it in the Gospels. But Helen was adamant that she and the boys were leaving immediately. Her mind was made up. Just like that, they were gone.

The following Monday at school, I found myself alone with few friends. That was bad enough, but things took a turn for the worse a few months later. A new student named Bill started at our school. The story was that he'd had some issues at his former public school. Apparently, his parents decided to enroll him at our Christian school thinking that this new, stricter environment would straighten him out. The irony was that Bill wasn't a Christian, but the school turned a blind eye and accepted him as a student.

Bill's "issues" at the public school quickly revealed themselves after he started at our school. A bully, he loved nothing more than intimidating and beating up smaller, more vulnerable students. He was a big, strong kid with a dedicated mean streak. Suddenly exposed without any friends to protect me—which Mike and Carl would have done—Bill decided that I was his next target. For the rest of that school year, I was on the receiving end of verbal and physical harassment from Bill. This was an entirely new experience for me, and I hated it.

Chapter Twelve

After months of suffering his abuse, when I couldn't take it any longer, I finally went to my parents and told them what was going on. They confronted the new principal about the harassment, but he claimed it was just Bill's word against mine. Nothing was done to stop the bullying, and it began to affect my mental health. I dreaded going to school each day, filled with anxiety over what might happen. Some days were fine, but others were a living hell. Thanks to Bill's intimidation, verbal abuse, and threats of violence, seventh grade was one of the worst years of my life.

I wondered how God could allow this to happen to me. I'd lost my close relationship with my dad. A few months later, Mike and Carl had been torn from my life. And then, things only worsened, with Bill's incessant bullying and antagonism the rest of that school year. Wasn't my Christian school supposed to be safe? I was seeking God's power to overcome my sins and live a victorious Christian life. I was trying to read my Bible and pray daily, but there was no divine help forthcoming.

Where was God in all this? After the principal refused to help me with Bill, my mom tried to comfort me. She put her arm around me and said, "We don't always understand why these things happen to us as Christians. God's ways are higher than our ways, the Bible says. I know this has been a tough year for you. As I understand it, suffering and hardship are God's ways of testing, strengthening, and refining our faith and trust in him. Someday, you'll look back on this time and thank the Lord for allowing you to go through this tough period. Trust me, when you come out the other side, you'll be stronger than ever."

But her words were cold comfort. I was the one who had to go to school each day, without my close friends, to face Bill's bullying and harassment. I needed help *now*, and I couldn't understand why God was allowing this to happen to me. What had I done to deserve this? Was the Lord punishing me for my many sins—my hidden pornography magazines, the swearing, and all the other things I was doing in secret? Was this the God I wanted to serve? Is this how he does business with his devoted followers?

Chapter Thirteen

Living Under God's Umbrella

According to Bill Gothard, to experience success in the Christian life, one had to follow seven immutable principles. He taught that these guidelines were clearly revealed throughout the Bible. By living up to these seven principles, you would develop character traits that would make you a successful Christian, and you would be blessed mightily by the Lord. Gothard provided many examples of people who rebelled against God's way of doing things, both from the Bible and his own experiences. Over and over, he showed how disobeying these principles led to terrible consequences.

The foundation of Gothard's "seven principles for success" was *proper submission to God-ordained authorities*. And he promised that every obedient believer was under God's big umbrella of protection, blessing, and covering. Underneath Christ was the husband's smaller umbrella, followed by the wife's umbrella. The children were under all the umbrellas.

Every individual is required to submit to the God-ordained authority above them. Failure to submit meant big trouble. The diagram on the next page demonstrates how this " umbrella of protection" concept worked.

From Gothard's point of view, this entire concept was all a proven biblical construct. He found ample textual justification for his theological system explaining exactly how families should work and thereby dismissed concerns that his understanding might be hindered by the fact that he was single and had no children. A stream of parenting and marital advice flowed from this man, and thousands hung on his every word at his seminars. Worse, like my parents, they modeled their marriages and child-rearing practices on his teachings.

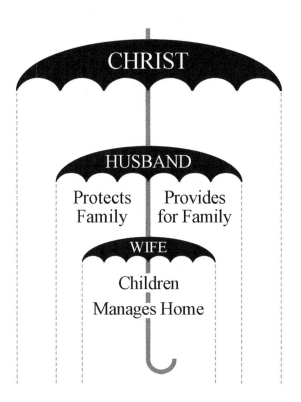

In the Gothard system, parents taught children that they were required to do everything possible to please the Lord, emphasizing such foundational activities as attending church regularly and faithfully worshiping God. Children needed to learn to obey God, and this obedience included diligently following all the Bible's teachings (according to Gothard's interpretation) and submitting to their parents. If they did all these things, the children would build godly character traits into their lives and would be perfectly safe under both their parents and God's umbrellas of protection. Moreover, in this "chain of command" structure, children would not only be safe, but God would also bless them.

What precisely this blessing entailed was never made clear, but Gothard envisaged a life including good health, safety, and material benefits bestowed by a generous God. Both personal and spiritual victory would inevitably follow from living your life according to Gothard's seven biblical principles. His was an evangelical formula for success, a new twist on the charismatic prosperity gospel, but without the supercars, flamboyant hairdos, and mega-mansions of the prosperity gospel preachers. However, Gothard enjoyed many benefits from the *Institute in Basic Life Principles* during his tenure as its head. Stories of Gothard and his brother Steve's misuse of ministry funds, facilities, and private jets for personal use broke in the early 1980s. Steve Gothard was credibly accused of grooming, controlling, and sexually abusing several female staffers, and the ensuing scandal nearly brought down the entire organization. Similar sexual abuse charges were made against Bill Gothard years later.

But those who followed Gothard's teachings didn't seem to be worried about his flying in private jets, and they did not—at least initially—know about the charges of sexual abuse. Nobody ever asked which authority Gothard was accountable to or where he stood in the umbrella scheme. He seemed to have a set of rules applicable only to him. People like my parents, siblings, and I were only interested in what would happen underneath the umbrella or away from its protective covering.

An obedient child would be safe, but what would happen next if a child made sinful choices and traveled down the wrong path? What if she started to rebel against her parents, and slid off into sin by not doing what they told her to do? Gothard stated that the consequences were dire since she removed herself from her parents' umbrella of protection by making these terrible choices. In so doing, she also moved out from God's larger umbrella. For biblical proof, Gothard cited the verse, "Rebellion is as the sin of witchcraft,"[1] to support this notion to demonstrate just how terrible even typical teenage rebellion was in the eyes of God.

The grievous sin of rebellion—tantamount to witchcraft—was an abomination in God's eyes and thus invoked his righteous wrath. The subsequent removal from the God-ordained umbrella system of protection would always lead to big trouble. Once this occurred, the wayward child was now fair game for Satan and his demonic hordes. Apparently, there was nothing the Lord could do about it. This child was now existing outside of God's umbrella of protection. Gothard unequivocally stated that if you made the foolish choice to step outside the umbrella of authority above you, at that point, there would be absolutely nothing to stop Satan from attacking your now-unprotected life.

The other, perhaps more disturbing, possibility was that God could do something about it. After all, wasn't he omniscient—all-powerful? Maybe he was letting the sinful individual get ripped to shreds by satanic forces to teach them a lesson about how wrong and sinful they were. In this way, the backslider would hopefully learn a painful lesson and return to the fold, duly chastened and repentant. As with everything within his system, Gothard provided extensive biblical precedent for his theology. In the Old Testament book of Job, for example, God allowed Satan free reign to destroy Job's entire life over a cosmic bet. It was clear that he could do the same to any of his children. Thus, evil and suffering in a Christian's life might be the result of demonic attacks, possibly sanctioned by the Lord himself. Perhaps the most disturbing aspect of Job's story is the fact that he never discovered the reason why he had endured such hideous suffering.

As a second illustration, the Old Testament makes it clear that God consistently punished the Israelites for failing to live up to the terms of the covenant every time they strayed into idolatry and other sins. According to this conditional contract, obeying the covenant brought blessing, whereas disobedience brought curses and judgment. Their covenant with Yahweh was essentially set up as a "reward and punishment" system. Ironically, a great many evangelicals view their relationship with God in the same way. Obedience should bring blessings. Sin and disobedience bring judgment. In this view, one's relationship with God resembles how Santa Claus operates. Good children get presents. Bad kids get nothing. The problem is this: What happens when that believer experiences suffering but has been a good Christian all along?

Such illustrations of how things work in God's economy aren't just drawn from the Old Testament. As a third example, in the New Testament book of 1 Corinthians, the Apostle Paul advised the Corinthian church to cast out a sinful believer from their congregation and to "hand this man over to Satan for the destruction of the flesh."[2] Apparently, it wasn't enough for Paul to give the man the boot and kick him out. Satan would now get involved in the situation, perhaps like he'd done with Job. Both the demonic assaults and the complete shunning he would experience from the congregation would convince the sinner of the error of his ways, and he'd come crawling back to God.

Gothard explained that God acts like a loving parent, disciplining and punishing those he loves. Therefore, it's for our own good that God brings suffering into our lives. Jesus taught in the Gospel of John that the Father is the wise and loving master gardener, pruning his children like a vine.[3] He's always busy, cutting out the bad parts of our lives, even if it's extremely painful at the time. We'll come to thank him for the suffering later when we understand why he did it. Hebrews 12:6 states, "For whom the Lord loves He disciplines, and He punishes every son whom He accepts."[4] God is portrayed as a loving father, and it's all for the good of his children. God does this to strengthen his children's faith and to teach them to trust him in tough times. Such teaching leads a great many evangelicals to have a genuinely warped theology of suffering. Everything that happens to them must have an explanation, a reason for why they are going through such a hard time–like I was with my dad, Mike and Carl leaving, and the bullying I'd experienced with Bill.

The story of the man in the church at Corinth, caught in a sexual sin, serves as a helpful case study regarding how this works. The shunning and demonic attacks he experienced were not the end of the story. There was a happy ending. According to 2 Corinthians, Paul's follow-up epistle to the church, the man had been shunned by the church and then apparently severely mauled by the devil. But hooray, after all that suffering and church discipline, he repented and wanted to rejoin the church! Given this new reality, it was now high time for the Corinthian congregation to welcome him back into the fold with open arms.[5]

Apparently, God conducts business by enforcing church discipline, hideous suffering, and demonic attacks upon his children to ensure they stay compliant and obedient. Like a cosmic mafia boss, these brutal methods appear to be the most effective way of forcing his followers to stay in line. It's a telling observation made by Dr Marlene Winell, a therapist and a survivor of fundamentalist religion, that for many evangelicals, their relationship with God is akin to that of an abusive partner.[6] The abuser beats and punishes his partner, inflicting great suffering on the other person. But in the end, the abuser always expects love, obedience, and blind subservience in return.

It appears to be a case of either carrot or stick when it comes to church discipline. If you are unlucky enough to be on the receiving end of church discipline, in addition to being shunned by your former friends and family in the church, Satan and his heavies will work you over until you can't take it any longer. Ideally, following this, you will repent and come crawling back, filled with regret and remorse. Then, and only then, should the church welcome you back. Until then, Paul advised the Corinthian church: "I wrote to you not to associate with any so-called brother if he is a sexually immoral person, or a greedy person, or an idolater, or is verbally abusive, or habitually drunk, or a swindler—not even to eat with such a person."[7] Utterly cut them out of your life. Shun the believer until they repent and beg to be allowed back into the church.

This is a clear example of Dr Robert Jay Lifton's markers of cults. He labels it "the dispensing of existence." It's all about how cultic or high-control religious groups engage in shunning a fellow believer. Once that backslider transgresses too far and breaks with the norms and teachings of the group or questions anything the leader says or does, he or she has no "right to exist." As a result, such individuals are often cut off from the group, shunned, or excommunicated.[8] Cult expert Dr Janja Lalich describes such practices as embodying a "self-sealing system." This is when a group or leader removes an offending member, but when they try to re-enter after expressing contrition, they discover the way is closed.[9] These are both are examples of how high-control groups and cults manipulate their adherents.

Making an example of a "backslidden" person, or anyone labeled a "troublemaker," is an excellent way to enforce control on those who stay within the system. Witnessing the brutal example made of the excommunicated sinner, the others vow that this will never happen to them. As a result, they remain compliant and rarely, if ever, question those in leadership, the teachings of the leader, or how things are done within the group—despite possible abuse and exploitation that may be occurring.

Such was the very abusive, controlling, and toxic theological system of my childhood. I can recall my mother explaining to me why Valerie was in the predicament in which she found herself in. By choosing to sin willfully, she had activated her own removal from underneath her umbrella of protection. She'd done this by engaging in the rebellious acts of sneaking out of the house, partying, and having unprotected sex with her boyfriend.

Getting pregnant, therefore, was nothing less than the divinely ordained consequence of her numerous transgressions. By removing herself from underneath the authority and protection of the umbrella system, she encountered the harsh reality of her sinful and rebellious activities. Satan's attacks on her unprotected life resulted in her getting pregnant out of wedlock and, by extension, shaming her loving family. One of the unintended consequences of her actions involved my dad stepping down as an elder at our church, which my parents interpreted as a significant win for Satan. Tempting Valerie into sin brought about the added result of taking a godly man out of church leadership due to the sinful activities of his daughter. Thus, for the devil, it was a win-win scenario.

To take it even one step further, Gothard cult theology majored on so-called "modesty culture." He taught that women are especially dangerous to men, tempting as they are with all their feminine wiles and sexual charms. According to the Apostle Paul in 1 Timothy 2:13-14, Eve, after all, had first eaten the forbidden fruit in the Garden of Eden and subsequently led Adam astray—and that hideous act of rebellion against God plunged all humanity into sin. Shortly before that statement, Paul mentions how important it is for women to dress chastely, a teaching picked up by Gothard and many others. Female modesty was a massive part of Gothard's teaching. Women had to be sure to dress and act decorously, or they would ultimately be responsible for leading a lustful man astray into sexual sin. Gothard called this "setting an eye trap" for a man. Thus, as Gothard interpreted it, the man who got Valerie pregnant wasn't to blame. Instead, it was her fault for inducing him into immorality.

Bill Gothard himself was eventually credibly accused of being a groomer and sexual abuser of numerous young women who worked for him at the IBLP headquarters. Although he stepped down as its head in 2014, to date, he has never been formally charged with these alleged abuses. Always blaming the woman encourages predators within churches. Nine times out of ten, the girl or woman will be blamed for "leading him astray" by allegedly dressing or acting provocatively. Such teachings create a culture rife with abuses, and sadly, we've seen it happen time and time again—as in, for example, the over seven hundred documented cases of clergy abuse within multiple Southern Baptist Convention churches nationwide.[10]

My parents manipulated the situation so Valerie would be forced to give up her baby for adoption. Part of their control was cruelly turning their backs and directing all the blame at her, booting her out of the house, and shoving her into foster care. The cruel, heartless decisions by my parents would all qualify as exposing her to hideous "punishment at the hands of the devil." Consistent with their literal biblical fundamentalist logic, perhaps they reasoned that once Satan finished with her, she'd come crawling back, duly repentant. She'd be just like the chastened sinner in the Corinthian church all those centuries ago, who had seen the error of his ways and wanted nothing more than to return to the fold.

According to the Gothard umbrella system, what should happen once Valerie had learned her lesson and paid the price for her sin? In the best-case scenario, she would voluntarily return to the safety of her parents' umbrella of protection. This would also place her safely underneath God's larger umbrella. Wouldn't that be the best place for her—or anyone, for that matter—to be? Gothard said this was the God-ordained situation for producing maximum spiritual success and divine blessings. Surely, the repentant sinner knew that being placed back under the umbrella of authority and protection was the best and the only place to be. And this is what Valerie was supposed to understand. Safely ensconced back under her parental umbrella of godly authority, she'd once again start to experience all the wonderful benefits that came along with it. And wouldn't her "loving" parents want Valerie to be back in such a position?

But one must ponder the question: Why would loving Christian parents knowingly remove their own daughter from underneath the umbrella of protection? If things were as bad out there as Gothard warned, rebellious sinners were open to satanic assault. Given this reality, then surely Valerie's loving parents would want to do everything in their power to keep her as safe as possible to spare her from horrific demonic attacks. Why would any genuinely godly parent want their child to be out from underneath their umbrella of protection for even a moment, let alone God's umbrella? What Christian parent, knowing that their child was out in the cold, would willingly and callously leave their child open to satanic oppression and assault? At the very least, on a human level, surely, knowing that this was their daughter unsafe out there in the unprotected world, they would welcome her back with open arms after the whole ordeal was done.

Speaking as a parent, I would want to protect my daughters as much as possible, despite what they may have done. But then again, the brutal, callous logic of church discipline applies here, too. Paul ordered the Corinthian church to shun the backslidden Christian as a means of chastisement that would hopefully lead to repentance. In addition to the dispensing of existence, this involves a third clear example of Dr Robert Jay Lifton's markers of cult practices entitled "doctrine over person." In other words, the doctrine and theology we are taught in our religion take precedence over personal relationships.[11]

Believers are empowered to close their hearts, ears, and eyes to the pain they are causing the other person so long as they can reassure themselves that they're doing what God expects. Whatever painful emotions the other person feels, the hurt and discomfort they're experiencing because of our cruel actions, are justified when we tell ourselves: "I'm doing the right thing. It's what God wants me to do." We reason that, like Paul's example of the shunned believer in Corinth, it may serve as an example to others. Surely, isn't it for the best that one person suffers so that others aren't tempted to be led astray and fall into sin?

What happened after Valerie gave up her baby for adoption? Did my parents welcome her back with open arms, like the repentant prodigal son of Jesus's parable? As loving and godly parents, why not take the first opportunity to tuck her back underneath that umbrella of their own—and perhaps more importantly—God's protection? Wouldn't that be best for all concerned? Why would any loving Christian parent leave their own child out in the cold, unprotected by God from the schemes and attacks of the devil?

One would surely conclude that this would be the logical application of the Gothard umbrella system of theology. As egregious as his initial sin was, 2 Corinthians makes it clear that even the church in Corinth welcomed that repentant man back into the community after he'd been shunned and then battered by Satan for a while. Surely, my parents would do the same and welcome Valerie back home after her traumatic ordeal. It would be the right thing to do, on every possible level, both as parents and as Gothard-style Christians.

Unfortunately, this was not what happened. Shortly after enduring the trauma of watching her daughter being whisked away to be adopted by new parents that she wasn't allowed to meet, Valerie called from the hospital to see if she could come back home. She had nowhere to live, no job, no money, and nowhere to go. She was eighteen years old. My mom's response was to inform her coldly, "You made your bed. Now lie in it." Then, Mom hung up on her.

Ultimately, Valerie's best friend's mother—who was not a Christian—demonstrated far more Christian charity and compassion than our parents. This woman took Valerie into her home, bought her new clothes, helped her land a job, and found her a place to live. While my parents continued to shun her, this non-Christian family assisted Valerie in the difficult task of getting back on her feet. My loving Christian parents, by contrast, continued to steer clear, giving Valerie nothing but the cold shoulder.

One must wonder what my parents thought their snubbing of Valerie would achieve. At no point did they appear willing to forgive and forget. I recall my mother once informing me that Valerie giving up her daughter for adoption was the best possible outcome since she'd gone to a good and loving Christian home. My niece's conservative Christian adoptive parents would give her a far better life than Valerie could ever hope, so things worked out for the best for all parties concerned. This was despite all the emotional damage and psychological trauma my parents inflicted upon their child through their cruel and heartless actions. From their point of view, the end justified the means. If a particular goal is morally important enough, any means of achieving it is justifiable.

1   1 Samuel 15:23, KJV.
2   1 Corinthians 5.5, NIV.
3   John 15:1-5.
4   Hebrews 12:6, NASB.
5   2 Corinthians 2:6-8.
6   Marlene Winell, "Religious Trauma Syndrome," JourneyFree.org, referenced July 29, 2024, https://www.journeyfree.org/rts/.
7   1 Corinthians 5:11, NASB.
8   Robert Jay Lifton, "Cult Formation," *The Harvard Mental Health Letter*, Volume 7, Number 8 (February 1981).
9   Janja Lalich, *Bounded Choice: True Believers and Charismatic Cults* (Berkely: University of California Press, 2010), 17.
10   Robert Downen, Lise Olsen, and John Tedesco, "Abuse of Faith: Investigation reveals 700 victims of Southern Baptist sexual abuse over 20 years," Chron.com, February 9, 2019, https://www.chron.com/news/investigations/article/Investigation-reveals-700-victims-of-Southern-13591612.php.
11   Robert Jay Lifton, "Cult Formation."

Chapter Fourteen

Holes in the Umbrellas

I was eight when my family learned that Valerie was pregnant. Even at such a young age I was convinced of the truth of Gothard's umbrella of protection theology, and I was terrified of removing myself from the protection of these divine umbrellas. I knew I could exit the umbrellas by rebelling against the authority of my parents and God. I witnessed first-hand what happened to Valerie, and I didn't want to go down that road. Beyond being shunned by my own family and my church, I feared leaving myself wide open to satanic attacks by entering into any form of rebellion. Alarmed that God would withdraw his hand of protection from my life, I knew that—above all else—I had to stay safe underneath the God-ordained umbrellas of authority above me.

If I did rebel, in the best-case scenario, I'd still be considered a Christian, but like Valerie, I would be vulnerable to the attacks of the devil. I would have no one available to protect me from demonic assault. At worst, if I rebelled enough to cross some possible unclear line that would cause the loss of my salvation, and was alive when the Rapture occurred, I would end up stranded on Earth to face all seven years of the tribulation and would ultimately spend eternity in hell. I didn't want either of those terrifying possibilities to happen to me!

As I sat traumatized through all those highly contentious meetings,

Chapter Fourteen

watching my family tear itself apart and then witnessing what happened to Valerie, I started connecting the dots. Don't let what happened to her happen to you. At all costs, I had to avoid losing the protection of the umbrella of authority! I had to do everything possible to keep myself under those God-ordained umbrellas that Gothard taught so convincingly, drawing on what seemed to be solid biblical principles.

When my mother explained to me why all the horrible things had happened to Valerie, she had stated matter-of-factly that it was because she had rebelliously walked away from our parents' umbrella of protection. By extension, she had also walked away from God's protective umbrella. At the time, this all made sense to me, and I could see how Mom's interpretation of events perfectly described what happened to my sister.

Despite the convincing arguments surrounding the umbrella theology and its practice in my family, I struggled with a glaring inconsistency. I had committed my life to Jesus. I had been baptized. But little or nothing had genuinely changed inside me. Life went on as it did beforehand. The only difference was that, at least some of the time, I could convince myself that I was a true Christian, albeit not a very successful one. I made a valiant effort to live a victorious Christian life, but I kept failing miserably. And following the pregnancy and adoption incident with Valerie, my family was divided and dysfunctional, certainly not an embodiment of victorious Christian living. God didn't seem to be helping any of us.

Why the lack of divine help? Just like the struggles I was experiencing in my own Christian life, I asked myself repeatedly why God didn't seem to care at all about fixing and healing all the trauma, hurt, and dysfunction so clearly on display in our home. Both Gothard and Christian psychologist James Dobson stated emphatically that family was the most crucial thing in God's eyes. But God didn't seem to be involved in helping us heal in the least. Following the teachings of these men to their logical conclusions, our family should have been the epitome of blessing, happiness, and joy bestowed from God's hands. We tried mightily to live up to Gothard's seven principles for success, but where was the divine blessing promised to follow such devotion?

It seemed to me that something about the promised formula wasn't quite right, but I couldn't pinpoint what was wrong. Was the problem to be found on God's end or ours? Who was to blame for the fact that our family wasn't being blessed?

The reality was that my siblings and I lived in a dysfunctional, anxiety-ridden, fear-filled, hostile, and often unsafe environment. We were all required to act a prescribed and promised part for our church family. From the outside, our family appeared to be loving, godly, and wonderful, but that was far from the truth, especially for us kids.

I remember many Sunday mornings when we were all getting ready for church while my mom shouted at us to hurry up. With a family of six kids, someone was always late getting into the car. Upset and angry, my mom would indignantly scold us all the way to church as we cowered in the back seat. "See what you've done because you were messing around? Yet again, we're going to miss the start of the service. Everyone will stare at us when we walk in late. I'm sick and tired of you kids embarrassing us every week!"

After finding a place in the crowded church parking lot, Mom would lean over the back seat, menacingly point her finger in our faces, and threateningly intone: "Now, all of you, turn those frowns upside down. Put on a smile because we're at church now." Still processing the berating we had received enroute, we would choke back our sobs, wipe the tears from our cheeks, and try to paste on a plastic smile. Taking a minute to compose ourselves at the front door, we would enter the church building fifteen or twenty minutes late, each of us desperately trying to look happy. As we attempted to find a pew with enough free space to fit our entire family, the rest of the congregation stared disapprovingly at us as we disrupted the service with our late and conspicuous arrival. Despite our occasional tardiness to church, the rest of our family image looked good on the outside, even though the reality was far different.

Come to think of it, that explanation seemed to fit what I was doing in my own life, too.

Chapter Fifteen

I Wanted to Admire Mark

T he New Testament describes the church as the Body of Christ. According to this metaphor, the humans who make up the church are empowered by the Holy Spirit to act as the hands and feet of Jesus on Earth. The church is God's ultimate human instrument for teaching, ministry, and fellowship.

But if Jesus was acting in and through Christians so empowered, why wasn't the "body of Christ" there for such a messed-up kid like me—especially given how teenagers routinely struggle with so many aspects of their lives? As far as I could tell, no help for my adolescent struggles was forthcoming from my local congregation.

Initially, I had high hopes that our Youth Pastor Mark might become my mentor. My spiritual life was like an airplane off course, flying dangerously low and running out of fuel. I needed someone like Mark with whom I could talk.

I was impressed with Mark. He was a good-looking, charismatic guy, and he carried himself with an air of confidence. In terms of fashion, he was cutting-edge. He sported a beard, which was risky in those days in church settings since beards were still associated with hippies. Mark also defied stuffy church norms for dress by wearing a suit jacket with jeans.

He could preach, but his forte was his musical talent. When Mark sang at church services, he pounded the piano keys and poured out his heart to God in song. He even wrote original worship songs and taught them to us in the services. He played the piano and sang at a level that could have earned the respect of the most famous Christian musicians of the day. In fact, Mark reminded me of Keith Green, a famous Christian musician whom I idolized for his passionate piano playing and singing. Mark believed his talent at the keyboard was a miraculous gift from God. He never took lessons. He just started playing the piano one day. He also played the guitar. He was a talented musician, singer, and songwriter. He felt he had received this musical gift for the purpose of glorifying God in worship.

In my view, Mark was both super-cool and super-spiritual.

Despite Mark's unmistakable charisma and musical talent, his preaching and teaching weren't the best. On rare occasions, he was allowed to preach on Sunday mornings, and his sermons always ran twenty to thirty minutes over his allotted time. Getting fired up on some topic, he would spend way too much time on a point he considered important. In the fall, all the sports fans in the congregation would be seriously annoyed because Mark's overtime preaching meant missing the start of the Sunday NFL games. This was long before VCRs or digital devices that could be used to record a televised sporting event, so if you missed the kickoff live at one o'clock, too bad for you! The church ladies weren't happy with the long sermons either. At a certain point, they would lose focus on Mark's sermon and begin to worry that the roast in the oven—timed to finish shortly after the service was scheduled to end—would burn.

Sunday School and Wednesday nights at youth group with Mark were no different. We sat bored while he would speak to us for over an hour about something from the Bible that he considered vitally important for our spiritual growth. Sometimes, he would go on and on about some life-changing spiritual insights he'd gleaned from the latest Christian book he was reading. He tried to get us to engage and discuss what he was speaking about but to no avail. Mark excelled at music, but when it came to speaking, he never learned the value of conciseness and brevity. And he didn't know how to connect with teenagers. So, typically, we would stop listening after a few minutes and start fooling around. Soon, whispering, talking, and giggling amongst ourselves, we had utterly ceased to notice whatever Mark was talking about.

Mark would eventually reach the end of his patience after telling us to shut up several times. He'd get angry, throw down the book from which he was teaching, and shout, "Hey! That's enough! You need to pay attention to what I'm saying." He told us we were acting foolishly. What he was telling us was extremely important— at least he thought it was important. He said he was trying to help us learn how to live victorious Christian lives. "You'll be sorry someday when your life falls apart!" he would angrily exclaim. "And why will your life end up in a mess? Simple: because you've foolishly failed to listen to these amazing spiritual insights the Lord has revealed to me." Wagging his finger at us, he would say mournfully, "Sometime in the future, when it's far too late, you'll have forgotten all these profound biblical truths I've worked so hard to prepare for you. You unappreciative spoiled brats!" If we still failed to listen, in despair, he would throw his hands up and ask plaintively, "Don't you guys even care?"

Unfortunately, Mark's one-to-one skills with teenagers were even worse than his speaking skills. He was extremely erratic about giving his attention to us teens. One week, he would act like your best friend, lavishing warmth and affection on you. That felt great! The following week, he might ignore you. You would see him approaching and expect a positive greeting like you had received the week before. But instead of welcoming you as he'd previously done, he would warmly hug the person he had disregarded entirely the week before. And this person was often standing right next to you as Mark walked toward them, ignoring you. This scenario would happen over and over, week in and week out.

Even though his treatment of us teens was inconsistent at best, I nonetheless admired Mark for his 70s-style hippy beard, "suit-jacket-with-jeans" look, and his Keith Green piano playing and singing style. Most of us in the youth group secretly thought Mark was cool, but we didn't want to admit it to anyone else.

When Mark was your friend, you were on top of the world. When Mark ignored you, it felt terrible. Mark's unpredictable behavior could drive you into depths of despair. When he ignored you, you would wonder, "What did I do wrong?" I can recall, on many occasions, feeling extremely upset and deeply wounded due to Mark's on again/off again behavior. And I wasn't alone in this reaction. Other members of our youth group felt it too.

I desperately wanted this young minister's approval but never seemed to get any consistent attention from him. As you might guess, Mark never became my mentor. After a couple of years of his hot-and-cold treatment, I managed to work up the courage to confront him. In my awkward way, I tried to explain what I thought of his inconsistent actions toward me, how they made me feel so insecure, and how badly they hurt my feelings. After I'd said my piece, he didn't acknowledge anything I'd said and instead blamed me for our difficult relationship. The problem he said was my "bad attitude." His response led to my trying to figure out how I could change my "bad attitude" to become part of Mark's accepted inner circle, but I could never work it out. All I knew was that when it came to Mark and the youth he seemed to like, I was always on the outside looking in.

Here I was, a teenager who desired acceptance from an admired authority figure, but he was unwilling—or perhaps unable—to give me that simple gift. Our youth group was stuck with someone who was supposed to be portraying the unconditional love and acceptance of God to a bunch of teens working through the normal but challenging issues of adolescence. But unconditional love and acceptance were hard to find where Mark was concerned. As an imperfect human like the rest of us, Mark had his own unresolved issues. But he could not, or would not, see how his erratic behavior affected the teens for whom he was supposed to set an example.

I desperately needed someone I could talk to about the problems I was having with my dad, Mike and Carl suddenly leaving, and the bullying at school. All I knew was that I needed spiritual help and mentoring from Pastor Mark, but once I understood who he really was, he became the last person I would turn to for help.

Once again, I felt that both the church and God were badly letting me down, just at a time when I needed it the most.

Chapter Sixteen

The Fear of Being a Goat

T hree years after my baptism, I was a thirteen-year-old increasingly tormented with feelings of unworthiness, guilt, and shame. As a means of coping with the trauma and anxiety, I had become addicted to pornography, which only added to my struggles in life.

What had begun as a few *Playboy* magazine swaps between my church buddies and me had grown into something more pervasive. I couldn't quit the habit, no matter what I tried. Like a drug addict craving a more effective high, I progressed to looking at more hardcore magazines like *Penthouse* and *Hustler*.

Thanks to my church upbringing and Bible memorization, I knew that God knew and saw everything. I was guilty of committing the sin of Onanism! Remember Onan? He was that unfortunate guy that God put to death in the book of Genesis for "spilling his seed on the ground"—a sin that many students of the Bible identified as masturbation.

I was on shaky ground, and deep down, I knew it all too well. No matter how successful I was at hiding my addiction from my parents, God knew what I was doing. And I knew he had to be tremendously disappointed in me. I knew that all sin is an abomination to God, and I assumed that secret sins were even worse. Hadn't Jesus proclaimed in the Gospels that merely looking at a woman lustfully was tantamount to the physical act of sexual infidelity? Even the sensual thought of having sex with someone you weren't married to was a crime against God.

Here we have another marker of cultic and high-control religious groups. I previously referred to Hassan's BITE Model™ of cults in which the "T" in the acronym stands for thought control. As a Christian, in addition to behavior and emotions, you must also control your thoughts to avoid committing a thought crime against God. And sexual sin violated the strict purity culture in which I had been raised, so I was really in trouble. My problem was that I was in the grip of a compulsive addiction. No matter how hard I tried to stop or control it, I couldn't seem to prevent myself from committing this type of sin over and over. As the frequency of my private sexual sin increased, I was terrified that I might be edging out from underneath the umbrellas of protection placed above me by God.

Looking back on it now, and having gone through counseling, I can see that, in some ways, my private sexual behaviors were a normal part of male adolescent development. But it's also true that my compulsive use of pornography was likely rooted in a need to self-medicate. I was attempting to ease the pain of living amid a torn-up and deeply dysfunctional family, as well as the pain of knowing that I was disappointing God with my actions. Porn was the only thing I had discovered that got my full attention and made me feel good, albeit for a few fleeting moments.

The entire time I was looking at porn, lurking in my mind was the dreadful thought of how sinful it was. I told myself all the time that I was a total failure. I didn't know what to do other than to beg God daily to take this addiction away from me. But he never came through. The compulsion only seemed to grow, and as I saw it, the situation became increasingly unmanageable.

I often wrestled with a thorny question. Why didn't God take a more active role in helping me kick this nefarious habit? I remember hearing a preacher at a Christian camp claiming that God had instantly and supernaturally taken away his cigarette addiction the moment he gave his life to Jesus and was saved. Just like that, with the seeming wave of a magic wand, all his craving for nicotine had vanished. Praise the Lord, he was instantly set free from decades of smoking! Hearing that testimony, I wondered why God wouldn't do the same for me. Why couldn't God immediately relieve me of my accursed affliction? Surely, he had the power to remove my desire for porn. But no matter how many times I prayed, desperately begging the Lord to relieve me of my crushing burden, no help was ever forthcoming.

I didn't feel it was safe to talk to my parents about my struggles with pornography. I could easily envision myself on the hot seat like Valerie had been in those traumatic family meetings. All my shameful misdeeds against the Lord would be aired in front of the rest of my family, and I would be profoundly humiliated. Given the likelihood that such a scenario might happen to me if I opened up about my struggle, I concluded that I had to keep this private behavior a closely guarded secret. But carrying all that guilt and angst, combined with the constant effort of having to conceal such a terrible sin, ate away at me all the time. I had a constant knot in my stomach from the stress of it all.

Making things even worse, I feared that I might have committed the "unforgivable sin" Jesus spoke about in the Gospels. Although this unpardonable sin had to do with blaspheming against the Holy Spirit,[1] nobody knew what Jesus actually meant or how one would know if they'd crossed this point of no forgiveness. The fact that you could cross this line without knowing it made it all the more threatening since there was no coming back after you committed it. I began to suspect I might be one of those "lukewarm Christians," like the members of that lackadaisical church that so enraged God in the book of Revelation. I constantly worried that just as God warned them of their potential fate, in the same way, he might "spit me out of his mouth" for not being on fire for him. My life was anxiety-ridden and filled with fears, both real and imagined.

Reflecting on my life now, as an adult who left both the church and the Christian faith years ago, I can clearly see that I was suffering from Religious Trauma Syndrome. Dr. Marlene Winell, a therapist and a survivor of fundamentalist religion, coined the phrase "Religious Trauma Syndrome" (RTS). She notes in a 2011 article in the British journal *Cognitive Behaviour Therapy Today* that the damage done by RTS is incredibly hurtful on numerous levels. She points out that "the actual teachings and practices of a restrictive religion can be toxic and create lifelong mental damage."[2] In another article discussing Religious Trauma Syndrome on her *Journey Free* website, she notes how RTS occurs in a person's life. She states that within controlling and fundamentalist religions,

> You are guilty and responsible and face eternal
> punishment. Yet you have no ability to do anything
> about it. (These are teachings of fundamentalist
> Christianity; however other authoritarian religions
> have equally toxic doctrines.)

> You must conform to a mental test of "believing"
> in an external, unseen source for salvation, and
> maintain this state of belief until death. You cannot
> ever stop sinning altogether, so you must continue
> to confess and be forgiven, hoping that you have
> met the criteria despite complete lack of feedback
> about whether you will actually make it to heaven.

Salvation is not a free gift after all.

For the sincere believer, this results in an unending cycle of shame and relief.[3]

This certainly describes me in my early adolescence. As I saw it, the "free gift" of salvation was anything but free. So many of us who grew up in a controlling religious environment were robbed of a normal childhood and the opportunity to develop and grow in healthier ways. Terrified of the dangers of hell, the Rapture, the threat of apostasy, and the fear of committing the unforgivable sin, I felt neither good nor safe. And, as Dr. Winell points out, there was no assurance of that salvation. God either didn't care or was incapable of giving me the type of feedback that would allow me to know for sure that I was indeed saved and on my way to heaven. Added to that was my struggle with sins from which I could not seem to be set free—despite begging God thousands of times to take the sinful desires from me.

I recall listening to a song performed by the famous Christian artist Keith Green. Titled "The Sheep and the Goats," it was adapted from the gospel of Matthew, chapter 25. In the song, Green describes those people who end up before Jesus's throne of judgment when they die. As Jesus relays the story in Matthew's Gospel, the goats were sent to hell, and the sheep went to heaven. Green somehow managed to make it funny, but the story is actually quite disturbing. As Jesus explains it, there's a vast group of professing Christians who live their whole lives thinking they're saved when, in reality, they're not saved at all. Strangely, the only discernible difference between the sheep and the goats is the good works they did or didn't do while on Earth.

In Jesus's parable, the "goats" discover the horrifying truth when they're being judged—and by then, it's too late to do anything about it. I was terrified that I was a goat! I didn't want to be consigned to the flames of hell. I wanted to be a sheep so I could spend eternity in heaven with the Lord, walking those fabled streets of gold.

The same tone applies to Jesus's parable of the "foolish virgins" in Matthew 25:1-13 who were unwisely unprepared when the bridegroom (Jesus) suddenly appeared and they were caught napping. Unfortunately for them, when the bridegroom arrived, the door to heaven was slammed shut in their faces, barring forever their entrance into the eternal wedding feast. Despite their desperate pleas to the bridegroom to let them into heaven as they banged on the door, his response was cruel and cold: "Assuredly, I say to you, I do not know you." Frighteningly, Jesus ends the parable by warning that everyone should always be on their guard, constantly watching and waiting, because no one knows the day or the hour when he might return to Earth. I certainly did not want to be either a goat or one of those "foolish virgins" sent off to hell with Jesus's words about not knowing me at all ringing in my ears.

I've come to see that these two passages portray a seriously messed-up theology, complete with a cruel and capricious God behind it. Why would God allow millions of people to go their entire lives thinking they're saved and bound for heaven when they're not? With the stakes so incredibly high, why wouldn't he invest more time, effort, and energy in helping them to get things right while it was possible? Sadly, for them, the only time they realize the truth is when it's too late to do anything about it. Another problem: The theology undergirding the parable of the sheep and the goats seems to be one of good works as the pathway into heaven rather than relying on belief in Christ alone for the promise of eternal bliss.

If I indeed was a goat or a "foolish virgin," then I needed to know now while there was still time to do something about it. But hang on a minute. I wondered about Paul's theology in 1 Corinthians 3:10-13, which refers to those apathetic believers with wood, hay, and straw representing their lifelong accomplishments. Didn't they barely squeak into heaven after the test of purifying fire? Were they the sheep Jesus referred to in his parable, or was this some additional category? What kept these lackluster Christians who make it into heaven—albeit without significant eternal rewards—from being the goats in Jesus's parable who were immediately consigned to everlasting hellfire? Why didn't Jesus use the purifying fire to test the works of the goats and at least give them a fighting chance? Who was right? Paul or Jesus?

These conflicting teachings confused me even more and added to my constant feelings of worry and anxiety. All in all, I was in pretty bad shape, and I desperately needed some answers. But the religious bubble in which I lived was less concerned about grappling with difficult questions of belief and more concerned about keeping me separate from the evils of the secular world.

---

1 Matthew 12:31-32.
2 Marlene Winell, "Religious Trauma Syndrome," *Cognitive Behavioural Therapy Today*, Volume 39, Issue 2, (May 2011). See https://www.journeyfree.org/rts/rts-its-time-to-recognize-it/.
3 Marlene Winell, "Religious Trauma Syndrome," JourneyFree.org, referenced July 29, 2024, https://www.journeyfree.org/rts/.

Chapter Seventeen

We're Just Trying to Protect You

To say my family was dysfunctional is putting it mildly. Ironically, the root of our dysfunction came not from a dangerous secular world but from extreme Christian teachers. Based on the child-rearing teachings of Christian teachers like Dobson and Gothard, my parents created an environment whereby we children were "sheltered from the evils of the secular world." Growing up under the teachings of the Gothard cult and following his "biblical" advice for godly parenting, we had no television in the house. We weren't allowed to listen to secular music of any kind. Christian or classical music was fine, but none of that devil rock n' roll music! Gothard warned that the drum beat in both secular and Christian rock would summon up demons, so we had to be protected from such evil threats.

As I began my teenager years, the "Satanic Panic" emerged.[1] In the view of those caught up in this paranoia, the devil was everywhere. He was lurking around every corner, waiting to pounce on any unsuspecting Christian and drag them down to the pit of hell. Secular heavy metal music was highly suspected to be an insidious tool of Satan. If you played a rock n' roll phonograph record backward on a turntable, you might hear some devil worship intentionally placed there by the godless musicians who created the music. Known as "backward masking," it was believed to be a demonic strategy designed to influence the subconscious minds of unwitting listeners to worship Satan—while the record was playing in the correct direction.

Another meme that made the rounds in churches those days was that the wizard and stars on the Procter and Gamble logo were demonic. Some Christian counselors specialized in helping clients recover suppressed memories of "satanic ritual abuse" that had taken place in secret devil-worshiping covens. Years later, many of these counseling clients had to seek help from other counselors to unravel what had and hadn't happened to them. And what had happened, they discovered, did not involve any kind of demonic worship. But at the time, everyone I knew within my Christian bubble fully bought into these conspiracy theory fever dreams.

I had a girlfriend whose fundamentalist parents were horrified when they discovered that my best friend, Guy, enjoyed the role-playing game Dungeons and Dragons, or "D&D" for short. Everyone in my Christian world knew that Dungeons and Dragons was a subversive tool of Satan. D&D taught unsuspecting young people to unintentionally cast real satanic spells as they innocently played the game. This practice would surely open the door to the world of the occult. Terrified of this evil influence being introduced into my girlfriend's life, her parents ordered her to break up with me, and she immediately did so—even though I had never played the game!

When I first played the drums in our church with some of my friends from the youth group, not everyone was pleased with our performance. After the service, one of the congregants—an older man who had been at the church since its founding—belligerently confronted our pastor. He lambasted the pastor for his foolishness in allowing such dangerous instruments into the building. Pianos, acoustic guitars, and organs were fine, but drums? That was a step too far. Everyone knew that drumbeats could summon up demons! The next thing you knew, he angrily stated, "We'll be having electric guitars in here!" Wagging his finger in the minister's face, he confidently declared that allowing drums in our worship services could open the doors of our church to Satan and his demonic hordes! Due to this man's threats to make trouble with the Elder Board over the incident, the pastor was forced to issue a public apology on the following Sunday. No more drums in the worship services!

At home, if my sisters or I were caught listening to rock music—which Gothard and many other evangelical influencers taught was satanic—we'd get an immediate spanking. Immediate punishment for such actions, in our parents' line of thinking, was a way of protecting us from the dangers lurking out there in the world. Looking back, I'm sure my dad and mom thought they were doing things right. We attended church multiple times a week. My siblings and I were safely ensconced in Christian school all week long. Christian camp had us covered during the summer.

My parents tried hard to shield us from the dangers lurking in the secular world. Because of their sincere and consistent efforts to protect us from evil influences, they thought we were safe. And if we did respond to temptation and go astray, part of the plan for protecting us from this evil world was implementing a swift and painful punishment to teach us how dangerous it is to sin.

As a result, spankings were commonplace in our house. There was a period when my sister Beth and I, who were fourteen months apart in age, were spanked a minimum of two to three times a day for various infractions of my parents' strict rules. Valerie received a spanking when my parents learned she was pregnant at the age of seventeen. This practice was also part of the Dobson and Gothard formulas for family success. Both men taught that this was all ordained by God and laid out clearly in the Bible.

Chapter Seventeen

Gothard instructed parents to spank their children with the aim of "breaking the will" of the recalcitrant child. Corporal punishment would eventually disarm the child's natural propensity toward sin. How did a parent know when to stop a spanking? The minute the child cried, the parent could know that the punishment had been successful. My mom and dad also subscribed to Dr. James Dobson's "strong-willed child" thinking. His books *Dare to Discipline* and *The Strong-Willed Child* were among their favorites. Dobson put a slightly different spin on corporal punishment, insisting that spanking was about "shaping the will" of the child but not completely breaking the child's spirit. To me, such distinctions did not matter. All I knew was that I was getting spanked, sometimes numerous times a day.

Both men taught that the strong will of a child was not a positive character trait but rather the result of our inborn sinful nature. Adam and Eve disobeyed God by eating the forbidden fruit of the Tree of the Knowledge of Good and Evil in the Garden of Eden. This act of disobedience is known in Christian theology as "original sin." Forming one of the core doctrines of Christianity, it means that every human is corrupted by the original sin of Adam and Eve. Many Christian groups understand original sin to mean that every child is born not only with a sinful nature but is also born guilty—as if they somehow participated in the rebellious act in the Garden of Eden. Other Christian groups understand original sin to mean that every child is born with a sinful nature but is innocent until they reach an age of awareness of accountability for sin and choose to disobey. Either way, virtually all Christians agree that our sinful nature is a powerful force. We can be easily tempted to do the wrong thing—over and over—and we are likely to succumb.

Given the stark reality of our fallen state, one of the main jobs of Christian parents is to combat the sinful nature within their children to set them on the path of righteousness. Dobson and

Gothard both taught that corporal punishment was the most effective way to do that.

"Spare the rod and spoil the child" is one of the foremost biblical "principles" cited in defense of spanking.[2] This same verse states that parents who fail to discipline their children actually hate them since, apparently, they don't really care about the child's moral development. Another go-to biblical citation states, "Foolishness is bound up in the heart of a child; The rod of discipline will remove it far from him."[3] Bible verses like these allowed my parents to believe that their practice of disciplining my sisters and me had God's blessing.

Each time one of my sisters or I was spanked, a ritual took place. First, my mom or dad would sit us on the bed and solemnly recite the plaintive line: "This is going to hurt me more than it hurts you." Despite hearing that statement numerous times just before being spanked, I never believed it. The spanking was next, which surely hurt me more than it hurt Mom or Dad. Since crying meant the lesson had been learned, we were always spanked until we cried. The tears had to be authentic. We tried fake crying, but that didn't work. The spanking continued until the punishing parent was convinced our tears were genuine. When the tears start flowing, that's when the parent knew they had successfully triumphed over the child's inherited sin nature.

If the goal is to make the rebellious child cry, the right instrument is required. My folks had a piece of kindling wood about eighteen inches long with masking tape wrapped around one end to create a handle. After about four or five solid whacks on the buttocks with this stick, the pain truly became unbearable. I'd always cry, despite resolving beforehand not to give in and shed a single tear. This eighteen-inch pain tool was excellent for producing real tears.

Through spankings, Gothard explained, God-fearing parents

safeguarded their kids from future foolish rebellion against their parents and the Lord. This was all to the good, from Gothard's point of view. This was another way of protecting the child from the evil in the world.

There was another aspect to this whole mindset. Simply spanking the child did not complete the ritual. Gothard taught that after the spanking, when the child is in physical and emotional pain, the mom or dad doing the spanking should immediately hug the sobbing child. The parent needed to explain that they only spanked the child "because I love you, and this is what God requires of us as parents to help you avoid sin." Often, the "spare the rod and spoil the child" verse would also be alluded to. This passage indicates that the parent must discipline the child because of their love for them. Statements such as these would supposedly comfort the distressed child and reinforce the message behind the spanking.

These highly stressful spanking experiences left a distinct mark of trauma on my life that I still feel today. I recall numerous occasions when I waited apprehensively in my bedroom to receive my punishment. Sometimes, this would happen several times in one day, and I wasn't necessarily alone when I got in trouble. If my sister Beth was spanked first, I felt a mounting sense of distress and dread. From my room down the hall, I could hear the resounding *whack* of the kindling stick hitting her backside until she started sobbing and begged my mother to stop. Next came the obligatory hugging and perfunctory statements by my mom, and Beth would be sent to her room to "think about what you've done." Then it was my turn. I could usually fend off the tears until the third or fourth hit. But after that, it hurt like hell, and I couldn't hold back the tears.

Looking back, I now realize that these ongoing punishments amounted to physical and emotional abuse, but that's not all. Being told by my parents that God was behind it all, that this is what the Bible taught, and that God was the one instructing my parents to hurt us children daily only added layers to the trauma we suffered. Thus, I consider such experiences to be not only physical and emotional abuse but spiritual abuse as well. How could I learn to love an invisible God who commanded my parents to abuse me and my sisters? No wonder I struggled so mightily to try and love this divine being who seemed to have a cruel and sadistic streak.

As an adult, I've read multiple accounts written by individuals raised in similar environments. Those of us who grew up in these types of abusive households, with parents who relied on corporal punishment, report feelings of shame, anxiety, dread, trauma, abuse, and more. Those who were unfortunate enough to be spanked on their bare bottoms speak of it as being akin to a form of sexual abuse. Luckily for my sisters and me, our parents never resorted to bare bottom swats, but we were spanked countless times. These traumatic experiences left a massive imprint on our psyches and profoundly affected our emotional, psychological, and spiritual development. I can personally testify that these emotions and traumas require a lot of therapy and counseling to work through as an adult.

My mom and dad certainly did not spare the rod, but the spankings did little or nothing to stop us from being extremely naughty children. Their approach to parenting didn't achieve the desired results. But I don't think either of my parents ever stopped to reflect on the strategy's efficacy or to ask the difficult questions: Why are these kids acting out so badly? Why aren't the endless spankings stopping them from constantly being naughty?

In the view of my parents, the lack of promised results could not have had anything to do with the family system dysfunctions ripping our relationships apart. Nor could it have had to do with their fundamentalist beliefs and blind obedience to the twisted "biblical" teachings of men like Gothard and Dobson. No, my parents' strategy was never to look in the mirror and reflect on whether they needed to do things differently. Instead, they would apply the rod of discipline even more and never concede a single inch. They were determined not to let us win, ever. This only led to an atmosphere of constant fear, anxiety, and dread. My sisters and I walked on eggshells, afraid of our angry mother and constantly expecting a spanking, which frequently did happen. Rather than being a loving and nurturing home, ours was a fear-filled, anxiety-ridden environment in which we constantly expected to get in trouble.

As a parent, I wonder why Mom and Dad never questioned this parental punishment game plan. I need to say again that I firmly believe this was physical, psychological, emotional, and spiritual abuse on their part. They were only following through on what they thought were biblical guidelines for child-rearing and this behavior was more culturally acceptable than it is today. But their strategy did not work. We were as naughty as ever. As a parent, if my plan for disciplining my daughters didn't work despite numerous attempts, I would then need to question my assumptions and procedures.

It is now my view that a parent must constantly adapt and come up with new and more effective strategies that don't involve physical abuse and corporal punishment. But my parents never questioned anything, blinded by the "biblical principles" behind the teachings of "experts" like Gothard and Dobson. Many evangelicals blindly followed Dobson, for example, because he had an actual Ph.D. in child psychology from the University of Southern California—so he had to be an expert!

Ironically, despite his massive popularity as a speaker and influencer on successful marriage and parenting, Bill Gothard was never married and never had children. But since he dispensed sage and authoritative advice about these topics from the Bible, hardly anyone seemed to question this obvious disparity.

We need enough fear to stay safe, but we also need affirmation, hope, and joy. I now understand that fear is the friend of leaders bent on control. Their mantra is: *Be afraid of this and this and this. And understand that only I can save you from the things you fear.*

---

1 Sparked by the Canadian book *Michelle Remembers* in 1980, the bestseller ostensibly revealed underground Satanic covens performing "satanic ritual abuse" on children, mainly infants. That led to a nationwide "Satanic Panic" about secular heavy metal music, tabletop fantasy games, and more. Even law enforcement became involved, training police officers to identify satanic ritual killings and demonic activities. For more on this see https://www.cbc.ca/arts/satan-wants-you-filmmakers-q-a-sean-horlor-steve-j-adams-1.6822213
2 Proverbs 13:24.
3 Proverbs 22:15, NASB.

Chapter Eighteen

A Lime Green Suit and the Christian Right

O ur leaders put the word out among Bible colleges and seminaries that we were seeking a new minister. The Elder Board formed a prayer chain to ensure that the Lord would send us a wise and godly pastor. They believed this vast amount of prayer coverage would help us find an outstanding leader. They put together a Pastor Search Committee to find and recommend God's man for the job. Confidence was high that God would send us an experienced man to guide the church forward into a new season of growth. Several ministers applied for the position and completed the obligatory weekend of visiting and being checked out by the church, which included preaching a trial sermon.

Working through the candidates provided by the Pastor Search Committee, the Elder Board settled on David. The church enthusiastically voted him in after hearing him preach. Pastor David was in his mid-sixties and had a long history of pastoring churches. Most of his pastorates had been in Southern states, and this new move marked his first foray into the Pacific Northwest. Despite his age, he was a dynamic, high-energy preacher. I don't recall much about his sermons other than a line he was fond of repeating: "America," he would pronounce as he dramatically held his Bible aloft, "is filled with scores of faceless politicians and voiceless preachers!" I think he meant "voiceless" in the sense that although they were speaking, they didn't have a voice that made any difference. I surmised that these bad actors—the politicians and inept preachers—must be busy doing their level best to ruin America. Each time Pastor David recited that line, I always wondered if those "voiceless preachers" were like that liberal preacher from *A Thief in the Night*.

The Christian Right was on the rise, including the blossoming of fundamentalist preacher Jerry Falwell's "Moral Majority" in 1979. Pastor David was in sync with Falwell's views and repeated many of Falwell's lines in his sermons. "We must fight against the scourge of secular humanism. That demonic philosophy has led the nation astray from its formerly Christian roots. It's time to clean up America!"

Along with the rest of the congregation, I bought into Pastor David's Christian nationalist sentiments which I later learned were based on a belief system called "Dominion Theology." I firmly believed that America had been established as a Christian nation by the Founding Fathers. Over the centuries our nation had wandered off the path of righteousness. The USA desperately needed to get back to its previous godly status. Liberal Democrats were a big part of why America was going down the tubes. I figured these must be the "faceless politicians" Pastor David referred to in his sermons. He claimed that along with godless atheists like Madalyn Murray O'Hair, "These people have successfully driven God out of our public schools and public squares!"

Pastor David claimed that these faceless politicians had been the ones driving evil moves to the left like the Roe vs. Wade decision handed down by the Supreme Court in 1973. The grievous national sin of this decision brought about two outcomes. First, it made abortion legal nationwide, and second, it made God furiously angry over the murder of all those millions of innocent babies. The liberals also promoted feminism, the ERA, women's liberation, and the so-called "homosexual agenda." Driven by our pastor's passionate rhetoric, we weren't always sure why we were against these things. We just knew we were against them.

All we knew for sure was that, taken together, all these unrighteous developments were bad omens for our country's future. Pastor David confidently asserted that these corporate sins explained why God wasn't blessing America any longer. We had violated the terms of our covenant with him. "The most effective thing you and I can do," he would solemnly advise us, "is to pray. We need to beg God that he may—in his infinite mercy—grant America a reprieve before his righteous judgment falls on our wicked nation." In the meantime, our pastor declared that we needed to get busy saving as many souls as possible before Jesus returned.

Apparently, evangelism and prayer weren't enough. There was more work for his flock to do. Pastor David handed out "voter's guides," provided by Religious Right political organizations, to ensure his flock voted for the correct candidates. Like my parents, I was a diehard Republican and firmly supported the Christian Right's agenda, which, over the years, has come to be more and more aligned with the GOP. I couldn't wait until I turned eighteen and was eligible to vote. In 1984, the first time I voted, I was ecstatic to cast my ballot for Ronald Reagan for president. He won by a landslide, thanks in large part to the evangelical vote. For years I voted straight down the Republican Party ticket and would never consider voting for a liberal Democrat. After all, it was our duty as good Christians to vote for Republicans since these godly candidates would help stem the tide of secular humanism. Moreover, it was always possible that placing these righteous men and women in office would restore America back to its former status as a Christian nation—exactly as 2 Chronicles 7:14 promised.

Despite his often-redundant lines and over-emphasis on politics,

Chapter Eighteen

I liked Pastor David. Along with many people in our church, however, I didn't like his loud outfits that didn't quite match. He'd regularly show up in the pulpit wearing a lime green polyester suit, a brown shirt, and a purple tie with a huge knot. To complete the ensemble, he wore Pat Boone white buck shoes. He sported a hideous dome-wrap comb-over hairstyle, and his wife wore old-fashioned, out-of-style dresses. He once confided to me that because pastoral jobs paid so little, he and his wife had often been reduced to shopping at thrift stores and charity shops for their clothes. It was all they could afford. But he was genuinely a nice guy despite his many fashion crimes.

Just as his fashion sense was out of touch with the times, so was his car. During the "gas crunch" of the 1970s, with lines around the block at gas stations, people started trading in their larger vehicles for economy cars. But Pastor David paid no attention to this trend. He drove a big, gas-guzzling powder blue Chrysler that matched one of his polyester suits. The car was a serious chunk of Detroit steel, and Pastor David loved driving that tank. He would never consider giving it up, although it cost him dearly at the fuel station each time he filled it up.

If our church was going to grow, we needed the right leader. Despite his questionable fashion choices, Pastor David seemed to be the right man for the job. Once again, the Lord had provided.

Chapter Nineteen

Playing Hooky in the Pastor's Study

When I turned thirteen, I was excited because it meant I could now join the youth group. We even had our own dedicated classroom in the new building. But it didn't take me long to discover that I hadn't escaped my issues with Pastor Mark. I was now stuck with him and the other youth group teens for an hour each week before the Sunday morning service. Since Mark rarely had a chance to preach, he unleashed all his pent-up pastoral energy on us. We were the unfortunate recipients of many long and boring lessons. I desperately needed a way to escape. When I heard a rumor that another church had bought our old building, I decided to investigate.

To avoid sitting through Mark's boring lectures in youth group class, some Sunday mornings, I'd head toward the bathroom instead of going to class. Once the coast was clear, I would quietly duck out the back door and walk up the street to attend the church now meeting in our old building. They were an ethnically mixed congregation with a high-energy African American pastor named Johnny. They had way more intensity than our fundamentalist, stuffy old church did! I had never witnessed such a service, and I was happy to bail out of our stodgy, boring meetings. At the Word of Life Church, I discovered a new way of worship and preaching. They had a gospel choir with a band—drums, bass, and electric guitars—that rocked the place. This was a whole new world for me, and I loved it. Pastor Johnny and his family were probably the first African Americans I'd ever gotten acquainted with. I felt an immediate respect for this pastor. I looked up to him as a friend and potential mentor. I couldn't afford to skip Mark's class too many times, but over the next six months or so, I tried to make it to the Word of Life Church at least once a month.

One Sunday, following my new routine, I quietly eased out of my church's back door and headed up the street to catch what now felt like more of my kind of worship service. But when I arrived, I was surprised to see no cars in the parking lot at the Word of Life Church. The lights were off, and no one was there. Dejected, I trudged back to my church and wondered what had happened. Later, I learned that Pastor Johnny had been caught having an affair with the church secretary. After the scandal broke, the Word of Life Church closed its doors for good. I was devastated to hear that this new church venture had flamed out so quickly. And "flamed out" was the perfect description. They shut the church doors, and everyone went their separate ways after being in the building less than a year. This sad and abrupt end to my cross-cultural church adventure meant that I was stuck back with our incredibly boring Youth Pastor, Mark, and a youth group where I felt like an outsider. I felt discouraged, unhappy, and caged. With nowhere to go on a Sunday morning other than youth group class, I was now resigned to my fate.

Mark assigned one chapter of reading a week from the latest Christian book he was fired up about. None of us read our chapters, which only increased Mark's frustration with us. Each week, during the lesson time before the service, Mark desperately tried to get us to talk about what we'd learned. He asked us to share any exciting thing God was doing in our lives. Awkward silences inevitably followed as we stared at the floor, uncertain what we should say in response. I wasn't interested in either his books or his preachy, boring conversations. The truth was, I couldn't share with anybody, let alone Mark, what was really going on in my life. My stimulation came from porn, and the only excitement God had shown me lately—the Word of Life Church—had disappeared. Now, I was looking for another way to break free from everything I disliked about my family's church.

To avoid these pointless youth group sessions, I devised another means of escape. A few months after the Word of Life Church closed its doors, once again, I started skipping out of Mark's class on Sunday mornings. Quietly moving past the youth group classroom door, I would continue down the hall and knock on Pastor David's office door. As a former pastor, I realize now that he was likely swamped trying to put the finishing touches on his sermon for the upcoming service. To his credit, though, he never booted me out or told me to get back to Sunday School. Somehow, he always found the time to stop what he was doing and talk to me. I always wondered why he did nothing to stop me from skipping out on Mark's class. Did Pastor David suspect or know that our youth pastor was not doing a super job? Did he say anything to Mark? Maybe Pastor David told Mark that my playing hooky was okay because at least I was getting some much-needed spiritual guidance.

These weekly meetings with my senior pastor became counseling sessions. Despite his loud suits and obsession with conservative politics, he did seem to care, and I felt like he was qualified to help me. Over a period of several weeks, it became clear to Pastor David that I was having a lot of problems. He could see that I was engaged in an intense struggle trying to put all the pieces of my life together.

Under his gentle questioning, I began to open up. I shared some of the most profound issues and problems I was facing. I wanted to know if Christianity was true. I asked him, for example, about reasons to believe the resurrection of Jesus actually happened. He faithfully provided what seemed like solid answers to my questions about the Bible. After several sessions, as my trust in Pastor David grew, I finally admitted that I was tormented with guilt and anxiety over the fact that I was a miserable sinner. I saw myself as a complete disappointment to God. I mentioned that I was afraid I would miss the Rapture and be left behind to face the seven years of the tribulation. I was terrified that I might not be a true believer and could end up suffering an eternity in the flames of hell. I admitted nothing about my porn addiction. I wasn't quite ready to be that vulnerable. I never said anything to Pastor David about our home life either, although our family dysfunctions added to my ever-growing list of traumas and anxieties.

Utilizing years of pastoral counseling skills, Pastor David began to diagnose my problems. Why did I believe I was such an appalling failure and so displeasing to God? Determined to discover why I felt this way, he assured me he would help. His understanding and empathy gave me hope and made me feel better. After many sessions in his office, he announced that he'd put his finger precisely on my problem. He told me that, despite the church's best efforts on my behalf, my first baptism didn't "take." He didn't want to get into all the theological finery or disparage Pastor Jerry, but he suggested that his speedy retirement looked suspicious.

As a proof of his allegations, he pointed to one major blunder that Jerry had made regarding my baptism. Allowing my father to baptize me had been a grave mistake. In Pastor David's opinion, this was a severe shirking of Jerry's duties as a minister. Who knew, he mused, maybe this type of laziness led to his suddenly abandoning his pastoral responsibilities and leaving his needy congregation to struggle along without him.

"But none of that matters now," he declared. "We can't change the past. What's done is done. The important thing now is that we've diagnosed the problem, and fortunately, we have time before Jesus returns to do something about it, but quickly." He then announced the obvious solution: "Clint, it's clear to me that you need to get baptized again." That hit me like a thunderbolt. Could it be that simple? Wait a minute, can I get baptized again? I had no idea that a person could even do that. I felt a sudden surge of relief once I realized that the answer might be simple and easy.

This second time around, we would do it right and not repeat the regrettable mistakes of the past. Pastor David emphasized that I needed to act quickly. "What if Jesus suddenly returns before you are re-baptized?" asked David. I agreed wholeheartedly. I didn't want to take the chance that I might be left behind if the Rapture occurred before my spiritual problem was rectified. Pastor David assured me by confidently declaring that this second baptism would solve all my issues with the Almighty, bring me that much-needed assurance of salvation, and set my troubled mind to rest once and for all.

I leaned back in my chair, relaxing for the first time since I first set foot in his office, and the knot in my stomach started to loosen up just a bit. Listening to his expert theological and pastoral diagnosis, I figured he'd finally cracked the case. Waves of relief washed over me. Just like I'd done three years earlier with Pastor Jerry, I walked out of Pastor David's office on cloud nine. I felt a whole lot better, relieved that things were finally going to work out. Through the wise shepherding of godly Pastor David, the Lord had indeed responded with a solution. I now felt that all those countless prayers for divine assistance had finally been not just heard but answered conclusively.

I felt a twinge of shame, knowing that the Lord had provided clear direction when I so desperately needed it. How could I have doubted God? At long last, a solution was at hand. Could it be that all those years of struggling through life and failing miserably time and time again, were simply God's wise way of refining and deepening my trust in him? Perhaps he had been using difficult circumstances to test and ultimately bolster my weak and ineffectual faith. Surely, it couldn't be his fault.

Chapter Twenty

Underwater One More Time

I was happy to follow Pastor David's spiritual diagnosis and treatment plan. And I expected that my re-baptism would solve every one of my problems. I had one of my sisters drop me off at the church the following Saturday morning. There was no reason to waste time. We needed to do this quickly in case of the Rapture. As I saw it, the stakes were incredibly high since my eternal destiny was on the line. Pastor David met me in the church foyer as I stepped through the door, warmly shook my hand, and said, "Are you all set? Great. Let's get this thing done!" I hustled into the sanctuary with him, relieved he wasn't wasting any time.

The baptistry, a large tank of water located at the rear of the stage, was about three feet deep, three feet wide, and six feet long. Steps led down into the tank for easy access, with a handrail for extra safety. In their wisdom, the Elder Board had chosen a cutting-edge baptistry for the new church building. It had a clear window at the front so the entire congregation could watch the new convert getting baptized. Pastor David had arrived early, and everything was all ready to go. The tank was filled to the brim—and luckily for me, the water was warm.

Looking back as a former pastor, however, there was one strange thing. Why, of all days, choose a Saturday rather than a Sunday during the regular service time? Most people I'd known who were baptized did it as part of a worship service, and it was looked upon as something to be celebrated by the entire church community. Even though my dad had performed my first baptism, it was at a Sunday service in front of the congregation. On this Saturday, there was no need for the clear window on the front of the baptistry that enabled the congregation to see the baptism.

In my twelve years as an elder and a pastor, I baptized numerous people, but never in an empty building. A baptism with no publicity and no audience would have seemed almost secretive, almost as if we were trying to hide it from the rest of the church. We always planned baptismal services as a significant event. That day, as I was baptized for the second time, it was just me and Pastor David—oh, and the cleaning lady, who just happened to be working that day. Yes, that's right. The only witness to the whole solemn affair was the cleaning lady. When Pastor David was baptizing me that Saturday, the only other person in the building was a woman from the congregation who volunteered to clean the church.

Seeing that something was taking place onstage, she stopped doing her chores for a few minutes, sat down, and watched the ten-minute ceremony with a bewildered look on her face. She was apparently confused by a baptism with no audience of witnesses. But after we were done, she seemed to have recategorized what she saw as a new way of doing baptisms. She went right back to her chores as if it were utterly ordinary that Pastor David would baptize a thirteen-year-old boy on a Saturday in an otherwise empty church building. Nothing weird about that at all.

From Pastor David's point of view, however, having witnesses on hand would have been superfluous. As he saw it from his expert pastoral perspective, we didn't need any audience to achieve the desired result. While the Bible commands believers to be baptized, it says nothing about having a mandatory audience.

Underwater One More Time

My Saturday ceremony involved nothing more than a dedicated pastor performing a necessary service for one of his parishioners. Onlookers were unnecessary so long as both we and God were in on the deal. That was all that mattered—one or a thousand witnesses wouldn't have changed the essential dynamic.

Looking back on it, I think Pastor David did it in this way as more of a "forensic baptism"—an operation defined by the act itself. According to his way of thinking, the number of witnesses was an insignificant factor. Just like the great detective Columbo solving a difficult crime, Pastor David had thoroughly observed the evidence. He'd completed his theological and pastoral assessment of the entire situation and cracked the case, coming up with the required solution to my pressing issue. As a needy parishioner, I had come to him with a specific theological and existential problem. We weren't entirely sure why my first baptism hadn't "taken," but it was clear to both of us that the first baptism somehow just hadn't been done right. What was necessary the second time around was to ensure that all the appropriate pieces were in place.

Pastor David had surmised that more than a few things were wrong with the initial ceremony. We uncovered some of these problems during our Sunday morning counseling sessions, but we also had a serious chat just before the deed was done. He stated that since my father had baptized me and not Pastor Jerry—the officially ordained pastor—maybe somehow the formula was off. Despite being a church elder, my dad was still an un-ordained layman, and he might have said the wrong thing before baptizing me. After all, he hadn't been to Bible college or seminary, and without such theological training, he could easily have made a mistake. And maybe I hadn't known exactly what I was doing at the time since I was only ten. David also reasoned that perhaps I hadn't reached the "age of accountability" yet. Perhaps I'd been too young, too intellectually immature, to commit to such a serious undertaking.

Chapter Twenty

My pastor uncovered another potential pastoral pitfall. He said he didn't want to disparage a good man, but there was a good chance that Pastor Jerry had severely let me down on at least two fronts. First, as he had already identified, Jerry had seriously shirked his responsibilities by letting a layman baptize me rather than doing it himself. Second, my first baptism had been something of a rushed job due to my fear of missing out on the Rapture, and Pastor Jerry had not adequately explained to me at the time how it was all supposed to work. Sitting in front of a picture of a smiling, white Jesus with little children sitting happily on his lap, David confidently stated that Jesus could and did explain the way of salvation simply and clearly to the little children. And it was possible that, since I was only ten, Jerry would not have been able to explain completely all the difficult theological complexities involved.

The diagnosis of my spiritual problem was clear: My first baptism hadn't worked for me. The solution was also apparent. I needed to be baptized again. "Are you now ready for this commitment?" Pastor David solemnly asked me. I said I was absolutely sure of what I was doing and understood the gravity of this decision. This time, I knew I was doing everything right, for all the right reasons, and with all the correct pieces of the theological puzzle in place.

According to Pastor David's theology, this second baptism would solve my problem. There was no need for spectators, a special baptismal service on a Sunday, or a celebration of any kind. This was simply a sort of business transaction being conducted between myself, Pastor David, and God. Skeptically, however, I wondered later if he didn't want any attention drawn to the fact that I had to be baptized twice—in the same church. After all, it was bad for the church to be seen as failing its parishioners. This oversight could easily be swept under the rug with a private re-baptism. Nobody needed to know about it. The only witness was the cleaning lady. At least the members of my family could have come. Wouldn't that have been easy enough to accomplish? Wouldn't having all my family members present have made the ceremony more meaningful?

Unlike the first baptism, this time, I sincerely believed that I understood exactly what I was doing and the implications. Furthermore, I had Pastor David's authoritative pastoral guarantee that everything was being done right and by The Book. As a duly ordained minister, he knew what to do. He'd been to both Bible college and seminary. He'd conducted hundreds of baptisms in his decades of ministry and knew exactly what should be said. He confidently assured me that of all those numerous converts he'd baptized over the years, there hadn't been a single person who had ever needed to get re-baptized. I felt a lot better just knowing that fact. With my new baptism, my problems would be solved, and I could go on my merry way, rejoicing and singing glad hallelujahs as I praised the Lord for my deliverance.

And so, for the second time, I was baptized. Pastor David pronounced the same trinitarian formula as my father did three years earlier: "I baptize you in the name of the Father, the Son, and the Holy Spirit." I did have a fleeting moment of doubt when I heard him say those crucial words exactly as my father had spoken them. Hadn't Pastor David questioned whether my dad had gotten the words right when he'd performed my first baptism? Yet here he was, stating the same formula. But it didn't matter, I told myself. Why should I worry? This time, a pastor had gotten the job done—not a layperson. This solemn ceremony took about ten minutes. Afterward, I was free to go with Pastor David's blessings ringing in my ears.

As I walked out of the building, drying my hair with my towel, I found my sister waiting patiently for me in her car. On the ride home, I explained what had happened in the church and asserted confidently that all my problems would surely be solved. I'd done everything right this time, and surely God was happy with me.

Chapter Twenty

I was definitely a Christian now, and there could be no doubt about it since this time, I could count on the authoritative word of an ordained and experienced minister of God to back me up. Baptized according to the proper formula this second time, I could forget about my unfortunate mistakes in the past. From this day forward, I fully expected to experience that victorious, supernaturally successful Christian life promised by preachers, teachers, and Christian parents. This time, I knew I'd ticked off all the boxes and done everything correctly and by the book.

Before climbing into bed that night, I happily thanked God for sending Pastor David into my life. I felt confident that I was now, as an old hymn states, "safe and secure from all alarms."[1] A tremendous burden had been lifted. I would no longer have to say that sinner's prayer that I had prayed countless times before—over and over—because now my eternal salvation was finally and forever safe. I slipped off to sleep with a clear conscience for the first time in years.

Now that I'd been re-baptized and was definitely saved, I knew for sure that I wouldn't miss the Rapture, even if Jesus suddenly decided to return that very night. If he did return tonight or tomorrow, or at any point in my life, I reasoned that it would be good news for me, not bad news, because most assuredly, I wouldn't be left behind. I would ascend through the clouds into heaven along with all the other true believers. I wouldn't even have to worry about the test of purifying fire to check the quality of my deeds on Earth. Saint Peter would wave me straight through the Pearly Gates, and I'd soon be walking along those streets of gold, heading for my heavenly mansion.

---

1   Anthony J. Showalter and Elisha Hoffman, "Leaning on the Everlasting Arms," 1887.

Chapter Twenty One

Living on a Spiritual Mountaintop

I was on top of the world in the months following my second baptism! Powered by what I believed to be a Holy-Spirit fueled Jesus high, I went about spiritually cleaning house. I threw away all my porn magazines, cleaned up my language, and made a special effort to be nice to my sisters. I did my chores at home without complaining and even did some extra tasks around the house without being asked. These changes got my parents' attention. They may have wondered if they were dreaming! I had turned over a new leaf now that the second baptism had finally and forever fixed my spiritual problems. Things were looking up for the first time in years. It was like I had been, well...born again.

One Saturday morning during this spiritually high period, I was chopping firewood in the woodshed. This was one of my daily chores, and I had always resented having to do it. My parents were constantly nagging me to ensure the wood box was full every morning before I left for school, and I frequently got into trouble because I failed to fill the box. But on *this* Saturday, fired with zealous righteousness and the desire to please God, I did much more chopping and stacking of wood than my usual half-hearted, bare minimum. And best of all, I did it without even being asked by my mom or dad.

As I chopped and stacked firewood that day, I reasoned that God would want me to do this. I was confident that God was more than pleased by my selfless actions. I firmly desired to be a faithful servant who happily toils away without complaining, not focusing on fleeting earthly rewards. As I chopped wood that was to be burned to keep my family warm, my goal was to build up treasures in heaven, rewards that God's purifying fire would not burn up! Indeed, this was what Bill Gothard talked about in his seminars. I was now building godly character traits into my life, attributes that would please God. I was now growing and maturing as a believer. As I sweated away chopping the ever-growing pile of firewood, I proudly told myself: "I'm *livin'* it, man!" I truly was a transformed Christian.

My mom was pleasantly surprised that she didn't have to ask me to do my regular chores, but as far as I could tell, she didn't attribute this to my newfound spiritual growth. As I recall, neither my sisters nor my parents asked me why I was suddenly being so nice. But I decided I was okay with that. I figured my new zeal for doing things right was just between me and the Lord. Hadn't Jesus taught that when you do good deeds for others, you should keep them secret, thereby building up lasting treasures in heaven? He said that your left hand shouldn't know what your right hand is doing and that compensation on Earth is meaningless compared to eternal rewards. Besides, the omniscient God I served saw everything, and he knew my heart was in the right place. That was all that mattered now.

Turning thirteen was a hallmark year for me not just because I was baptized that year. Being thirteen meant that I could attend the Bill Gothard *Institute in Basic Youth Conflicts* weeklong seminar. I'd been looking forward to attending this seminar for some time. All my older sisters had started attending when they turned thirteen, the minimum age for attendees. Held in our area at the Seattle Center, there were typically three to four thousand people in attendance each year. I attended all the sessions and paid close attention to everything Gothard said. I filled in all the blanks in the large notebook provided for participants. I remember the uplifting feeling I had after that intensive week ended. I knew that I had accomplished something significant, both for myself and for God.

Freshly baptized, and now seeing myself as a true believer, something about that week made me feel I was beginning a new stage of my Christian life, one that would be characterized by spiritual maturity.

Chapter Twenty Two

The Great Commission Right Next Door

The year before, when I was twelve, my Aunt Suzy, Uncle Rick, and their kids had moved into the house next to us. Two of their four children, Andy and Dan, were near my age. I was delighted to find myself with two new buddies. Not only were they good friends, they were also family!

There was one problem, and it was far from insignificant. Our relatives who moved in next door were not Christians. Well, it was our opinion that they were not Christians. As my mother informed me, they were *Catholics*, and thus, they weren't truly saved. When I asked Mom why they weren't truly saved, she replied, "Well, sadly, they mistakenly pray to Mary and the saints, but not to Jesus, like we true Christians do. A person can only be saved by believing in Jesus. Although they seem to believe a lot of the same things we do, unfortunately, they're not really Christians. It's truly heartbreaking because they're going to hell with a Bible in their hands."

The image of family members that I loved "going to hell with a Bible in their hands" really stuck with me. How could the Catholic Church have gotten it so wrong? Satan must have done a fantastic job of convincing all those millions of Catholics that they were truly Christians. The shocking truth was that, in reality, they were all bound for hell.

My uncle Rick was an atheist and never went to church. Aunt

Suzy went to Catholic Mass occasionally and forced my cousins to accompany her. I couldn't understand how they could be bound for hell if they went to church. One day, I posed a question to my mother. "Isn't going to the Catholic church the same as us going to our church?" "No," my mom confidently replied. "Like I said, Catholics aren't true believers. They're what I call 'counterfeit Christians.' Although they look and sound like us in many ways, they don't have a personal relationship with Christ like you and I do." I wondered how my next-door relatives—atheist or Catholic—could be so spiritually blind. As a result of their tragically lost condition, my mom was always praying for my uncle's family that they would see the error of their ways, repent, get right with God, and follow Christ. After that sobering conversation with my mom, I also started praying diligently for them, hoping that one day they would all get saved.

Knowing they were lost and bound for hell, I always tried to be a good Christian witness to my cousins Andy and Dan. I would drag them to our church youth group activities whenever we had a fun event planned, hoping the cool experience would convince them that we Christians weren't all fuddy-duddies who couldn't enjoy ourselves. "See, we can be normal and have a good time too!" Try as I might, neither of my cousins seemed to be convicted about repenting and getting right with God. They were having too much fun! As non-Christians, they did things that I believed were sinful, and their parents didn't even seem to care what they did.

My cousins had radios and record players in their bedrooms and were allowed to listen to whatever music they wanted. Unlike our home, they had several TVs in their house, with no restrictions on their viewing. Uncle Rick even paid for cable, which, back in the early 1980s, was a big deal—not everyone could afford it. Having cable allowed my cousins to check out all kinds of adult content late at night on HBO, and their parents didn't care. Andy and Dan had numerous porn magazines, which they didn't need to hide, and they gleefully watched R and even X-rated movies. They smoked marijuana, drank alcohol, and used foul language. Uncle Rick didn't care if they enjoyed a few of his beers when they watched a game with him on TV, even though they were minors.

Neither Andy nor Dan was a virgin. They bragged about sleeping with girls and mocked me for having no sexual experiences. It seemed to me that they were having a lot of fun living their secular, godless lives, certainly more so than my now squeaky-clean Christian existence. I loved hanging out with them, but I always felt deeply conflicted if they started to do something sinful and invited me to participate. My mom always warned me of the dangers of peer pressure leading me astray, and this was the height of peer pressure—coming from my relatives who lived next door!

They'd crack open a beer and offer me one, but I always refused, claiming I hated the taste. I knew that drunkenness led to all sorts of debauched behavior, so alcohol was best avoided. They might light up a joint, but I never partook because I'd been warned that marijuana was a gateway drug that would inevitably lead you into harder narcotics like cocaine or heroin. One toke of that joint, and the next thing you knew, you'd be a junkie out on the streets, desperate for your next fix. One of my cousins would tell a dirty joke, and I'd try my hardest not to laugh because that was sinful, too. Rock n' roll was their favorite kind of music, so I always made sure to leave if they played a forbidden album.

Knowing how important it was that they should get saved and go to heaven with me, I always felt pressured to set a godly example of Christlike living for my lost cousins. One thing I knew for sure: I couldn't let them drag me down with them. It was clear to me that God had placed them in my life so I could save them.

I remember once I was hanging out in their living room, and Andy put a porn movie that he'd rented from the local video store into the video player. He did this by mistake, thinking the tape was a different film we were all going to watch. But suddenly here I was confronted with naked people having sexual intercourse. Secretly, I wanted to stay and watch the forbidden video with them. I felt deeply conflicted. Thanks to my newfound spirituality following my second baptism, I had made great strides in overcoming my porn addiction. If I stayed, not only would I be sinning against God, I would also be a lousy witness by participating in this sinful behavior. I caught myself and made up a weak excuse. I suddenly remembered I had something else I was supposed to be doing right then, so I had to go. "What's your problem, man?" Andy mockingly shouted as I slunk out of the room, feeling like a foolish prude.

What they didn't know was that this good Christian kid already had years of experience with pornography. I'd watched many X-rated movies with one of my Christian buddies, so my cousins' video was nothing I hadn't seen before. But I felt that I couldn't admit my old porno habit to my cousins without destroying my witness as a believer.

Being a Christian made you *different* somehow. That's what we were told, and I had heard that line in Sunday School, church, and summer camp countless times. We're in the world, but not of it. Weren't we set apart for Christ to be unstained by the evils everywhere prevalent in our godless, secular society? Despite feeling embarrassed for my uncool behavior that day, deep down, I knew I'd done the right thing. I hadn't given in to temptation! I congratulated myself for setting a good and godly example before my unbelieving cousins.

There was always that nagging feeling in the back of my mind that I needed to do more to get them saved. My old, familiar pattern of guilt resurfaced, and I always felt as if I was letting God down.

I was continuously wracked with shame and anxiety, agonizing over the fact that if either one of my cousins died suddenly, they would face an eternity in hell. And it would be my fault because I hadn't tried hard enough to convince them of the gospel's truth. Their horrendous eternal destiny, tormented forever in burning agony, would be forever on my conscience.

I once heard a preacher discussing the prophet Ezekiel in the Old Testament. He said that God had told Ezekiel that the blood of the unrighteous man would be on his hands if he failed to warn him about the impending judgment day, when God would judge the world. I hoped and prayed that my cousins would someday get saved because I didn't want their blood on my hands if they died suddenly before they had repented and gotten right with God. There was no way I could live with myself if they passed away and ended up in hell, and it would be my fault for not leading them to the Lord. I did not want to shirk my responsibilities as a budding evangelist, so I was always on the lookout for ways to steer them in the right direction.

No shortage of opportunities existed for Andy and Dan to get saved and come to Christ. One summer, I convinced Andy to attend Christian camp with me, but the week turned out to be a disaster. What happened could have been straight out of a Hollywood movie about summer camp shenanigans. Taking an immediate dislike to Tom, our cabin counselor, Andy spent the whole week tormenting the poor guy. On the first day, he hung Tom's mummy-style sleeping bag from the rafters with a rope fashioned into a noose. Each day, when he was supposed to be at Bible study, Andy would sneak into our cabin, open Tom's suitcase, and hide his clothes around the camp. After a few days of this, Tom resorted to locking his suitcase in the trunk of his car.

Tom had a prized plastic Seattle Mariners batting helmet he'd gotten when attending a home game, and he wore it all the time—

backward—so he'd look cool for the female counselors. But every time Tom was in the shower, Andy took sadistic pleasure in hiding the batting helmet in places where Tom couldn't find it. It finally reached the point where Tom took his plastic hat everywhere— even when he took a shower or went to the toilet—for fear of it getting stolen or hidden.

Later in the week, when Tom was at the point of complete despair, Andy found a new way to annoy him. He ran a pair of Tom's dirty underwear up the camp flagpole in front of the lodge. This stunt delighted all of us campers, but it enraged that week's camp director, a massively obese pastor from a church in Oregon. He looked just like actor Chris Farley, when he played the role of Matt Foley, motivational speaker, in the classic sketch from *Saturday Night Live*. The camp director and Tom were at their wits' end, frustrated with Andy's disruptive behavior. Other boys followed Andy's lead and started pranking their counselors, making things worse.

The week culminated with all of us boys being dressed down in the lodge by the director on the final day of camp. He was red-faced, furiously angry, and sweating profusely as he berated us for being such incredibly poor Christians. "How could you set such a bad example by being so childish and rebellious this whole week? I know you're only boys now, but when you grow up to be men, you'll be leaders both in the church and in your families. But after this week, God is surely disappointed in every one of you. All of you should be ashamed since you know better. This isn't how your parents raised you. That much is for sure!" For our part, we stared at the floor, not making eye contact with him, and tried to suppress our giggles.

Finding out why he was so furiously angry with us didn't take long. After suffering through all the outrages of the week, one other thing happened, and it was the straw that broke the camel's back.

One of the toilets in the men's bathroom, located in the lodge, was clogged and overflowing with toilet paper, feces, and urine. "Clearly," the enraged director asserted, "this was no accident. One of you has deliberately done it!" All he wanted, he angrily declared, was for the offender to do the right thing and identify himself. He gave us about ten minutes for the culprit to confess, but no one said anything. The lack of an honest response made the director even angrier. "Well, it doesn't matter," he finally declared after nobody admitted to the crime. "Since none of you is man enough to acknowledge what he's done, you'll all be punished—together." Nobody knew what that meant, but it didn't sound good.

We soon found out what he meant by his threat. The exasperated director lined us up at the bathroom door and commanded us to unclog the offending toilet. Each of us boys had to take something solid out of the toilet with our bare hands and deposit it into a five-gallon bucket before being allowed to wash our hands and go. Angrily glaring at us, the sweating director stood beside the toilet to ensure nobody shirked this foul and disgusting job. Since I was near the front of the line of involuntary toilet cleaners, I had some choices as to what I would remove from the clogged commode. As I stared into the filthy, overflowing bowl, my first thought was, "I'm not picking up a turd!" After a careful search, I finally pulled out a tiny piece of toilet paper, held it up for the director's approval, and dropped it into the bucket. I raced to the sink and scrubbed my hands vigorously with soap and hot water for at least five minutes. I felt sorry for the guys in line behind me. As each of us chose what repulsive item we would remove from the toilet, the choices remaining for the guys behind us worsened. The whole experience was vile, disturbing, and disgusting.

To this day, I'm convinced that Andy stopped up that toilet with wads of toilet paper, but he never confessed, even privately to me. That week at Christian summer camp did not result in Andy finding salvation. Because he'd been such a troublemaker all week, he was forever banned from returning to camp. So much for making a nonbeliever feel welcome.

As for Dan, he was never interested in going to camp with me after hearing about Andy's experiences, even though I invited him the following summer. Despite this setback, there were still other ways to get through to him. I convinced him to come with me to a few Christian rock concerts, hoping that he would experience something in one of those concerts that would lead to his salvation. My anticipation was high one year at a Resurrection Band gig. I knew that following the show, there would be a rousing gospel message followed by an altar call—an invitation to come forward and accept Jesus as your savior—presented by Glenn Kaiser, the lead singer of the band. I reasoned I could lure Dan along because he loved rock music, and then at the end, he would be confronted with the gospel. To my delight, Dan responded to the invitation at the concert's conclusion. I was ecstatic that he wanted to get saved, and I went with him up to the front, hoping this would be a life-changing moment.

Despite going forward and praying the sinner's prayer at the concert, nothing ever came of Dan's conversion experience. For weeks, I prayed that he would start attending church or youth group with me. Despite my prayers and my repeated invitations, he went right back to his old sinful ways. Occasionally, in an effort to convict him, I'd try to remind Dan of his commitment to follow Christ at the concert, but it seemed that he had forgotten all about it.

I often wondered why his conversion experience didn't take. Why didn't God do more to ensure Dan stayed on the narrow path of righteousness? Moving forward, I operated on the assumption that neither of my cousins was saved. Wanting to avoid blaming myself if either one of them went to hell, I tried my hardest to get them to see the light. I remained puzzled at the lack of positive results. Surely, I reasoned, God should have blessed my efforts in evangelizing them and directed the Holy Spirit to open their spiritually blinded eyes to the truth before it was too late.

Tragically, in his late twenties, Andy was killed in a drunk driving accident. A few years after that, Dan put a gun to his head and committed suicide. I felt awful that both had died without me leading them to the Lord. For years after they died, I was tormented with guilt and remorse about the fact that I hadn't done more to save them. Their blood, I reckoned, would be on my hands forever for failing to do my part. I had not done a good enough job warning them of the eternal torment they faced in hell if they did not repent and get right with God.

Chapter Twenty Three

Falling Off the Mountaintop

I once heard some Christian sage proclaim, "The problem with mountaintop experiences is that you can't live on that mountain forever. Eventually, you must come down and rejoin the real world." Summer camp was always a mountaintop experience, and I think it was one of the preachers at the camp Andy and I attended who spoke those words. On the other side of every mountain is a valley. As the preacher predicted, I eventually descended from the mountaintop, and it was a very dark valley that I found myself in.

Six months or so following my second baptism, my spiritual high began to evaporate. The grim realities of life were staring me in the face. Over the next couple of years, despite my best efforts, I gradually slipped back into the life of sin I thought my second baptism had conclusively ended.

The problem was that the evil, secular world was always on hand to offer up novel and enticing temptations. Once again, I found myself trading porno magazines with my church buddies. To my shame, sometimes I would even sneak into my cousin Dan's room and steal a few magazines out of his closet. I felt even worse about that because not only was I stealing, which was a grave sin, but I was supposed to be evangelizing him by setting a godly example of victorious Christian living. Yet here I was, acting like a total hypocrite, lustfully fantasizing over stolen porn.

Dan asked me a couple of times if I had taken his magazines, but I always swore that it hadn't been me. Now, I was committing the additional sin of lying. I was compounding my sins one atop the other, all of which surely were a significant disappointment in the eyes of God. I knew from reading tracts at the Christian bookstore where my mom worked that God witnessed everything we did and said and kept detailed records of every sin we committed. This included sinful *thoughts,* such as looking at a woman lustfully—something I did every time I viewed the beautiful naked women in my pornography magazines. According to the teachings of Jesus, this sin was equal to having physical sex with a woman, so I believed that looking at porn was just as bad as engaging in illicit sex with a real person.

I reckoned that God's angels must have been extremely busy cataloging my sins. Maybe there was a whole angelic department working overtime dedicated to the task! I also knew that someday, at God's final judgment, I would stand before his throne like a guilty criminal in the dock before the judge. To my eternal shame, all those stacks of books would be brought in, and every sin I'd ever committed against God would be read aloud for everyone to hear. The knowledge of my potentially humiliating fate constantly gnawed at me, but even that didn't stop me from engaging in sinful behaviors.

All those swear words I'd learned from a neighborhood friend, purged from my vocabulary during my "spiritual mountaintop" time, came creeping back into regular usage. The fits of anger toward my sisters returned with a vengeance, and it was no more *Mr. Nice Guy.* All those good intentions slipped away like sand through my fingers, and it wasn't long before I was right back in the shit. Only this time, it was even worse because I was right back where I had started. Once again, I was in desperate need of help.

A year after my second baptism, when I was fourteen, I thought perhaps I could seek some pastoral guidance from my old mentor, Pastor David. But that same year, when I was thinking of asking him for help, he was unexpectedly fired due to ugly church politics—just when I needed him the most. He was run out by a faction who had turned against him because he was deemed too embarrassing for our up-and-coming congregation. His tacky, inelegant image wasn't what the church wanted to project, so the Elder Board cut him loose.

David's departure closed what had been a meaningful avenue of counseling and ministerial support for me. Pastor Mark was still around, and for a few weeks, I thought about approaching him for guidance, even though it was the last thing I wanted to do. But one Sunday, shortly after Pastor David left, Mark announced that he had accepted a head pastor role across the state. Suddenly, all the old familiar faces were gone, and our church started the arduous process of replacing two staff members. Without either David or Mark to turn to for godly spiritual counsel, I was left feeling adrift and lost.

I felt sorry for Pastor David. He was a genuinely lovely guy. Just as before with Pastor Jerry, his departure was one more exposure to the nasty and cruel side of church politics and how Christians frequently treat their fellow believers so severely. My parents disagreed with the way the whole thing was handled, and in protest, left the church, which cut me loose, too. For months, we spent Sundays church shopping. This involved looking for a new church home that ticked all the boxes our old one did, but we couldn't seem to find the right one.

My parents finally settled on a very conservative Baptist church.

Chapter Twenty Three

The senior pastor was a real piece of work, a hardcore Calvinist[1] who had graduated from The Master's Seminary, and had been deeply influenced theologically by its founder, John MacArthur.[2] I instantly disliked him and his hardline, dogmatic, fundamentalist sermons. There was no chance I would join my parents' new church. Occasionally, I'd tag along with some of my Christian buddies to their churches, but I would mostly drift in and out, without a place of worship. I sometimes worried that I might fade away like those coals Pastor Jerry had pulled from the campfire. But I couldn't find a good church I wanted to join, even though I knew the importance of genuine fellowship.

Despite my lack of regular church attendance, starting in ninth grade, I enrolled in a Christian high school. Once again, just like I'd done in church, I looked and sounded the part. Thanks to years of church indoctrination, I knew all the correct answers, and I excelled in Bible class. I knew how to play the game of Christian living to perfection.

I reasoned that maybe the fellowship of being around other Christian kids and attending chapel each Thursday would help keep me from fading away like those coals Jerry pulled out of the fire. But that did not happen—the community in our Christian school just did not seem to be the same as what a church could offer.

To the untrained eye, I was a great young Christian guy with his life on track, serving God by going to a Christian school and attending church as often as he could. At school, I was heavily involved in several wholesome activities. I sang in the choir, and we often performed in churches doing worship music. We all felt that singing in the choir was a great ministry opportunity, and it also demonstrated just how dedicated we were. I played varsity-level soccer and was on both the track and baseball teams. As far as anybody could see from the outside, I had my life together.

But I didn't have a true church home. I occasionally attended a local FourSquare church just south of Seattle that Lewis, one of my high school soccer buddies, attended. He played bass, and together with a couple of guitarists from school we formed a Christian metal band. The FourSquare church let us practice in the sanctuary on Saturdays. I felt obligated to participate every so often as a sort of payback, so I attended services whenever I could. As an added bonus, the church had a swimming pool. After Sunday service, in the summer, a bunch of us teens would spend hours splashing around and having a blast. But after I had been enjoying this activity for several months, the Elder Board decided the pool represented a safety hazard. They didn't just close the pool—they had it filled in! No more swimming after church. My interest in the church waned significantly after that, and I found myself attending less often.

During the summer, I still attended the Christian camp I had gone to as a kid. The difference was that now, I was a camp counselor in charge of groups of kids for an entire week. They looked up to me as a shining example of a good Christian young man. No stopped-up toilets on my watch! No kid would prank me by running my dirty underwear up the flagpole!

But life wasn't so great because I knew the truth. I was a hypocrite, and the omniscient God I claimed to serve knew everything I did. I wore the Christian mask but felt terrible about it. This was a repeat of what had happened after my first baptism. Only now, it was compounded by some festering questions. My chief concern was this: What had gone so badly wrong the second time? Hadn't Pastor David explained it clearly and done all the right things according to the correct formula, solving all my problems? Like a rerun of an old movie, my existential guilt and dread of hell returned and wouldn't go away, nor would my fear of missing out on the Rapture and being left behind.

And where was God in all of this? Once more, I wondered why he didn't come to my aid. As before, over and over I begged him for help. I desperately prayed asking for guidance, but none seemed forthcoming. In high school Bible classes, I was reminded of what I had been taught growing up in church: The power of the Holy Spirit is always available to assist believers with the process of sanctification—the lifelong journey of becoming more and more like Christ. But nothing remotely like that was happening in my life, despite my repeated and heartfelt prayers for help. Perhaps God wasn't listening because I was sinning too much, or maybe I just didn't have enough faith.

Once again, I couldn't see any compelling evidence that I resembled Jesus in any area of my life.

---

1   "Calvinism" refers to the theological system of John Calvin and his successors, as laid out in the context of the 16th century Protestant Reformation. It develops Martin Luther's concept of "justification by faith" but centers on the notion of "predestination," in which God chooses or "elects" those who will be saved, and the non-elect who will go to hell.

2   Located in Los Angeles, The Master's Seminary was founded by John MacArthur in 1986. Well-known as the head pastor of Grace Community Church since 1969, MacArthur has also courted controversy due to his dogmatic Calvinist views, anti-Covid mask mandates, and promotion of Christian patriarchy. He is vocally anti-LGBTQ, and staunchly against the ordination of women and same-sex marriage.

Chapter Twenty Four

The Brother I Never Had

Halfway through my freshman year at the Christian high school, I discovered a soulmate. Guy was the brother I never had, and I filled the same role for him, since like me he had only sisters for siblings. My new best friend quickly became the one bright spark in my otherwise dark life.

Guy came out of a messed-up, dysfunctional home like mine. When we met, his parents had divorced a few years earlier, which screwed him up badly. Not long after his divorce, Guy's dad went sideways, turning his back on his former Christian faith. Becoming an agnostic, he walked away from the church and abandoned himself to what Guy considered a lifestyle of sin and debauchery. He watched his dad circling in a revolving door of sexual partners. Prior to ditching his Christian faith, for decades Guy's dad had been a staunch believer. He led Guy's mom to become a Christian shortly after they got married. For years he had been an elder in their charismatic church, where he preached, led Bible studies, and performed other leadership roles.

Guy was thirteen when his parents divorced, and we could relate to the fact that both of us had lost our relationships with our fathers around the same time, albeit in different ways and for different reasons.

I wondered if Guy's dad's leaving his faith was an example of what happens to one of those coals that left the fire and disappeared in the darkness. It seemed like a clear-cut case of what could happen to someone who appeared to be a steadfast believer. Guy's mom went in the opposite direction and doubled down on her Christian commitment. Not long after the divorce was finalized, she married an avid fundamentalist Christian named Don. Neither Guy nor I could stand Don. He was a prison chaplain who purportedly had led scores of hardened inmates to Christ, using a method of evangelism he claimed worked without fail. Don was also into charismatic Christianity—speaking in tongues, interpretations of tongues, miraculous healing, and divine words of knowledge. Don claimed that God revealed things to him that nobody else could know, and therefore professed to "operate in the supernatural realm of the prophetic." He once claimed that he could feel the wind from angels' wings around his ears when he prayed. Despite Don's proclaimed closeness to God, the shabby ways he treated Guy and his two younger sisters was at odds with any true piety.

My close friendship with Guy had multiple connection points. We were both the only boys in our families, were social misfits, and came from dysfunctional homes. We could also relate in terms of our spiritual struggles and our ongoing failure to live the promised but elusive "victorious supernatural Christian life." But our friendship wasn't all roses. The first time Guy came to stay at my house, our burgeoning friendship nearly ended right then and there.

Guy's stepdad dropped him off at our house Saturday morning, and we had a great time messing around all day. At one point, I took Guy into my parents' bedroom and showed him all the hideous ties my dad had hanging on his tie rack. Most of them were polyester, and in 1970s fashion were tied with huge knots. Dad's ties were a lot like the ones Pastor David wore. He even had one polyester suit that could have been purchased at the same clothing store where David shopped. It was bright green and yellow plaid, and we were embarrassed every time he wore it to church.

My dad was extremely private and didn't want anyone going into their bedroom, but we were momentarily safe to venture there because my parents were downstairs making dinner. I darted downstairs to see when dinner would be ready, leaving Guy alone in the forbidden room. I didn't notice my dad heading upstairs until it was too late. Walking down the hallway, my dad approached the bedroom, and to his surprise, Guy stepped out the door proudly wearing one of my dad's ties knotted around his head. Guy thought it was me coming down the hall and that the tie on his head would get a big laugh. Instead, he was confronted by my dad, who was standing there, shocked by what he saw.

They just stared at each other in stunned silence for a moment or two. My dad was upset at Guy being in his bedroom without permission, but he was probably even more angry about the grievous insult to his fashion statement. To his credit, Dad kept his cool. He put out his hand, and politely asked, "Can I have my tie back, please?" Sheepishly, Guy removed the tie and handed it to my dad. Without a word, the two went their separate ways, but from then on, the damage between Guy and my dad was irreparable.

The next day, Guy went to church with us. Coming from a charismatic church background, this was the first time Guy had ever experienced another Christian tradition. Pastor David preached on the supernatural "gift of tongues" spoken of in the New Testament book of Acts. He argued forcefully that these miraculous gifts no longer functioned in today's world. Theologically, our Church of Christ held to what is termed a "cessationist" viewpoint, teaching that all those miraculous supernatural gifts in the book of Acts had ceased after the first century. Sitting in the pew with my Bible open, I agreed wholeheartedly with every point Pastor David advanced to bolster his argument that morning. It's what I'd been taught from day one, and I saw no reason to question what he was teaching. I'd never been exposed to alternative theological points of view, safe as I was within my little Christian bubble.

As I followed Pastor David's line of argument closely, I didn't realize that Guy was seething with anger as he sat beside me. He was from a charismatic church tradition where they regularly practiced speaking in tongues, miracles, healings, prophecies, and words of knowledge. From Guy's point of view, Pastor David was twisting Scripture to suit his own ends. Misusing the Bible and manipulating his listeners into believing lies, he was spewing nonsense—and was therefore most likely a heretic.

When we got into the car after the service, Guy told me how upset he was and how completely wrong Pastor David's sermon had been. Angrily, I defended not only my beloved pastor but the theology behind his argument. The entire way home, Guy and I debated whether the supernatural gift of tongues was still operative today. The disagreement intensified, becoming more and more heated. It got to the point where we were almost shouting at each other, and several times, my mom had to tell us to keep it down.

Desperate to prove that I was right in my views, I listed as many biblical citations as I could think of to uphold my point. I mentioned 1 Corinthians 13, the chapter I memorized and recited to my dad years earlier. I pointed out that Paul taught that one day, all tongues would cease![1] What additional scriptural evidence could one ask for to make an airtight case? Ironically, there was no love coming from my position, even though I was quoting from "the love chapter." All that mattered was that I was correct in my biblical interpretation, and Guy was wrong.

Guy vehemently disagreed with me and pushed his pro-tongues perspective just as firmly as I argued my point of view. He cited several proof texts to prove that the gift of tongues is still operative today. I had never heard this line of reasoning, and I started to feel unsettled. I didn't admit it to Guy that day, but the thought crossed my mind that my cherished theological position might somehow be incorrect. Ironically, that twinge of doubt prompted me to double down, go on the offensive, and fight all the harder for my cessationist position. As our argument escalated, it became personal and ugly, devolving into accusing each other of being heretics. We were utterly convinced that the other held aberrant views on the subject. Surely, we both couldn't be right.

When we arrived back at my house, Guy was so angry that he immediately went upstairs and packed up his belongings. Without saying a word to anyone, he slipped out of the house during a torrential rainstorm. He planned to walk all the way home, which was more than twenty miles away! About a half hour later, upon discovering that he had left the house quietly, my dad jumped in his car and went searching for him. Fortunately, Dad found Guy a few miles down the road, soaked to the bone. Guy agreed to come back to our house with my dad. We were able to patch things up, and after this experience that nearly ended our friendship, we decided not to fall out over doctrinal matters ever again. We agreed to disagree and as time passed became best friends.

Looking back, I realize how indoctrinated we were in our theological traditions. We had almost been willing to end our new friendship over the issue of speaking in tongues. We had placed our relationship in jeopardy over differing interpretations of the Bible. This relates to a third aspect of Lifton's categories of cult markers: "doctrine over person."[2] Many Christians are more than willing to hurt a fellow believer or destroy a relationship, correcting the other person harshly when they firmly believe they're "wrong" about something the Bible says. Many Christians have ended personal relationships over disagreements about theological differences, biblical interpretation, or cherished church traditions.

For many devout Christians, being right is all that ultimately matters. What the other person feels is unimportant in the grand scheme of things. Believing the exact right things and hammering others with your "Truth" (with a capital T), based upon your interpretation of the Bible, can easily take precedence over interpersonal relationships, especially in more conservative Christian churches. What happened between Guy and me fits another of Lifton's categories: "sacred science."[3] Every religion has its sacred text, and Christianity is no different. Ironically, both Guy and I would have agreed that as the Word of God to humanity, the Bible is inspired and inerrant— without error in all that it affirms. However, we strongly disagreed over how the Bible was to be correctly interpreted when it came to the speaking in tongues debate. Later, I wondered why God didn't make things more explicit in his infallible Word. It would solve many doctrinal disputes, arguments, and church splits if, for each issue, there was but one clear, simple, and correct interpretation on which all believers could agree.

Fortunately, in this case, Guy and I patched up our doctrinal squabble and became best friends. Unfortunately, despite both claiming to be good Christians, we weren't the greatest influences on each other. Sometimes he'd stay at my house, or I'd go to his. We'd sneak out late at night after everyone was asleep, prowling the streets, engaging in petty vandalism, and playing pranks on our long-suffering neighbors. One of our favorite tricks was to swap all the deck furniture between two houses a few blocks away from my house. We must've played that prank a dozen times, but the neighbors never caught us. I liked to imagine what they said when we pulled this stunt: "Damn those kids! Next time, we'll catch them in the act." Fortunately for us, this was decades before the *Ring* doorbells and other surveillance equipment now commonplace in so many homes.

Once or twice a year, we'd stay the night with another high school buddy, John, when his parents were out of town. We'd smoke cigars, swap dirty magazines, and get blind drunk on wine stolen from a neighbor's wine cellar. We were always careful only to steal one, or at the most two, bottles. They either didn't notice or didn't care, but we felt fortunate that, for whatever reason, their wine cellar continued to be unlocked. Had we been caught, we would have instantly been booted out of our fundamentalist Christian high school. We had violated many other legalistic rules that could have gotten us kicked out. The three of us made a solemn pact: Never speak about our late-night activities to anyone else for fear of being snitched on by someone outside our triad.

Our concern about being ratted out was not ill founded. Toward the end of my senior year, five schoolmates were betrayed by a "friend" for sharing *one* beer at a party. Ironically, Guy and I had attended the same party earlier that evening and had been offered a drink by the same guys who ended up getting into trouble. Since I hated the taste of beer at the time, I refused the offer. If I'd taken just one sip, I would have been busted alongside the guys who got caught.

The principal's initial response to the drinking incident was to expel the offenders immediately. But their parents intervened, begging the school administration for the tiniest bit of leniency. They argued that kicking their sons out of school would be pointless since they were only weeks away from completing all their academic work. In the end, the parents got the sentence reduced: The five could finish their senior year but would not be allowed to attend graduation ceremonies. However, it turned out a surprise was in store.

Despite sharing that same beer with his friends, the guy who ratted out his buddies was allowed to participate in the graduation ceremony. From the school's point of view, even though he'd sinned, he had eventually done the right thing by turning his friends in. The other four suffered the consequences of their infraction and missed their graduation ceremony.

Chapter Twenty Four

Sitting on that stage at my high school graduation, I breathed a sigh of relief that Guy and I had been smart enough to keep our mouths shut. We'd done far worse things than those guys, but the school administration never discovered our wicked ways. We were smarter at playing the game than the guys who got caught. Fortunately for him, the night of the party, the stakes had not been so high for Guy. He had escaped our Christian school after tenth grade and transferred to a public school. He preferred the secular environment more than the strict and legalistic atmosphere where I was stuck.

But moving to a public school didn't solve all his problems with religion, shame, and guilt. A few years later, when his girlfriend Lisa became pregnant, they decided to have an abortion. Tormented by guilt that he had "murdered his child," as he confessed to me afterward, at eighteen, he convinced an unscrupulous doctor to give him a vasectomy. He told me that he felt so badly about being part of the grievous sin of abortion that he didn't deserve to have a child. He never wanted to get another woman pregnant and risk facing the decision to abort. Such was the immense hold that his religious upbringing had on him.

In addition to all the bad stuff we were into, both of us were addicted to pornography. We swapped dirty magazines. When we were finally old enough to drive, we rented porno movies from the local video store. Looking back, I think this behavior was primarily about self-medicating to ease the pain of being such disappointments to God and having such dysfunctional families. At least we could share how messed up we were, but we didn't have a clue what to do about our emotional pain other than to keep on self-medicating.

I vividly recall going on many a late-night walk down darkened streets, smoking cigars and baring our souls to each other. We'd talk for hours about our deeply flawed families, how much of a disappointment we surely were to God, and what we could do to get our lives back on track. At least Guy and I could be honest with each other. We acknowledged freely to ourselves and to each other that we were complete screw-ups. Despite propping each other up emotionally and, perhaps in some unorthodox manner, spiritually, neither of us could figure out what to do about our problems. We both tried praying and begging God for help, but as always, no divine answers or help ever arrived.

In my junior year of high school, I was struggling mightily to achieve that victorious Christian life I had been promised after my second baptism. Things weren't getting any better, and it didn't help that Guy had switched to a public school the year before. As a result, we barely saw each other. I made a few new friends through playing sports, but there was no one at the Christian school who I was as close to as I was to Guy. I missed hanging out with him every day. Without his support, I had no one to tell my deepest, darkest secrets, and things were getting very dark.

Three years after my second baptism, at the age of sixteen, I could not ignore the reality of my spiritual condition. I finally admitted that my second baptism hadn't worked its promised magic. Pastor David's confident prediction that my problems would be solved had not come true. I felt I was far worse off than after my first baptism. I had convinced myself *twice* that I was a genuine Christian based on these simple acts of immersion in the baptismal waters. Once again, I had been dunked in a tank by someone and had the same formulaic statement pronounced. Other than getting wet, nothing had happened besides convincing myself that I'd been saved and a short burst of "changed" behaviors. The results I had expected from both baptisms were starting to look like magical thinking.

That feeling that I was a fraud and a phony was ever present. It would only be a matter of time before someone found me out. I was wearing a mask, playing the part like an accomplished actor. Although I was adept at the role, my religious self and my authentic self always competed. Which one was I? Which one was my authentic self? I didn't even know at this point, and I suppose I was trying to live out the words described by Paul in the book of Romans, as he seemingly struggled with some unnamed sin problem like I was.[4] I truly believed that my "sinful nature," the "old man" to which Paul refers, had to be suppressed and put down so that my spiritual "new self" could have ascendancy. I reasoned that I'd be pleasing to God if I could just do that, but I struggled mightily to work it all out.

I firmly believed that my old sinful nature was thoroughly evil. As a result, I had to battle with it because it constantly attempted to drag me back into a life of sinfulness. I also had to admit that Guy and I were probably not very good influences on each other, as we egged each other on into committing worse sins. I heartily agreed with Paul later in that same passage in Romans when he agonized, "Oh, wretched man that I am! Who shall deliver me from this body of death?"[5] Although he went on in the very next verse to claim that it was Christ that helped believers to become victorious over a life of sin, I was unable to make that supernatural connection. I had not been able to overcome my sins. Quite simply, this promise didn't work for me at all.

Now, I see my prolonged spiritual struggles, doubts, and guilt during my adolescence as horribly damaging psychologically. For years I suppressed my authentic identity in favor of a religious one. It's a false dichotomy that does incalculable damage on multiple levels. Once again, I'm reminded of Lifton's description of "doubling"—the creation of a religious self alongside our authentic self. Unfortunately, when this happens, our true identity can become damaged or even lost in the process. Surely, this is what I was doing, but it was all "normal" at the time. That is, it was normalized within the evangelical world in which I lived. Virtually all the other Christians I knew spoke of enduring the same struggles with sin in their lives, and the need to "remove the mask" and be real. They all faced similar difficulties as they tried in vain to overcome sin and live a life of victory. Despite all the late-night conversations focusing on how to get past our spiritual defeats, and the countless prayers begging God for help, Guy and I could never work out how to live that victorious Christian life.

I remember a preacher at summer camp talking about how critically important it was for believers in churches to "remove their masks" and reveal their true selves since the omniscient God knew who we were all along. I agreed with his argument in principle but couldn't imagine becoming that vulnerable. As one of my buddies wryly commented afterward, most churches weren't safe places to be vulnerable. The sad truth of the matter is this: In many, if not most, congregations, if a believer opened up about their actual struggles, life complications, adulterous affairs, addictions, mental health problems, and other secret issues, they would likely be roundly rejected and shunned by their fellow believers. If every believer in a church engaged in this action, it's hard to imagine what would happen. I guess there would either be a revival, or the church would close its doors like the Word of Life Church I had been drawn to years earlier.

So many self-righteous and judgmental Christians are involved in secret sins they would never admit—and certainly not at church. This was all so ironic to me. Weren't churches supposed to be "hospitals for sinners, and not museums for saints?" I suspected that almost everyone in church was wearing some kind of mask. And church didn't feel like a safe place to take off your mask and reveal who you are. I recalled how the Elder Board had treated Pastor Jerry so badly when he told them he needed some time to rest and recuperate from the rigors of ministry. Later, Pastor David was run out of the same church because of his questionable fashion choices. He liked his loud polyester suits and mismatched shirts and ties, but this wasn't the image the church wanted to portray.

I had no reason to believe that I would be accepted if I removed my mask and revealed my true self to my church. At least with Guy, I could be authentic, and he could do the same with me. Our relationship wasn't the healthiest, but we could each share our deepest, darkest secrets without fear of judgment and rejection from the other. With Guy, there was never any need to wear a mask.

Later in my junior year, it seemed that there was a potential lifeline to grasp as I flailed spiritually. Dennis, a friend of the family, was one of the few people my parents had stayed in touch with after we'd left our church. He and I chatted one night after he and his wife had invited us all over for dinner. Sensing I was struggling in my Christian walk, he kindly offered to disciple me. I thought this was just what I needed. It would be a great way to mature and grow spiritually. Together over the next few months, Dennis and I worked through a Christian spiritual growth workbook, filling in the blanks with answers to questions from the Bible. But in reality, I only liked going over to Dennis's house each Saturday because his job involved filling up vending machines. He always had a great store of candies in his hall closet, and I'd gorge myself on these tasty treats while we did our Bible study.

Week by week, I would forget to fill in most of the blanks in the workbook, which I was supposed to do at home in preparation for our meetings. Shortly before Dennis would arrive to pick me up, I'd search my room for the workbook, which I had ignored all week—just like my dusty Bible. In the last seconds before Dennis arrived, I would frantically try to whiz through answering all the questions, but I never had enough time to finish them. I just wasn't into it. We managed to finish the first book and started another, but the sessions with Dennis eventually stopped. It didn't matter to me when the sessions ended, because the truth was that I hadn't received much help from them.

Now that I barely saw Guy since he had left my high school, other than Dennis, there was nobody who could help me. And the help Dennis offered didn't help. Where could I turn for guidance and direction? I weighed my options. I couldn't talk to my parents about my problems, since I imagined I would receive the same treatment Valerie had gotten years earlier when she was pregnant. We had long since left our old church after Pastor David had been forced out, and I had not followed my parents to their new church. I was unmoored, without a church home. I refused to talk to the fundamentalist pastor at my parents' new church, since I couldn't stand him in the slightest. After the FourSquare church had filled in its swimming pool, I had quit attending and had lost my connection there. I didn't trust any of the teachers at my Christian high school, since I figured that if I confessed my sins, there was every chance I'd be booted out for violating their rules.

With no one to talk to and nowhere to turn for assistance, it seemed that my only option was to continue struggling through life as a dismal failure in the eyes of God. I was now wracked with even more guilt and shame. I felt like my life was pathetic.

---

1   1 Corinthians 13:8.
2   Robert Jay Lifton, "Cult Formation."
3   Robert Jay Lifton, "Cult Formation."
4   Romans 7:4-25.
5   Romans 7:24, KJV.

Chapter Twenty Five

Giving Up on God

O ne thing always bothered me. I could never figure out why God could not or would not help me with my problems. God seemed distant at best and downright unhelpful at worst. Was this what a loving heavenly father should look and feel like? I wondered if God and I had fallen out at some point—like my dad and me—and I just hadn't noticed when he left. Had my sins finally reached the point where God was so disgusted with me that he had checked out of our relationship? I didn't know for sure, but God seemed to be absent. He certainly didn't seem to be the helpful, loving father that I'd been taught about growing up in Sunday School.

What about all those Bible promises that my life would improve after I committed myself to God? I was supposed to be on the promised path to sanctification—becoming "holy" or set apart, becoming Christ-like. I understood that this process was a lifelong journey. I thought the Holy Spirit was part of the deal too, there to empower me to live a pure, holy, and righteous life of godly victory. It wasn't just God the Father who had switched off. Both Jesus and the Holy Spirit seemed to be out of touch as well. It seemed to me that the whole Trinity had bugged out and left me in the lurch.

Despite the silence from heaven, I prayed a lot, hoping that due to the sheer amount of my prayers, perhaps one might reach his ear. I begged God to deliver me from my pornography addiction thousands of times. If that sin was the cause of God turning his back on me, then I reasoned that he should have a major interest in helping me kick the habit. If he would come through for me, then perhaps our broken relationship could be restored. Despite all my prayer requests for help, there was never any miracle, no supernatural assistance of any kind that I could see. The preacher at summer camp who shared the amazing story about how he had been divinely delivered from his smoking habit sure sounded good, but I wasn't seeing any similar response in my own situation. Why couldn't God provide me with a similar "overnight" victory?

I continued to struggle with my porn addiction, tormented with the knowledge that I had moved beyond merely being a disappointment and was now actively making God angry with me. I was pretty sure by this time that I was way outside that Gothard umbrella of protection. Maybe my struggles with sin and the failure to live a victorious Christian life were the result of demonic attacks on my now-unprotected life. That explanation at least made sense to me and offered a plausible explanation for my lack of spiritual success.

By my senior year I was fed up with what felt like a hopeless situation. I came to a major crossroads and made a momentous decision. I'd had enough of years of trying and failing to make it as a believer. I decided that if anybody asked me, "Are you a Christian?" I would answer, "No." I wouldn't go out of my way to advertise the fact, but at least I was trying to be honest with myself and God about my spiritual condition.

One summer day my cousin Dan and I headed out to see a movie. I had gotten my driver's license, and I picked Dan up in my dad's car. On the way, as we chatted, I casually dropped some swear words. Dan—who I'd been trying to evangelize since he and his family moved in next door—turned to me with a surprised look. "What's going on, man? I've never heard you swear before. You've always been a good Christian boy. What's this dirty language all about?" I responded,

"Well, it's like this. I'm not a Christian anymore. I've decided that this is my true self, and that's how it's gonna be from now on." Dan took the surprising news in stride. "Hey, I get it, bro," he said, slapping me on the back reassuringly. "I really do get it. I totally understand what you're talking about. It's always best to be true to yourself." I felt relieved. A huge burden had been lifted off my shoulders. I no longer had to pretend to be someone or something that I wasn't.

My conversation with Dan marked a major milestone. That was the first time anybody who knew me well learned that I no longer considered myself a believer. I couldn't afford to be open about my newfound unspiritual state at my Christian high school. Had I done so, I would have been kicked out immediately. But otherwise, my intention—if asked directly—was to admit the truth. I'd say honestly, "I don't buy into Christianity anymore. I tried my hardest to make it work all my life, but at least for right now, Christianity simply isn't working for me."

As resolute as I sounded in my response to Dan, I was inwardly ambivalent. Part of me hoped that in the future God and I could be reconciled. And despite my resolve to answer honestly when asked about my spiritual state, I didn't advertise the fact that I felt like one of Pastor Jerry's blackened coals outside the fire. The truth was that I had no idea how to get back into the "heart of the fire" and rekindle my lost relationship with Christ.

Despite my status as a clandestine non-Christian, in June of 1985 I managed to graduate from Christian high school. Publicly, I went through the motions of obeying the legalistic rules of the school while successfully keeping my outside-the-lines behavior a secret. When it came to my high school, it seemed that they were more interested in my external appearance than my actual spiritual condition. It was more important to look and act the part.

At our school, it was assumed that "good Christian boys" had short hair that didn't touch the ears or collars. I hated the hair code and was always getting warnings that I needed a haircut. Jeans were allowed for both boys and girls if they were clean, not too tight, and didn't have holes, but boys couldn't wear T-shirts during the week. On Thursdays for mandatory chapel, there was an even stricter dress code—slacks and collared shirts for boys, minimum knee-length dresses for girls. Anyone not conforming to the strict dress code on Thursdays got into trouble. Removed from the chapel service, they had to sit in the principal's office during that hour. In that time, they were required to write a short paper giving biblical reasons why God was not pleased with their choice to rebel against divinely ordained authority.

The school administration never explained to us exactly how any of the external-appearance rules made us better Christians, but such was the nature of the evangelical culture. Once again, I'm reminded of Hassan's BITE Model™ where the "B" acronym stands for "behavior control."[1] We certainly had to conform to multiple rigid rules that gave the school a large amount of control over us. Anyone caught flouting the rules one time too many would proceed through the disciplinary stages, ending with being kicked out if they continued to rebel.

What the teachers and principal didn't know was that despite our clean-cut appearance, many of us were into secular music, drinking, smoking, pornography, premarital sex, and all kinds of other sinful activities that would have devastated their delicate sensibilities. All they seemed to care about is that we obediently followed their rigid policies, always looking and acting the part while on campus. The rules were not to be questioned, much less broken. After all, isn't that what good Christian kids do—follow the rules without questioning them? For our part, we simply learned to put on our masks and play the game. And by this time, nearing my graduation, I was really, really good at acting the part and keeping up appearances, even though I no longer considered myself a Christian.

Giving Up on God

I never got into much trouble at my Christian high school, but many of my classmates did. My closest friends and I were simply sneakier about our sinful activities, and smart enough to keep our mouths shut. And the culture of the school never even came close to being a safe place whereby we could talk about our very real problems and spiritual struggles. In that way it closely mirrored what most conservative churches are like. All we knew was that there was no chance we'd ever admit to doing anything wrong or sinful, since one literally could not afford to be vulnerable, open, and honest. The best course of action was to play the game, try not to get caught breaking any rules, and survive each day.

The call of the Christian summer camp preacher to "remove our masks" in church, to open up to each other, and to become genuinely vulnerable sounded appealing in some ways. But I'd seen too many times at the Christian school that if you did confess your sins to someone in authority, you'd get punished or quite possibly expelled. Thus, in a weird way, their zero-tolerance policy for sin actually forced us to keep them a deep dark secret, but all the while we feared getting caught—and kicked out.

The bottom line was this: Christian school, like so many churches, wasn't a safe place where we could be real or vulnerable. We'd seen this verified when students had been caught drinking or were accused of having a "bad attitude" toward authority when they questioned what they were taught or stood up to the system. One example was my buddies who weren't allowed to participate in our high school graduation ceremony because they'd shared one beer among five guys at a party. Theirs was far from the only example. I recall a girl, a couple of grades behind me, who had unprotected sex with her boyfriend and became pregnant. She did the right thing and confessed her sin to the principal. But if she thought she'd receive grace or mercy, there was a nasty surprise in store. She was made to stand up in front and confess her sin to all the assembled students at a Thursday chapel service. Shortly thereafter, she was kicked out of the school, and then disappeared from the scene. I often wondered what became of her, but since she was a pariah, everyone just moved on and forgot about her.

My ex-wife Lisa attended the same school a few years after I finished. She became pregnant at seventeen in her junior year and was devastated over the mistake she'd made. But upon hearing of the other girl's story and knowing how the school treated students who messed up, she kept the potential scandal a closely guarded secret. She chose to have an abortion, which only compounded her shame and guilt. However, hiding the truth allowed her to graduate a year later. Better to keep a dark secret, and deal with the psychological impact later, than be publicly named, shamed, and kicked out.

Observing how students were treated when they sinned and confessed, most of the rest of us learned to put our heads down, keep our mouths shut, and play the game. This meant publicly abiding by the rules, looking and acting right. What we did in secret never came out, except for those unfortunate individuals who were unlucky enough to get caught.

As I neared my graduation, I felt fortunate that I had figured out how to keep up appearances, doing just enough to get by and escape. But privately, there was another far more pressing issue. Despite my decision to answer no when asked if I was a Christian, I wondered where I actually stood with God. Was I still a Christian, albeit a backslidden one, or had I crossed the line into full-blown apostasy? Had I lost my salvation, and become one of those blackened coals that Pastor Jerry spoke of? Or was there a chance that if I could somehow "get back into the fire," I could be rejuvenated and brought back to life spiritually?

---

1   Freedom of Mind Resource Center, "BITE Model™ of Authoritarian Control."

Chapter Twenty Six

Drifting Into the Navy

After graduating from Christian high school in June of 1985, I drifted along for a while, working dead-end jobs here and there. I finally picked up a full-time job at the Christian bookstore where my mom was the manager. It was a minimum-wage position covering for a woman on maternity leave. I stayed busy in the back room, unboxing and sorting product deliveries while blasting Christian music on the radio.

In addition to working in the back room, part of my job was to stock the shelves with the products my mom irreverently referred to as "holy hardware." Most of it was cheap stuff like crosses, rings, pencils, erasers, and plastic rulers with inspirational Scripture verses printed on them. Along with the holy hardware there was plenty of other Bible-branded trivia that the evangelical shoppers loved to buy. We sold Bibles, Christian music, and a wide variety of evangelical books that promised to help the reader live a victorious Christian life, have a happy marriage, or learn how to raise godly children.

I found it funny to watch shoppers argue vehemently with my mother about how they deserved a steep discount on the merchandise we sold. Why? Simply because their church had an account with the store. This happened regularly, and my mom grew adept at gently—but firmly—explaining that if they weren't on the church staff, merely being a member of their church did not entitle them to a discount. It was commonplace to see these frustrated Christians storm out of the store in a huff, leaving their merchandise on the counter.

I didn't realize that when the woman on maternity leave returned to work, my sweet little gig was done. I walked in as usual one day, only to discover she had reported back that morning. My boss came into the back room, thanked me for helping out for the last few months, and then announced that my services were no longer needed. Just like that, I was out of a job. He didn't even let me finish the day. Discouraged, I packed up my stuff, said my goodbyes to everyone, and drove home. Later, I regretted that I hadn't given my boss the Johnny Paycheck response: "Take this job and shove it!" I had the rug pulled out from under my feet, and I had no plans for the future.

I mooched around for the next few months—out of work and doing little to nothing. I slept late each morning and spent hours either playing video games on my Nintendo in my room or watching daytime TV. Shockingly, we now had a television in our house.

Losing my job so abruptly sapped my motivation, and I wasn't really trying to find another line of work. Frustrated with my laziness and lack of drive, my dad started hounding me every chance he got. "Get a job or join the military, you bum! No more freeloading in my house. I'm the one paying all the bills since you aren't working any more. This ain't a free ride!" My close relationship with my dad had ended with the lawn mowing incident several years earlier and was now shaky at best. But this was a new level of antagonism, and our relationship only deteriorated further.

I didn't know what to do. Once September passed, I had missed all the college entry deadlines. My high school grades were good enough to enroll in a community college, but by now, it was too late to start. Looking back, I wonder how much Gothard's teachings had influenced my lack of life choices. His view was that there was little point in going to college since Jesus was coming back soon. It's better to spend your time serving God and saving the lost rather than wasting your life on pointless secular pursuits! I think a lot of Christians missed out on education, careers, travel, or skill training opportunities due to such awful advice.

Even though I no longer called myself a Christian, there was always that pull to "get back into the fire" and avoid the fate of being one of those blackened coals Pastor Jerry had spoken of. I tried praying about what I should do, but I could find no clear sense regarding God's will for my life. No answers seemed to be forthcoming, and since I wasn't a member of any church, I couldn't ask any pastor for assistance either. By now, I considered myself to be out from underneath my umbrellas of authority due to my sinful lifestyle. This meant that God wasn't on speaking terms with me. Of course he wasn't answering my prayers for guidance. My relationship with my dad was broken and so was my relationship with God.

I was drifting through life, just waiting for something to happen. I had no job or marketable skills, no prospects, and no plan for what I should do.

All that changed in October of 1985. I made a snap decision that changed my life. I was hanging out next door with my cousin Dan and we were talking about our plans for the future. He caught me off guard when he mentioned that he'd recently signed up for the Navy. Within a few weeks, by early November, he was shipping out to boot camp in San Diego.

On the spot, I decided to enlist along with Dan. Of course, this was provided that the recruiter could guarantee that we would both go through the same boot camp. That afternoon, after talking to the recruiter on the phone, I rushed to his office. Minutes later, I was scribbling my signature on the numerous papers he had strewn across his desk. Signing my life away, I enlisted for eight years in the "Sea and Air Mariner Program," known as the "SAM Program." The enlistment entailed six years of weekend reserve duty and two more years of inactive duty. I had no idea what I was signing up for. All I cared about was that I could go to boot camp with Dan. After boot camp, I'd get some apprenticeship training and then, as I understood it, would have to report one weekend a month somewhere. I didn't get all the details, but it sounded like a fantastic plan!

The Naval Reserve Units were top-heavy with personnel who had served in the fleet on active duty. Upon fulfilling their service requirements, they had decided—rather than reenlisting or leaving the service entirely—to join the Naval Reserve. This required them to serve one weekend a month and two weeks in the summer. By the time they joined the Reserves, most were higher ranked and above doing the more menial but essential jobs. That's where Dan and I came in. The SAM Program was created to backfill the Naval Reserve Units with recruits who would start at the bottom of the ladder.

Little did the Navy brass know that this plan would backfire on them. A few years after the program's inception, the "SAM exodus" occurred. Thousands of disaffected young people in the SAM program switched services to get out. It was a long-term commitment, and the one weekend a month tied you down.

Two years into my enlistment, I started experiencing that same frustration. All I could think about was that I had six long years left in what had begun to feel like a prison sentence. Six years felt like an eternity, and I began searching for a way to escape. After speaking to an Army recruiter, my best friend Guy and

I devised a scheme that would seemingly help both of us. Guy, currently a civilian, would join the Army, and I would switch from the Navy to the Army. I wouldn't have to go through Army boot camp. After Guy finished his basic training, we would meet up at an Army carpentry school. We had a guaranteed assignment for three years in Germany after graduation. After serving the three years in Germany with Guy, I would get out five years before my original eight-year Navy Reserve enlistment would have ended. Unfortunately, on the way to the Military Processing Center to have our physicals and sign all the Army papers, Guy chickened out at the last minute, so I did not follow through either. I was stuck fulfilling all the terms of my seemingly endless Navy enlistment.

My cousin Dan hated the Navy assignment as well. After boot camp and apprenticeship training, he sat twiddling his thumbs at the Seattle Navy Reserve Center one weekend a month. Months passed as he waited to be assigned to a unit, but for nearly a year, nothing happened. After going AWOL and failing to report to his weekend duties for a few months, the Navy activated him to full-time status in the fleet as punishment. He ended up serving eighteen months on an oiler, which, according to him, was one of the worst assignments in the Navy.

After returning from a six-month Western Pacific voyage on the oiler, Dan went AWOL again. On his return a few weeks later, he failed a urinalysis after smoking a joint on the way back to the ship. He thought he would immediately be kicked out once he failed the drug test. But that was not to be. Hauled before the ship's Commanding Officer, he did get booted out of the Navy— but not until he'd been confined to the ship for six months doing menial jobs. After half a year of hell, he finally received an "Other Than Honorable" discharge. At least it wasn't a Dishonorable Discharge. Dan was out and free. I, on the other hand, was left plugging away while he had returned to civilian status. I still had three long years left to serve.

At the time of our enlistment, this was all in the distant and unknown future. On day one, all we knew was that we were both excited about embarking on our new adventure. As impulsive teenagers, neither of us seriously considered what we were getting ourselves into. We might not have signed all those legal documents if we had read them, but the recruiter dismissively waved his hand over the stack of papers and said not to worry. It was all standard legalese boilerplate jargon. And that was good enough for us.

Although my parents were shocked at the suddenness of my decision, my dad gave his approval. He served in the Army between the Korean and Vietnam wars and had been stationed in the Philippines. As a veteran, he figured that some military discipline was just what I needed. Besides, he knew that as an eighteen-year-old, I could make my own decisions. My mother was tearful, worried that if a war came along, I could end up in combat. But she, too, recognized that I was an adult and had to start taking responsibility for myself.

Chapter Twenty Seven

Life with Petty Officer 1st Class Hobbs

T he trip from Seattle to San Diego was the first time I'd ever been on an airplane, so the mere experience of flying was an exciting and significant event. Less exciting was the extremely unsettling feeling of having my head shaved and instantly losing my identity. Upon graduating from my Christian high school, chafing against their ridiculous hair code, I'd started sporting a mullet, that iconic look of the 1980s. Business in the front, party in the rear! Fed up with keeping the external appearance rules of my former school, I prided myself on finally being able to grow my hair long for the first time in my life. But now, mere minutes after the unsympathetic barber went to work on my head with his clippers, my beloved hairstyle lay in an undignified little heap on the barbershop floor. I was left with a completely shaven head. Leaving the barbershop, our entirely bald company of young men donned regulation Navy-issued uniforms, and our total loss of identity was underway.

Beyond the humiliation of a shaved head and the loss of individuality, I had never been screamed at by anybody like our company commander, Petty Officer 1st Class Hobbs. He ran our company with an iron fist, but we secretly admired him because he drove a 1977 candy apple red Corvette Stingray with side pipes and California wire wheels. Unfortunately, as we were to discover, having an immaculately clean and shiny killer ride didn't make him easygoing.

Chapter Twenty Seven

Hobbs took great pleasure in ruthlessly dressing you down in front of the entire company for the slightest infraction of the many rules. No matter how hard we tried to learn all the rules, we could never master them. For example, we struggled to learn how to tie the "knot of the day" using a rope hanging from our beds, or as we learned to call them, our "racks." Any recruit who couldn't tie the knot correctly received an instant ass-chewing from CC (Company Commander) Hobbs. "God damn it, recruit, you're worthless and weak. You're lower than whale shit! How the hell did you ever get into this man's Navy, you beady-eyed maggot? Talk about a clusterfuck. I'll kick your ass so hard, I'll break my foot off up in there! You'll have a size ten suppository. Now drop and give me twenty, dirtbag!"

The slightest mistake could get you into big trouble and often did. I once had to do what seemed like hundreds of push-ups and sit-ups for failing to straighten my pillow one morning. Even though I'd made my rack with regulation hospital corners, and you could bounce a quarter off the tight blanket, I was called out by CC Hobbs as he performed his morning inspection. I had stepped outside for a minute and returned to the barracks only to hear the CC screaming, "Where's Heacock? Dammit, sailor, your pillow is off-kilter. Don't you know, this is a clear violation of the Navy's rule of paying attention to detail? In combat, that careless lack of attention could get you or somebody else killed!" Even a seemingly trivial mistake was enough to earn our CC's displeasure, and I paid the price while all my fellow recruits watched my forced exercises in pained sympathy. After all, it could have been any of them—and if the CC felt especially sadistic on a particular day, he might make us all pay for one recruit's mistake.

At no point could you afford to let down your guard and relax. Whether day or night, some luckless Seaman Recruit could be called on to recite any one of the eleven General Orders we were supposed to memorize. Heaven help that poor guy if he got even one of the orders slightly wrong. Without the slightest warning, no matter what we were doing at the time, CC Hobbs might turn to a hapless recruit and shout out, "What is General Order number seven?" Make a mistake, and he would have you doing endless exercises until you got it exactly right.

We also had to know who the Secretary of the Navy was, the name of the Commanding Officer of our base, and any number of Navy-related pieces of trivial information. These were all fair game for CC Hobbs, and if you couldn't instantly come up with the correct answer, push-ups and sit-ups were your lot.

And it wasn't just our own CC we had to watch out for, either. Other CCs kept a keen eye out for any Seaman Recruit doing anything even marginally wrong anywhere on base. If you screwed up and got caught, you'd end up doing EMI—Extra Military Instruction—a barbarous exercise session, more akin to torture. Several SEALs, the Navy's elite special forces unit, would relentlessly harass those unlucky recruits assigned to an EMI session. This would go on for two non-stop hours, from ten to midnight every Saturday.

Screaming obscenities in their faces and blowing ear-splitting referee whistles throughout the entire session, the SEALs would relentlessly force the unfortunate recruits to do jumping jacks, sit-ups, push-ups, and other exercises until guys were puking their guts out and sobbing for their mamas. That happened to me only once when I was in trouble for some trivial mistake I allegedly made. The CC of another company called me on an error but wouldn't accept my explanation for what I had done. After the relentless EMI session, as I struggled back to my barracks at midnight, I fervently vowed never to get in trouble again.

As new sailors, life was often bewildering, as our usual way of referring to everyday things required changing per longstanding Navy tradition. The military phonetic alphabet replaced the standard alphabet, so A became "Alpha," B was "Beta," C was "Charlie," and so on. Time even changed so that the 24-hour clock system referred to everything. For example, 8 PM became "twenty-hundred hours." After noon rolled around each day, I could never figure out what time it was. Even more confusing—CC Hobbs would order one unlucky Seaman Recruit to "stand fire watch at eight bells tonight," which meant nothing to us. And what did it mean when you were supposed to stand the "Dog Watch?"

We also had to learn a baffling array of military acronyms and Navy rank systems, different from all the other armed services. It was imperative to know who we should and shouldn't salute and the difference between the orders "fall in" and "fall out." Soon, we felt like our heads were spinning! Whenever an officer entered the room, somebody would shout, "Attention on deck!" Immediately, everyone had to leap to their feet and stand at attention. That rigid pose would continue until the officer was satisfied that we were all "shipshape and squared away," at which point he would command, "At ease!" Following that order, we could resume whatever we'd been doing before the disruption. Whenever CC Hobbs ordered the entire company to do something and asked if we understood, we all had to shout "Aye-aye, sir!" in unison. If we got it wrong, we would have to do it again or risk doing numerous push-ups and sit-ups as a unit.

In addition to Navy lingo, everything we'd known before in our civilian lives suddenly received new and highly confusing terminology. For example, the bathroom was now called "the head." Stairs and the floor were called "ladders" and "the deck." Walls were transformed into "bulkheads." Left and right were now "port and starboard."

Our ragtag unit slowly mastered marching in lockstep as a

company of eighty men, while CC Hobbs screamed at us to turn to port or starboard. At first, none of us knew which direction to turn, leading to many pileups. Every morning, our company was rousted out of our racks by CC Hobbs at 0500 hours as he rolled an empty garbage can down the middle of the barracks. Following that rude awakening, we had what seemed like minutes to perform the "three S's"—shit, shower, and shave—to prepare for whatever the day had in store for us.

On the bright side, Dan and I got to stay together, and both of us ended up in Company 232. Despite the rigors of boot camp, with all the marching, classroom sessions, and daily Physical Training sessions, we enjoyed the beautiful winter sun of San Diego. There was snow, sleet, rain, and ice back home in Seattle. Yet, here we were, getting tan in sunny southern California in December and January.

There was one slight downside to the gorgeous weather. One could always tell a Seaman Recruit who'd been to basic training in San Diego by their "grinder reminder." This was a tan line across the forehead caused by wearing our white Navy "dog dish" sailor hats. All the marching and standing for hours at attention in the blazing sun on "the grinder," the massive square used for drills and marching practice, created a butt-white line above and a darkly tanned face below. It took me months afterward to even out my tan!

Chapter Twenty Eight

A Not So Religious Religious Petty Officer

E ven in the harsh atmosphere of basic training, there was a religious component in my life. Despite my decision not to admit being a Christian, I still considered myself a nominal believer. And despite my lapsed spiritual state—a blackened coal out of the fire—I always felt a nagging sense of shame that I could and should do better. I needed to be a faithful witness for Christ. Despite the many failures of my Christian life, I felt trapped in the same weird dynamic I had been in most of my life when it came to being around unbelievers. Like all those times with my cousins, I had the urgent sense that I needed to stand out and set an example of what a Christian should or should not be doing in every circumstance.

From what I could tell, virtually all my fellow sailors in Company 232 were far from being Christians. Despite being a lapsed believer, I strove diligently to act differently. To set a godly example, I didn't swear, didn't participate in the dirty jokes with everyone else, and tried my hardest to be a good witness for Christ. I reasoned that perhaps as God saw me taking this new opportunity seriously, I would improve spiritually, and maybe he would finally help me to "get back into the fire." There might just be a way to revitalize my lost relationship with God.

At the same time, this was a new and alien environment, with guys from all over the country, and I didn't know anyone other than my cousin Dan. I desperately wanted to fit into the group, so I always struggled internally. I didn't want to be the one weird religious nut in the company, citing random Bible verses to try and save everyone but always ending up on the outside looking in. Worse yet, I was also a virgin, thanks to my evangelical purity culture upbringing. The other guys constantly bragged about their sexual experiences, and I was ashamed of my lack of such experiences. It seemed as if everyone in Company 232 was sexually active except for me. I kept my mouth shut and never admitted my virginal status, hoping that none of my fellow recruits would find out and publicly mock me for it.

A few weeks into basic training, the scuttlebutt making the rounds had it that a position in our company had not been filled. The unfilled role was the Religious Petty Officer, or RPO. I asked CC Hobbs about the position, and he informed me that the RPO had the responsibility of taking the other recruits to chapel each Sunday. I told him I wanted the job, and since nobody else was even slightly interested, I immediately got the gig. Any recruits from the company who wished to go to chapel would be assigned to my detail, and I had to ensure that we all made it back to the barracks in time after the service ended. I figured that even though I was a backslidden Christian, being the RPO of the company would set me apart as a religious person. I reasoned that I could help my fellow sailors should they seek spiritual guidance.

I faithfully attended chapel each Sunday morning and usually took along two or three other recruits. Their parents had probably ordered them not to skip church while away in boot camp. It's ironic that even in my erstwhile Christian state back then, I still had that religious conscience and guilt that I wasn't doing enough to evangelize my fellow sailors.

A Not So Religious Religious Petty Officer

Despite my "exalted spiritual status" as the RPO, no one ever asked me about my faith, nor did I ever have the chance to lead anyone from my company to Christ. But at least I felt good that I was doing my part to stand out and be different for the Lord. If anyone *did* have any deep spiritual inquiries, I figured they'd head to me first, and I would try my best to steer them in the right direction. Based on my lifetime of church indoctrination, Sunday School, Bible memorization, and the like, I felt confident that I could handle any question tossed at me regarding God, the way of salvation, or the Bible.

Chapter Twenty Nine

Navy Planes and The Driftwood Lounge

A fter graduating from boot camp in January of 1986, I was shipped to Millington Air Base in Tennessee to attend a four-month Aviation Structural Mechanic A School. There, I would learn a trade and be given what the Navy calls a rating. In the Navy, a rating is essentially an enlisted person's occupational description that denotes the specific skills of that sailor. Thus, after graduating from A School, I'd be "AMS AN Heacock" which stood for "Aviation Mechanic (Structural) Airman Heacock," rather than just "AN Heacock" standing for "Airman Heacock." Other rating designations include AMH (Hydraulics) or AME (Electrical) depending upon one's specialty and training.

While attending the school in Millington, the fragile Christian veneer I'd tried to maintain in boot camp started to slip away. Nobody needed an RPO, so I had nothing to differentiate me from the other sailors regarding religious commitment. Rather than pursuing godly activities, I gave in to peer pressure and fell in with new friends doing the typical sailor thing. The first weekend after arriving, I let some new friends—one of whom had a van—talk me into going out into town for a night of hard partying. They pressured me into wearing civilian clothes, which was against the rules. All new arrivals to A School had to wear their regulation Navy uniform for the first six weeks, after which you could start wearing your civilian clothes again. It showed how impressionable

Chapter Twenty Nine

I was, letting these guys talk me into flouting multiple rules within hours of my arrival on base. So much for setting a godly example.

As I changed out of my uniform in the back of the van, the next thing I knew, we pulled into a local strip club. This was the first time I'd ever seen naked women in the flesh, although I'd seen plenty in my porn magazines and X-rated movies. Not only did I get plastered at the club, but somehow, on the trip back to base, I lost my military ID as I drunkenly struggled to change back into my uniform. That little mishap restricted me to base for the rest of the weekend until I could get a new ID the following week.

Soon, my thin Christian veneer had vanished. I got over my dislike for the taste of beer and started enjoying myself as much as possible. Once the weekend hit, my buddies and I would walk the short distance to a local dive bar and get hammered while listening to local rock and blues cover bands. The Driftwood Lounge had never seen a piece of driftwood since Millington was hundreds of miles from the nearest coastline. It was also far from a lounge, offering an all-you-can-drink beer night for the bargain price of five dollars on Tuesday nights. I tried the all-you-can-drink special only once but paid the price the next day, struggling off to class with a roaring hangover. Although admittedly not the classiest watering hole, the Driftwood Lounge was the bar closest to the main gate. This convenient location meant you could stagger back to the base on foot after a rough night of drinking without paying for a taxi—a meaningful savings on our meager salaries.

Reveling in my newfound independence away from the strictures of church and parents, just like a typical sailor, I also got my first tattoo in Millington—a small black panther head on my left arm. It was done at a rough-looking tattoo parlor by an even rougher-looking tattoo artist, but I didn't care then. I had saved my money for months and scraped together the sixty dollars required for the piece, which only took about thirty minutes to complete. Despite being inordinately proud of my new ink at the time, I regretted this poor choice several years later and got it covered up with a much larger piece. But at the time, all my A School buddies were green with envy since I was the first one to get inked up.

Despite all my unspiritual behaviors, there was always that religious element, that feeling of righteous conviction, gnawing at me. I reckoned that it was the influence of the Holy Spirit working on my seared conscience and sin-hardened heart. A month after arriving at A School, feeling increasingly guilty about skipping church, I located the chapel on the base and set my alarm for early Sunday morning. I wasn't impressed with the chaplain's sermon, which seemed to go on for an eternity. I couldn't follow along since it had neither a discernible point nor clear structure. Plus, the service itself was incredibly dull, so I felt fully vindicated in deciding never to return. Despite my rationale for not returning to the chapel, I still felt guilty that I wasn't reading my Bible or praying daily. I didn't even have a Bible with me. As time passed, the guilty feelings began to subside, and life went on.

My life now reflected the reality that I was an out-and-out nonbeliever. I made no attempt to hide the fact that I did not identify as a Christian. Like the stereotypical sailor, I had a kickass tattoo and smoked cigarettes. Each weekend, my buddies and I got roaring drunk at the Driftwood Lounge, and my foul language could shock even the most hardened old salt. Saving up my money, I bought a Sony Walkman and began amassing a collection of secular rock and heavy metal cassette tapes. I also had my share of *Playboy* and *Penthouse* magazines. Only this time, I didn't have to hide them under my mattress like at home because all my other Navy buddies had them too.

For the first time, I was living in an environment where I didn't have to conceal what I was doing or wear a mask to hide my authentic self. This new experience felt strange yet freeing. For the first time in my life, I began to wonder if perhaps this was the real me after all.

In April of 1986, I finished my four months at A School. I received my AMS rating, and was assigned to VP-69, a P3 Orion squadron known as "The Totems." Built by Lockheed, a P3 is a four-engine turboprop anti-submarine warfare and surveillance aircraft that the Navy has been using since the early 1960s. We were based out of Oak Harbor, a small town on Whidbey Island in Washington State. Ours was an anti-submarine warfare squadron designated as a "TAR" unit, which stands for "Training and Administration of Reservists." About half the squadron consisted of full-time Navy men and women. The other half was made up of SAMs like me, who only reported for duty one weekend a month.

Upon arriving at VP-69, I was assigned to the Line Maintenance Workshop, where every newbie started. This was the bottom rung and involved simple tasks like washing the planes, minor routine maintenance, and parking returning aircraft. After several months of this, a job—what the Navy refers to as a "billet"—finally opened, and I was transferred to the Airframes Shop. This was a much better assignment because I could utilize the skills I'd learned in A School, working on airplanes as I'd been trained. We changed tires and brakes and serviced hydraulics. We also performed more advanced maintenance tasks, worked on sheet metal repairs, and conducted regular inspections on our aircraft to make them mission-worthy.

There were pros and cons to being a Naval Reservist. At the time, all I could think of was getting out of my enlistment, but looking back on it now, the experience proved to be more than beneficial. Since the Navy was desperately trying to fill out the ranks of the reserve fleet, those of us signed up for the SAM Program didn't have to serve the typical full-time four years in the fleet before transferring into reserve units. Instead, they sent us to boot camp, and after that, most went through a short apprenticeship training program that was only weeks long. I was fortunate enough to earn a rating in A School, a rarity in the SAM program.

Following our initial training, we SAMs were attached to reserve units nationwide to bolster the ranks of junior enlisted personnel. We only had to serve one weekend a month and two weeks full-time in the summer. Meeting these requirements, we could receive limited GI Bill educational benefits. I took immediate advantage of this, and in September of 1986, I started attending a local community college in the Seattle area, training to become a carpenter. I still draw on this skill set as a carpenter and a teacher. I've always been able to make a living as a contractor, carpenter, and carpentry teacher. I think learning these skills is one of the most priceless bits of training I've done in my life, although I didn't see it that way then. This skill has also served me well since I left church ministry behind.

The fact that I could get training virtually for free, thanks to the GI Bill, was a valuable bonus. The downside was that I had signed up for eight long years in the Naval Reserve. After a few years, this proved to be increasingly difficult. As civilians, we had to transform into sailors two days a month. On Fridays before weekend duty at Whidbey Island Naval Air Station, I'd shave off my growth of beard, get a regulation haircut, and scramble to find all the parts of my uniform. This frantic activity would be followed by a two-hour drive to the base on Friday night. We'd work all weekend on our squadron's P3 Orion airplanes, then make the long, weary drive home Sunday night after our shift ended. It was typical to arrive home around 8 PM or 9 PM. Exhausted, we'd head back to our civilian lives—jobs, school, or whatever else we usually did.

This routine started to grind on me after a while, and all I could think about was how to get out.

But being in the Navy wasn't all bad, and there were a lot of good times alongside the grueling schedule and long hours. Beyond learning some valuable skills and military discipline, summertime provided a chance to get paid to travel the world for our two-week summer stints. Our squadron deployed to fascinating locations like Japan, Korea, Guam, and the Philippines to locate and track Soviet submarines. This was all within the context of the end of the Cold War, the final years of the Reagan/George H.W. Bush American military, and the showdown between the American Eagle and the Russian Bear.

If it weren't for the Navy, I'd never have been able to travel to such exotic places—and get paid to do it, no less. On the weekends and in the summers, our routine was what most military personnel get up to. We'd head straight to the enlisted club after a long day of hard work. For the first few years, I did what everyone else was doing. I'd get blasted on pitchers of beer at the club as we all sat around talking about all the Navy's many problems. We'd passionately describe how they would all be solved if they listened to us. Of course, no one listened to us, but that didn't stop our constant bitching—a common pastime for military personnel.

When we flew to Japan during the summer, the first stop after disembarking from the military transport plane was heading to the PX on base, the military's version of a supermarket. Loading up on cases of beer, we'd then check into our barracks and immediately start drinking. We spent many hours at the enlisted clubs on base, pounding down pitchers of beer, sandwiched between twelve-hour shifts working on airplanes.

My Christian witness? There wasn't one at this point. I had

progressed beyond being a secret nonbeliever to openly acting as a non-Christian—swearing, drinking, smoking, consuming secular heavy metal and porn. I was your typical military man. Having finally dispensed with that thin Christian veneer, I felt this was likely my authentic self.

My lost condition was proven to my satisfaction not long after returning to Seattle from A School in September of 1986. I started attending community college on the GI Bill, training to be a carpenter. An ex-girlfriend of mine, with whom I'd gone to Christian high school, helped me land a job with her uncle Mark, a custom home builder. As a laborer, I started on the bottom of the rung, cleaning up the job site and doing all the menial jobs nobody else wanted. I earned the princely sum of five dollars an hour, which wasn't too bad then. I needed the extra cash to pay for college expenses the GI Bill didn't cover.

Onsite, I usually worked with a journeyman carpenter, Big Steve, a Navy veteran who had served as a cook in the fleet in the late 1970s. He told me some crazy stories about his time in the Navy. In those days, shortly after the Vietnam War ended, you could get away with smoking dope—seemingly everyone on the ship was doing it. Following a crackdown on this severe drug problem in the military, by my time, they had instituted a zero-tolerance policy toward drugs. As part of their effort to curtail drug abuse, our squadron conducted regular urinalysis tests on us. Anyone caught with drugs in their system was immediately booted out of the Navy. If you came clean and confessed beforehand, help was available—the Navy would put you through rehab if you struggled with a drug or alcohol addiction.

Back in the 70s, things weren't so tight when it came to uniform regulations either. Sailors wore blue jeans instead of regulation dungarees and stole tools off the ship left, right, and center. They'd also shove their long hair underneath their sailor hats while on duty, then go into town and party after work, literally letting their hair down. Nobody seemed to care too much in those days. But things were vastly different during my years in the Navy during the 1980s and 1990s.

"Big Steve" was a fitting name since my new carpenter friend stood at six-foot-six and had a big, booming, James Earl Jones voice. One day, not long after I'd started, we were working together, and in typical Navy fashion, I was cussing a blue streak whenever I made a mistake, which was often. Steve heard that I'd gone to a Christian high school, and halfway through my tirade, he turned to me with a strange look. He asked, "Aren't you supposed to be some kind of Christian or something?" Although I laughed it off and said I wasn't, I felt a momentary pang of remorse. Just then, it struck me exactly how far I'd slipped away from the Lord.

I no longer identified as a believer. At least I felt I'd "taken off the mask" and was living consistently as my authentic self. The problem was that deep down inside, I knew God was still disappointed with me. I had allowed the "old man," that sinful nature the Apostle Paul wrote about in the book of Romans, to win out over my Christian self. I hoped there was some way for me to return to God's good graces. But if I was one of those coals that Pastor Jerry had pulled out of the fire all those years ago at summer camp that had faded away, could I ever "renew my fire?" If only there was a way back.

One day, an odd and unexpected pathway back to my faith appeared–*heavy metal music.*

Chapter Thirty

Christian Heavy Metal Band-Aid

O ne advantage to being a reservist was that I was home most of the month. I'd been in a Christian metal band in high school, the one that practiced at the FourSquare church, but that ended when I left for Navy boot camp. After I came back home in the Spring of 1986, we tried to restart the band, but things quickly got ugly when I began dating the lead singer's girlfriend. To avoid unnecessary drama, I quit the band, and they replaced me with a new drummer.

Still wanting to be a rock n' roll star, in the Fall of 1986, I placed an ad in a local Seattle music magazine called *The Rocket*. My ad stated that I was searching for fellow rockers interested in starting a Christian metal band. Not long afterward, Steve, a Christian and a solid rhythm guitarist, contacted me. Steve and I hit it off right away since we were both into the same type of music and liked many of the same bands. Like me, he was a rock and metal guy who wanted nothing more than to get a Christian metal band together.

Even though it was just the two of us, we started jamming two nights a week at my parents' house. We practiced in my bedroom for about a year, where I'd built a drum riser—a short stage on which the drums sit—using my newfound carpentry skills. My parents must have been annoyed as we played the same three or four songs endlessly at near max volume. But they liked Steve and probably figured that as a Christian, he'd be a good influence on my life. As time passed, Steve and I wrote a few original numbers and learned a lot of cover tunes. We played songs by Christian metal bands like Stryper, one of the most popular Christian metal bands of the day. We idolized Stryper for making it big in the secular world as an overtly Christian band, unashamed as they boldly proclaimed their faith.

One night after practice, Steve and I were chatting about my experiences in the Navy and what I was doing with my life. I was about halfway through carpentry school at the community college. I felt optimistic that not only was I learning valuable skills and a trade, but I was accomplishing some positive goals. As we talked, one question from Steve caught me off guard. "Are you a Christian?" I was still answering no to that question, and that's how I responded. Then, Steve challenged my answer with a follow-up question. "But if you're not a Christian, then why are you trying to put together a Christian metal band? That makes no sense. What's the point? Why are you doing all this?"

What Steve said made me realize that something I was doing didn't make sense. What motivated me to run the ad that brought Steve and me together? Why, indeed, did I want to be in a *Christian* metal band to spread the gospel into secular clubs and bars when I wasn't even a Christian? I reflected to Steve that even though I wasn't a true believer, since I'd grown up in the church and loved playing drums, being in a Christian metal band made the most sense. I had no desire to be in a secular band since part of me still desperately wanted to believe that Christianity was true, even though it hadn't worked out for me.

Steve's response was to ask, "Why don't you come to church with me? I think you'll like it. It's in downtown Seattle, very nontraditional, and has a great Christian music scene. Plus, our pastor, Wayne Taylor, is a laid-back guy. He's not one of those hellfire-and-brimstone preachers. Why don't you come along this Sunday and check it out?" I figured why not since I didn't have Navy duty that weekend. What's the worst that could happen? So, at the age of twenty, I headed back to church for the first time since the last chapel service at A School in Millington.

That Sunday, I went with Steve to check out the Calvary Fellowship near the University District in Seattle. They met in the former Lincoln High School building just off 44th Avenue in the Wallingford neighborhood not far from the University of Washington. As we pulled into the parking lot, I suddenly recognized that this was the same church where we'd seen Mike Warnke perform his Christian comedy act years ago.

After the service, Steve took me to a Seattle area landmark—Beth's Café, located near Green Lake. Over a pancake breakfast, he enthusiastically peppered me with questions. "So, what did you think? Was the service alright? Did you enjoy the music? What do you think of the building? Isn't it cool that we meet in an old high school? What about Wayne's sermon? I told you he was alright." I had to admit that Steve had been correct about all of it. The music was good. They had a full band with drums, electric guitars, and a decent sound system. I wondered what it would take for me to become part of the worship team there and if they had any slots open for a drummer.

Pastor Wayne was indeed laid-back, as Steve had indicated. In contrast to former Pastor David's awful choice of outfits, this pastor wore a suit jacket with jeans. How postmodern! I was reminded of Pastor Mark, at my old church years ago, rocking the same look back in the late 70s. But, unlike Mark's sermons, Pastor Wayne's message felt relevant to my life. It was a point-by-point, biblically-based sermon following the classic Pastor Chuck Smith tradition. Smith founded the Calvary Chapel movement in Southern California in the mid-1960s, and Calvary Fellowship Seattle was part of that tradition. Back in Smith's day, hippies and surfers had gotten saved in the hundreds on the beaches and went on to start the "Jesus Movement." I also knew many Christian rockers I loved listening to emerged from this tradition. Many of them had been secular rockers before they got saved. As believers, they started rockin' for God, and Christian rock was born.

If I did attend a church, I figured Calvary would be the place. They had the same open and inclusive attitude as Calvary Chapel had back in the 1960s. I'd noticed guys with long hair and tattoos and women with dyed pink Mohawk haircuts sitting beside a strait-laced couple wearing their Sunday best. Despite looking like a square with my regulation Navy haircut, I felt right at home. Aside from my haircut, I fit right in with my black Levi's jeans, black panther head tattoo, leather jacket, and Harley-Davidson t-shirts. I decided then and there that I'd start going to Calvary with Steve and let the chips fall where they may when it came to my spiritual journey. Although I no longer considered myself a Christian, this decision somehow felt right. Was this God leading me into the next step along the path of righteousness? Perhaps he wasn't finished with me, I reasoned, so why not just go with the flow?

I attended Calvary Fellowship with Steve for the next year or so, but without becoming a Christian. A few months after I started attending there, we picked up a bass player and a lead guitarist. With a complete lineup, our band finally started making progress, writing more originals until we had a complete set of our own songs. We still needed a lead singer, one of the hardest slots to fill in a band. I was able to patch things up with my buddy Tony when, by chance, I ran into him at a supermarket where he worked. Upon seeing him, I was apprehensive because I didn't know how he would react to seeing me.

Tony was the lead singer in that Christian metal band we formed in our Christian high school days. I had stolen his girlfriend and subsequently left the band. But Tony had moved on and had found a new girlfriend. They were now engaged and a few months away from getting married. We decided to let bygones be bygones. Just like that, we had a lead singer and a full lineup for the band. We all interpreted this miraculous meeting as a "God thing." Not only did Tony and I reconcile when he forgave me for what I'd done, but it appeared that the Lord had gifted us with a great lead singer as part of this package deal! It seemed like a clear case of a "divine appointment," and further proof that God was indeed working mysteriously in my life.

With Tony handling lead vocals, our vision of that Christian metal band we'd worked so hard to achieve finally began to take shape. Could this be a providential move of God, I wondered, finally putting all the pieces of my life together? Even though I wasn't a believer and considered myself a seeker more than anything else, I still believed that God was firmly in control of everything. Nothing happened apart from his will and plan, so I reasoned that our finally getting a complete band together must be the result of his almighty guiding hand at work.

It certainly did seem as if God was blessing our efforts. Our band rehearsed a couple of nights a week. I was in my second year of carpentry training at the community college, enjoying learning new aspects of the trade and other related skills. I did a lot of carpentry work with Big Steve as he branched out independently. I felt like he was a great mentor as a carpenter and friend. Plus, he played bass and sang in a local covers band, so we had music in common too. Even though I wasn't a Christian any longer, I had to admit that one thing seemed abundantly clear: *God was working in my life.*

Chapter Thirty

When I wasn't doing my monthly Navy weekend, I usually attended Calvary with Steve. However, the sheer size of the congregation served my plan to avoid any accountability. The church had thousands of people attending, which allowed me to blend into the congregation unnoticed, answerable to no one. If I attended by myself, I would go to the first morning service and sing the worship songs, joining in heartily with everybody else. With my Bible open, I'd faithfully listen to Pastor Wayne's sermon and take notes, but I would immediately duck out afterward. Being just a face in the crowd was fantastic since I didn't have to speak to anyone or answer any awkward questions about matters of spiritual accountability. If Steve went with me, we'd hit the first morning service, head over to Beth's Café for a late breakfast, then come to my folks' house for some jamming. On the positive side, I was faithfully attending church weekly. On the negative side, I was answerable to no one, and that was precisely the way I wanted it.

Chapter Thirty One

Sex and Run
Accident with Karma

E very source of Christian training in my life taught that sex outside of marriage is forbidden. When I enrolled in community college at the age of nineteen, I was still a virgin. Given that I had been raised in the evangelical purity culture and influenced by Gothard's modesty teachings, my virginity wasn't surprising. But it was surprising given the peer pressure of fellow sailors who constantly boasted about how they'd gotten lucky the night before. They encouraged me to sleep with any available woman, but I always resisted the temptation. Even though I wasn't a Christian, I still tried to hold on to the notion that I should remain a virgin until my wedding night.

While attending community college, I finally crossed the point of no return. I slept one time with a woman, the sister of a classmate with whom I was close friends. Although the sex blew my mind, not long afterward, I came up with some pretend reason to break up with her. I felt horrible that I'd foolishly given up my virginity. It was terrible to let the young woman down in such a cowardly way. But I lied my way out of the relationship and vowed never to let "it" happen again as long as I was unmarried. Even though I wasn't a believer, I still had that sense of guilt and shame dogging my steps. I couldn't tell my Christian bandmates about what had happened either, let alone my parents, so I kept the whole thing a closely guarded secret. I figured that moving forward, the only way to make up for my mistake was to please God by staying celibate until my wedding night.

Despite my best intentions, meeting Linda[1] at the community college about halfway through my two-year program threatened to throw me off the righteous path again. My then-brother-in-law Jim, who was married to my sister Beth, introduced us, and I immediately fell for her. Not only was she gorgeous, but she was also into the same music I was—rock and metal. She wasn't a Christian, which was a problem for me despite my lapsed Christian state. I felt deeply conflicted. Just when it seemed clear that God was working mysteriously in my life, calling me back to him, dating a nonbeliever might lead me off the path of righteousness. But because I liked her so much, I needed a way to justify our relationship. I convinced myself that I could witness to her, and eventually, she'd get saved. Not long after we started dating, to try and evangelize her, I talked her into coming along with me to see Bloodgood, a Seattle Christian metal music icon.

The concert was held at Calvary Fellowship, and I figured I would kill two birds with one stone. Not only would she see a Christian metal band for the first time in her life, but she'd also find out where I went to church. I figured Linda would be impressed with any church willing to put on a full-on metal band. That would show her how hip and cool Christians could be. I inwardly rejoiced when the lead singer delivered a persuasive altar call at the show's end. Unfortunately, Linda didn't go forward to give her life to Christ, but I figured that a few more opportunities like this would soon set her straight. I didn't consider myself a Christian, so why was I so uptight about the whole thing? I should have gone forward that night in response to the evangelistic invitation.

A few months into our relationship, I began spending the night at her house while lying to my parents and telling them that I was at Guy's. I had to ring him first to give him the heads-up just in case they called his place to check on me. I felt terrible about lying to my parents and even worse about the fact that Linda and I had started fooling around, although we hadn't had intercourse yet. I wanted to make love to her in the worst possible way, but because of my earlier mistake in losing my virginity, I vowed not to cross that line again. As they say, the best-laid plans of mice and men often go awry. In the summer of 1988, our Navy squadron was just about to head out for two weeks to Misawa, an American airbase located in Japan. I knew I'd miss Linda terribly during that absence. So, the night before I shipped out, my newfound celibacy vow went right out the window, and we made love for the first time. The following day, I reported to NAS Whidbey Island, joined my squadron, and caught the C-141 military transport bound for Japan.

Desperately missing Linda and feeling like we had something special after just one love-making session, I tried calling her from the base in Japan a few times. However, back in the late 80s, before the Internet and smartphones, that was a difficult and expensive proposition. Despite my best efforts, I was never able to contact her, so I spent the entire two weeks missing her like crazy. I was a nonbeliever, but I still struggled with trying to set an example for my fellow sailors, so I tried not to get too drunk with my buddies at the enlisted club. It seemed that there was always that thin Christian veneer, the feeling of being conflicted, when it came to my lapsed spiritual state.

When I returned home, the first thing I did was ring Linda. There was no answer. I tried to reach her for two days. Sick with worry, I left several messages, but she never called me back. With no smartphones, all we had to rely on back then were landlines and answering machines. I drove by her house several times, but the lights were off, and nobody appeared to be home. I was getting very concerned. Where was she? Didn't she want to meet up with me? What in the world was going on?

Chapter Thirty One

On the third day, she finally answered the phone. After chatting for a bit, she told me to meet up with her later that day after she finished going on a walk with a friend. I didn't understand why I had to wait so long, but I raced to meet her when it was time. Her friend was there when I arrived, so we couldn't discuss why she'd been blanking me. She was acting weird and cagey. After the walk, her friend went home, and we returned to her house. She said we needed to talk, and I became even more worried.

Linda sat me down and told me she was breaking up with me. No reason was given other than the classic line when someone is being dumped: "It's not you. It's me." I tried reasoning with her, attempting to understand her sudden decision, but she kept repeating that we'd be better off apart. Broken-hearted and devastated, I drove home, wiping the tears from my eyes. That breakup affected me deeply. I hadn't realized how much I cared for her until that moment, and I was torn up about it for six months. I couldn't see why she'd changed her mind so quickly when things had been going so well. How could she have been so insensitive to dump me like that so unceremoniously?

But my Christian buddy Steve spun the whole thing positively, viewing it as good that I'd been cut loose from the relationship. He'd met Linda several times and warned me to be careful because she wasn't a Christian. I hadn't told him about us sleeping together, but he must have had his doubts. He and I had talked many times about my lapsed spiritual state, and he was convinced that the Lord was leading me back to him. Steve was worried about our relationship in case she led me astray. Patting me on the back, he offered this consolation: "Honestly, if we look at it objectively, I think God's hand was in this. Even though things seemed to be going so well, he broke you two up because Linda was a bad influence on your life. She was nice and all, but let's not forget that she is a nonbeliever. The Bible says you shouldn't be 'unequally yoked.' You should be thanking God right now—even though I know it hurts."

Although his words were cold comfort, I realized that he was probably right. Eventually, I came to believe that God had indeed engineered the breakup to steer me away from sexual temptation and sin before it was too late. God was working to get me back on the narrow path of righteousness I'd been on before I met Linda. Since we'd gotten along so well up to that point and had been so compatible, there was no other logical reason to explain her inexplicable change of heart. I was deeply wounded but finally saw that the breakup was for the best. Although I wasn't a Christian, I believed that God was still actively working in my life, lovingly and providentially guiding me to help avoid making foolish, thoughtless mistakes that would ruin my life.

I'd heard often enough the old saying that "God loves you and has a wonderful plan for your life." Reflecting on the situation months later, after the pain had subsided somewhat, I started asking myself some hard questions. What if I'd gotten Linda pregnant? I felt like I'd dodged a bullet there since we didn't use protection. Would I have married her? If she never became a Christian, we would have been "unequally yoked." I didn't consider myself a Christian at this point either, so this demonstrates how conflicted I was at the time. Why in the world was I so hung up on this issue?

If Linda and I had gotten married, it would have made things far worse because we'd probably do nothing but argue about whether our kids should attend church. Should they be raised as Christians or in a secular home? Christian or public school? Perhaps there was a good reason behind the biblical principle of two people not being unequally yoked. Maybe God was in this thing, as Steve had sagely pointed out. Despite my lack of faith, the Lord seemed to be working in my life, drawing me back to him.

I was still living at home, but things weren't going well. Shortly before I finished my degree at the community college in June of

1988, my dad and I had a huge argument one night after band practice. It all boiled over as I vented my anger and pain over Linda dumping me. I was also upset with my dad over what I perceived to be his heavy-handedness and how unfairly he'd treated me for so long. Our disagreement over the lawn-mowing incident had never been adequately dealt with, resulting in our relationship being almost nonexistent. Added to that were all the years of poisoning from my mother's private complaints about my dad to me.

As my dad and I quarreled, things grew more and more heated. I made a snap decision as Steve looked on in shock and confusion. Announcing that I'd had enough of my dad's inexcusable treatment, I would not stay one more night in that house. I angrily announced that I was moving in with Steve right then and there. I told my dad I wanted out from under his thumb, and it was high time I struck out alone. With my mother's voice ringing in my ears, pleading with me not to go, or at least not to end it like that, I resolutely packed up my stuff and walked out the door for good.

Living with Steve was great. I was out from under my dad's thumb, but one downside was that we had lost our practice space at my parents' house. A few months later we decided to rent a house together in West Seattle. The full basement in our new bachelor pad was the perfect place to hold band practice. We didn't inform the landlord upfront about our plans, because we felt sure he would never have rented to us otherwise. We soundproofed the basement, moved in our gear, and kept the band chugging along. After six months of practicing twice weekly, we finally had enough material for a gig, combining a few covers of Christian metal bands like Stryper and our material. Things were looking up, and our dream of being rock stars for God was finally taking shape.

---

1   Linda was not her actual name.

Chapter Thirty Two

If You Were to Die Tonight

Although everything seemed to be going well now that God had engineered my breakup with Linda, the only problem that I could see was that I still wasn't a Christian. I suppose I was sort of a "seeker" in spiritual limbo. To all appearances, I was a believer, but I hadn't crossed the line yet. I attended Calvary Fellowship regularly and played in a Christian metal band to share the gospel message in secular clubs and bars. However, there was still the nagging question: Why was I doing all this when I wasn't a Christian?

Steve and I used to talk late into the night about my spiritual condition, and what I should do about it. I told him about my two baptisms and how neither one seemed to work, so I was understandably skeptical about how to move forward spiritually. For the time being, I was content to attend church and keep jamming with my bandmates, but at this point—as at other times in the past—I seemed stuck and lacked direction.

We had many long conversations, but we never seemed to reach any satisfactory conclusions about my next move. I hoped the Lord would intervene in some supernatural way and fix everything. I certainly did not know what to do, other than to wait and see what would happen.

One night after band practice, what looked like a divine opportunity presented itself. As Steve and I once again pondered my spiritual condition, he announced that he was going to attend an evangelistic service on Sunday evening. The service was in North Seattle at the church he'd grown up in. Steve wasn't in need of hearing an evangelistic sermon, but he asked if I would come along with him and see what happened. What did I have to lose?

If the Lord had indeed been working in my life like I believed he was, Steve reasoned that maybe I just needed to hear the gospel message one more time from a new perspective. With nothing better to do, I agreed to go along with him. If God's hand was in it, I figured, what's the worst that could happen? Looking back over the last few years, it seemed clear that God had been subtly steering my life, keeping me headed toward salvation on that narrow path that leads to righteousness. Engineering the breakup with Linda, he'd gotten me out of the trap of sexual sin. Perhaps this new opportunity was just what I needed to get my life back on track and "get back into the fire" once again.

At first, nothing about the service that night seemed unique. I'd heard the gospel message all my life. There were only about thirty to forty people in attendance. We sang worship songs I had sung many times before. However, as the service went on, I began cynically harboring doubts, wondering if I'd made a mistake in coming out on a Sunday night when I could have been doing any number of better things. I began to suspect this idea was likely a waste of my time.

The speaker that night wasn't the regular preacher. Instead, the youth pastor was allowed to fill in because, he stated as he began his sermon, "I felt a special call from God to deliver this message. He's laid this on my heart. Someone here tonight needs to hear what I'm about to say." I wondered if he was referring to me since all the people in the place were regular church attendees. For the first time since arriving for the service, I considered the possibility that God might have put me in that church to hear this preacher's sermon that very night.

I can't recall everything the youth pastor said, but as he neared the end of his sermon, he started talking about "the conviction and calling of God on a person's life." The thought came to me that perhaps God had been working in my life in the last year or so. I'd met Steve and, through his influence, had started attending Calvary Fellowship regularly. And I had started playing in a Christian metal band, aiming to evangelize the lost. It was clear that God had intervened to break up my relationship with Linda at the exact moment when my life was about to veer off the rails completely. Maybe I did have a call on my life. As I listened to the young pastor, I began to feel convinced that something needed to change. I could no longer deny the fact that I'd been ducking and hiding from God, living an anonymous life at Calvary, a life in which I avoided spiritual accountability. It was time for a reckoning with God. There was no escaping my divine appointment that night.

The youth pastor seemed to be speaking right to me as he described a person who had once seemed close to God but had slipped away from the truth. "It happened through no fault of your own," he declared. "Satan doesn't want us to come to the light and see the truth. He and his demons are working overtime, trying to steal those good seeds of the gospel from the stony ground of our hearts." This explanation seemed to explain why my first two baptisms hadn't taken hold.

"Don't burden yourself with guilt over what's happened in the past," the preacher stated authoritatively. I felt reassured when he said that, because I had indeed beaten myself up for years about how *I* was the problem. It surely couldn't have been God's fault, and perhaps it was in fact the work of Satan and his demons, snatching up those gospel seeds from my heart. The preacher went on to say, "God has a call on your life. God has a purpose for your life despite your countless mistakes. None of that matters now. Like a loving gardener, Jesus is always there to replant those gospel seeds in your heart. The Holy Spirit will water and protect them so that they will grow."

I knew the youth pastor was speaking directly to me. There was no escaping that fact. As he brought his sermon to a close, he made the classic tent revival preacher's move, a sure-fire way to close the deal with a hesitant listener. "Every head bowed and every eye closed," he solemnly intoned. "I'll make just one simple request of you tonight. If you feel the calling and conviction of God in your heart, and you know that tonight is the night to get right with God, I ask you to look me in the eyes. That's all you have to do." My head was bowed, and my eyes were closed; I felt a burning sense of conviction deep in my soul. Was tonight the night that I should get right with God? No more running, no more hiding! But I didn't dare look up.

As I stood there in agony, wrestling with my stubborn conscience and obstinate pride, the young preacher kept up his evangelistic appeal. "Don't put this critical decision off. Don't procrastinate another day. If you were to walk out of here and die tonight in an unrepentant state, you would end up standing before the judgment throne of God. And he would ask you just one question: 'Why should I let you into my heaven?'" Startled, I suddenly realized this was the same question Pastor Jerry had asked me all those years ago, before my first baptism when I was ten. Back then, I had shamefully admitted that God wouldn't let me into his heaven because I had not made my commitment to him. Tonight was no different. I knew that if I died tonight, there was no way Saint Peter would wave me through the Pearly Gates and point me to a heavenly mansion.

"When he asks you why he should let you into heaven, you'll have no excuse," the preacher continued. "You'll have absolutely no good answer as to why, in your foolish pride, you knowingly and stubbornly turned your back on the truth. Tonight may be your final opportunity to get right with God. Who knows? You could walk out of this building and get struck by a car. You could have a heart attack in your bed while you're sleeping tonight, and it's all over, just like that. The bottom line is this: If you were to die tonight without salvation, you'd end up facing an eternity of conscious torment in the flames of hell. And sadly, it would be your fault because you closed your ears to the truth. Don't miss what may be your last chance!" I was flooded with an awareness that I could die suddenly. I knew what the young preacher was saying made sense.

He continued with his persuasive gospel message. "No one else here needs to see or know of your decision. It's only between you, me, and God. But know this: Your eternal destiny is at stake at this very moment. Will you spend an eternity of torment and agony in the flames of hell, or will you spend it celebrating, walking the streets of gold in heaven with Jesus forever? God may not give you another chance to get right with him!"

That final statement connected in a powerful way. I was deeply convicted and decided there would be no more running and hiding. Looking up, I felt an electric jolt shoot through my body when my eyes made contact with the preacher's eyes. Was this it? Was I truly saved? I felt that something profoundly different had taken place. Even though I'd prayed the sinner's prayer thousands of times as a kid and as a young man, those heartfelt petitions had accomplished nothing. I told myself I didn't know what I was doing then. I had responded out of sheer terror at the prospect of being left behind in the Rapture and ending up in hell. But now, at the age of 22, I knew what I was doing. I made a sincere and informed decision to become a Christian, to give my life to Jesus, no holds barred.

As the sermon concluded, the worship team began to sing, "I have decided to follow Jesus." I'd sung it a thousand times in Sunday School, worship services, Christian school, and summer camp, but now the words seemed different. This time, I *had* decided to follow Jesus—no turning back. The cross was indeed before me, and the world was surely behind me.[1]

I was on a spiritual high when I walked out of that Sunday night service with Steve. I felt that I'd made an informed decision without peer pressure or unreliable advice from pastors with a hidden agenda. I hadn't seen a movie that scared me into getting "fire insurance" to avoid hell or missing the Rapture. This time, I felt sure things were going to be different.

Praise Jesus, I was saved!

---

[1] Simon Marak, "I Have Decided to Follow Jesus," Public Domain.

Chapter Thirty Three

Listening to Radio Preachers

In the months following my conversion experience, things were different. A skeptical part of me expected my newfound salvation high to evaporate within a few months as it had following my second baptism, but that didn't happen. I knew I'd experienced another mountaintop spiritual experience, but this time, I wasn't a young, impressionable kid who hadn't understood what he was doing.

Convinced this was a genuine conversion, I felt I was on much safer ground than before. I was "building my house on the rock" instead of building on shifting sand. I continued to attend Calvary Fellowship where I received solid Bible teaching each week from Pastor Wayne. I stopped ducking out of worship services the moment they ended and hung around afterwards to fellowship with my fellow Christians. I decided to find ways to be of service at the church. I began tithing, at least every time I remembered, which was something I had never done before. My giving pattern had always been hit-or-miss, and usually, it was a miss. But this time, I was determined to give the Lord my "first fruits" out of gratitude for my salvation.

About six months after my conversion, I joined a home Bible study group. I also signed up for a six-week Inductive Bible Study class taught by Pastor Wayne to learn how to study the Scriptures for myself.

Chapter Thirty Three

I bought a set of highlighters and began underlining critical verses in my Bible as I made key observations and applications to my life. I wrote a heartfelt letter to Pastor Wayne, thanking him for helping me develop the skills to dig into the Word of God more effectively.

Although I never made it onto the main worship team as the drummer for Sunday services, there was another way to use my musical talents for God. Together with Tony, our lead singer, we assembled a worship band for the children's Sunday School service. We had a blast getting the kids riled up before class as they enthusiastically sang many of the same songs I'd sung growing up in church.

I even attended evangelism training by Hank Hanegraaff, the new "Bible Answer Man" who had replaced Dr. Walter Martin after he passed away. I wanted to learn how to share my faith confidently and effectively with my non-believing friends, family members, and coworkers. I felt like I was finally doing my part for the Lord and the church. It felt good being a valuable member rather than skipping out unnoticed each Sunday as I had done for so long.

At the time of my conversion, I was working as a warehouse delivery driver. I worked a Tuesday through Friday shift. Each workday, I was alone in my truck for up to twelve hours. I took advantage of the time to listen to famous Christian radio preachers all day. I saw this as time well spent. It was a form of Christian education, like attending Bible college or seminary but at no cost. What a blessing that God had gotten me this job with such a welcome side benefit! I marveled that I was getting paid to listen to Christian radio all day and learn about the Bible. That *had* to be God at work, opening doors in my life.

Listening daily for a period of months, I'd go through entire books of the Bible with these radio preachers. I felt that, for the first time, I was genuinely learning the Word of God for myself. It was like being in church all day, listening to these great pulpiteers break down the text, even delving into the Greek and Hebrew to explain the meaning clearly. They would always conclude by practically applying these nuggets of truth to their listeners' lives. For the first time, I began to see the relevance of God's Word to my day-to-day living. I was digesting the "meat of the Word" daily. No more milk for me! I was going to grow beyond being a baby Christian.

As I listened for months, learning the Bible and picking up lots of theology, I started to believe that God was calling me to be a preacher or teacher. I began asking myself whether I had a divine calling to attend Bible college. There, I could learn to be a pastor, a missionary, or a Bible college teacher. At this point it was just a dream, but I chose to believe I would be sitting in a Bible college class one day, studying the Scripture and learning theology from godly teachers. I couldn't see how it could happen, but I'd already come to believe that if God had a plan for your life, he would reveal his will to you and would provide the resources required. It might take time, but I believed it would happen.

Listening to their shows daily, I began to copy the speaking styles of famous preachers like Dr. J Vernon McGee, Dr. David Jeremiah, Dr. Charles Stanley, John MacArthur, and Dr. David Hocking. I noticed that most sermons stuck to the time-honored "three points and a poem" structure—explain the text, have no more than three points, and conclude with some emotional appeal to the listeners. Later, in homiletics (preaching) class in Bible college, the countless hours of listening to those preachers made putting sermons together something I did with relative ease.

Because I listened to these men so faithfully, I knew exactly what time of day each preacher was on the radio. I didn't need a timepiece in the cab because I listened religiously to their shows. I also devoured books on Christian apologetics by authors like Josh

McDowell and Dr. Walter Martin. I loved listening to Dr Martin, then later Hank Hanegraaff, on the "Bible Answer Man" radio show daily. After months of faithful listening, I felt I could answer most of the questions listeners asked. They tended to ask the same or similar questions over and over, and soon, I had the answers down pat. I was becoming an expert on the Bible and Christian theology and as a result, I felt more and more confident about sharing my faith without fear or hesitation.

As I worked in the warehouse preparing deliveries, I tried everything I could to evangelize my workmates. I openly read my Bible in the break room, hoping it would spark long discussions about my faith during lunch hour. With my newfound apologetics skills, I was always ready to provide what I considered solid reasons proving Christianity to be the one true religion. On my reserve weekends, I had a few long chats about God with some of my Navy buddies and tried to exemplify what a good Christian should be. No more swearing, no more drinking and smoking. Gone was the lewd talk about getting laid or looking at pornography. This was the new me!

As the months went by, I could see more and more that all that study and reading, the hours spent listening to sermons on Christian radio, were paying off. Although none of my work colleagues or fellow sailors became Christians because of my proselytizing, I nonetheless felt good that I wasn't ashamed of my faith. Everyone knew I was a Christian "on fire for God." I attempted to set myself apart by doing my best to be inoffensive in my witnessing efforts.

I proclaimed the gospel at every opportunity, witnessing to everyone I knew about Jesus and what he'd done for me. But one thing bothered me. Nobody I evangelized was getting saved. I felt much pressure when I read the Apostle Paul's command in 2 Timothy 4:2 that believers must "proclaim the word; be persistent whether it is convenient or inconvenient."[1] I knew many evangelicals who struggled with guilt and shame because they had never led anyone to the Lord, much less spoken about their faith. I wondered why the Holy Spirit didn't help them more. The stakes were so high! I needed an answer as to why more people weren't being saved.

One day during my daily quiet time—a period of prayer and Bible study—there came a flash of insight as I examined Jesus's "parable of the sower" in Matthew 13 using my newfound inductive Bible study skills. Jesus explained that although it was the job of believers to *sow* the good seed of the gospel to every heart, it was the responsibility of *God* to bring forth the harvest. That was a massive breakthrough of spiritual insight at the time, and it lifted a weight off my shoulders. I reasoned that even if they didn't get saved immediately because of *my* witness, at least I'd done my part in planting the seed of the gospel in their hearts. I had no control over the status of their "heart condition," as it were. That part was clearly up to God, not me.

After all, I reflected, hadn't the same thing happened to me? I had resisted for years, yet undeniably, the Lord had brought forth the harvest in my life, and I'd been saved. Hadn't Steve's faithful and diligent efforts to plant the seeds of the gospel in my life ultimately paid off? He certainly never gave up on me, and neither had God, despite my years of sinfulness and backsliding. But why hadn't he saved my cousin Andy, who had been killed in a drunk driving accident two years before? I'd done everything in my power to reach him for Christ but could never work out why those seeds hadn't "taken" in his heart. Perhaps it was because I wasn't truly saved back then, which may have affected my attempts at evangelism.

All I knew was that in witnessing to these unbelievers now, as a true believer, I was faithfully doing my part. It was up to God to see the work through to completion. I knew that non-Christians are spiritually blind, as the Apostle Paul taught in 2 Corinthians

4:4. They couldn't perceive the truth of the gospel because Satan was at work in their lives, preventing them from seeing the light of the glory of Christ. It was up to the Holy Spirit, not me, to remove the "scales from their eyes." I confidently believed that lost individuals would come to a saving knowledge of the truth at some point in the future—all in God's perfect timing. For my part, I felt good that I was doing my best as a faithful believer should. I knew I wasn't guilty of "hiding my light under a bushel," and was justifiably proud that I wasn't ashamed of the gospel, since it represented the power of God to save humanity.

As time went on, however, what I considered an inoffensive approach to preaching the gospel, whether convenient or inconvenient, must have been incredibly annoying, if not downright offensive, to those around me. I came to believe that it was necessary to be an unapologetic witness for Christ all the time, regardless of whom it might offend. After all, as the Apostle Paul explains it, the good news of the gospel message itself is an "offense" to nonbelievers. They would undoubtedly be offended when confronted by the undeniable fact that they were bound for an eternity in hell. Knowing it was my responsibility to tell them the truth, I felt that they needed to find out what was in store for them after they died if they failed to get right with God while they still had time. I certainly didn't want their blood on my hands for failing to warn them of their eternal destiny.

After I quit my warehouse job in 1990, I worked off and on for a guy named Brian. He ran a roofing and gutter company, and I worked for him until 1993 when I moved to Portland. For the most part, I enjoyed the job—except when it rained. When I heard he needed a second employee, I talked Brian into hiring our band's lead singer, Tony, and we interpreted this job offer as a definite "God thing." Tony and I were determined to be bold and effective Christian witnesses on the job site to demonstrate just how unashamed of the faith we were.

Listening to Radio Preachers

Like clockwork each day, regardless of what we were doing, from 11:30-12 noon, we'd put down tools, stop working, and take our lunch break. Setting up the radio in a strategic spot where other workers could hear it, we'd play the same Christian radio station I'd always listened to in the delivery truck that featured preacher after preacher. During lunch, we listened to Dr David Hocking's "Biola Hour" show. Later, the name was changed to "Solid Rock Radio," which I liked because it was named after one of my favorite classic hymns. I always loved singing in church, "On Christ, the solid rock I stand, all other ground is sinking sand."[2] Hearing that refrain every day took me back to my days of growing up in church and singing those old worship songs with such gusto in Sunday School.

Hocking was one of my most admired preachers, and Tony and I were excited to attend one of his week-long preaching events in the Seattle area that same year. He was speaking on the topic of "Israel and Bible prophecy." One night, I was able to convince a Muslim friend of mine I'd formerly worked with at the warehouse to attend. He was interested in the topic because he was from Palestine, and we had argued endlessly about the differences between the Qur'an and the Bible and the role Israelis and Arabs would play in the end times. Unfortunately, he wasn't convinced by Hocking's sermon. Still, I felt good that I was faithfully evangelizing the lost—and since he was a follower of Islam, I considered him to be a nonbeliever. Later, I comforted myself, knowing that despite his refusal to accept the offer of salvation, the gospel seeds had still been planted in his heart and would come to fruition someday.

On those job sites where Tony and I worked, I sometimes wondered what the other construction workers thought of these two rough-looking gutter guys playing Christian preachers and music on their radio all day. Although we received some strange looks at times, nobody ever asked us why we were listening to Christian content all day long. Why weren't we blasting rock music, as typical construction workers did? For our part, we were simply proud that we were unashamed of the gospel and were more than ready to share our faith with anyone who asked us.

Another job around this time was at a bottled water plant, filling office cooler bottles. I got the job through a friend named Rollie, a fellow long-haired Christian rocker whom I'd met at Calvary Fellowship. I worked on the machine next to him, which filled one-gallon bottles with distilled and spring water. At the beginning of our shifts, we each had our radios at our workstations tuned to the local Christian music station in Seattle, KCMS. At 11:00 AM, we'd switch radios over to catch John MacArthur's "Grace to You" program followed by Hocking's "Solid Rock Radio" sermon. We had the volume turned up high to drown out the cacophony of our machines.

Again, I often wondered what the other guys working in the warehouse thought of this, but nobody ever complained to our boss about our open displays of faith. From our point of view, Rollie and I felt proud that we were unashamedly proclaiming our faith, doing our part to help get the Word of God out to all those nonbelievers in the bottling plant. Looking back on it now beyond belief, if I were in that situation, being forced to listen to someone else's radio playing Christian content all day, I'd be the first one to raise the issue with management. I think it also demonstrates the point about Christian domination in American society, making employees hesitant or afraid to challenge expressions of belief that they find personally offensive. But back then, we were just doing our best to be faithful witnesses for Christ.

---

1   2 Timothy 4:2, NABRE.
2   William B. Bradbury, "Solid Rock," 1863.

Chapter Thirty Four

Experimenting with Critical Thinking

D uring this time of heavy listening to preachers on the radio, for the first time, I began to form doubts and questions about some of what I was hearing. It was also one of the first times I started to think critically by comparing varying theological traditions and weighing the arguments for and against all sides. Ironically, even though I considered myself a good evangelical, after a few months of daily listening, I grew tired of Pastor John MacArthur's rants on his "Grace to You" show. He preached a four-or-five-week sermon series on the gift of tongues, giving his authoritarian interpretation of this allegedly miraculous sign from God. His core thesis was that the spiritual gift of tongues, in which a believer empowered by the Holy Spirit suddenly starts speaking in a language unknown to them, had ceased operating after the first century.

His was not a new perspective for me. This was the same cessationist argument I'd grown up hearing from the pulpit at my Church of Christ decades earlier. Both Pastors Jerry and David taught that when the book of Acts concluded, so did the "signs and wonders" spiritual gifts. As a kid, I'd bought into the doctrine uncritically and thought all charismatic Christians were strange because they didn't follow clear biblical teaching when it came to the gift of tongues. They might even be edging into heresy. At the least, though they might be true believers, they were theologically off base. As teenagers, my buddy Guy and I had even fallen out over the same issue all those years ago, the first time he came to stay at my house.

But since my conversion, I'd been faithfully studying my Bible with my inductive skills and had picked up several books on systematic theology. The few years I'd spent at Calvary Fellowship had demonstrated that there were a lot of sincere Christians who believed the opposite of what MacArthur taught. Calvary was technically considered a "charismatic" church, although they didn't push tongues and miracles.

In 1991, when I was 24, I started dating Lisa, our bass player's sister. Along with her parents, she attended the FourSquare Church I had participated in before they filled in their swimming pool. Since we were dating, I figured it was a perfect time to switch churches and go with her and her parents, who were heavily involved in the church and its ministries. It was a definite change from the laid-back style of Calvary Church. My new church was firmly within the Pentecostal tradition and was into all the miraculous signs and wonders. Their services featured exuberant, rockin' worship with a full band, healings, prophecies, tongues, and interpretations of tongues.

This exposure to the supernatural realm opened my eyes to a new experience. By then, I wasn't so confident about the belief system of my earlier church and its hardline "signs and wonders have ceased" theological stance. As my horizons widened, I met many Christians in the charismatic tradition who seemed like sincere believers. I had a hard time believing they were somehow in league with the devil every time they spoke in tongues. But this is precisely what MacArthur taught. According to his fundamentalist view, allied with his literalistic and sectarian biblical interpretation principles, he added a new twist to the cessationist argument. Every single one of these charismatic Christians was being duped by Satan. More specifically, all believers speaking in an "unknown miraculous tongue" were being misled by demonic spirits. It wasn't a gift of miraculous tongues, he asserted confidently, but rather, these behaviors were prompted by Satanic deception. These poor, deluded individuals only thought they were speaking in tongues inspired by the Holy Spirit. In reality, it was demonic activity.

To me, MacArthur's position was a bridge too far. Although I have never experienced speaking in tongues, I could not agree with MacArthur on this dogmatic point. I found his voice to be shrill, and his opinions rigid and narrow. His stance was angry, judgmental, and strident. Moreover, his interpretation of Scripture offended me because he gave no credit to other Christian faith traditions and instead relied solely on his own sectarian Calvinist views. After a few weeks of listening to him belabor his argument, I informed Rollie that I couldn't take it anymore. Surprisingly, he responded that he was also getting sick of MacArthur's grating tone. We agreed that we'd skip his sermon and listen to Hocking instead.

I only lasted another couple of months at the bottling company and ended up going back to work for Brian hanging gutters. I left the bottling plant job with my head held high, knowing I'd done my best to proclaim the good news of salvation in yet another spiritually dark place. Having done my part as a loyal believer, I'd faithfully planted those gospel seeds, and it was now up to God to bring home the harvest.

Chapter Thirty Five

Christian Rock and the IRS

My music career was moving along on track while the events I described in the previous chapter unfolded. Back in 1990 our Christian metal band had finally started taking off. I interpreted this as a sign that God was blessing us due to my newfound spirituality. Calling ourselves "Angel 7," we finalized our set list and hooked up with a manager named Brad, who promised to get us gigs. Representing some three hundred rock and metal outfits, Brad had connections in rock clubs and bars all over Seattle. Fortunately for us, he was as good as his word, and soon, we were playing gigs all over the Pacific Northwest. Priding ourselves as good Christian witnesses going *into the world* as Jesus commanded, we rarely performed in churches or did explicitly Christian shows. Instead, we chose to play in rock clubs and bars, driven by the philosophy of ministry that musically, we'd try to be as good, or better, than any secular rock or metal band out there.

We believed we could hold our own onstage with any other band on the Seattle music scene in those days. But it was the *lyrics* to our songs, we believed, as well as our Christian witness offstage, that set us apart. Each song had a message about God, spirituality, Jesus, or the Bible, but not in blatantly obvious ways. We worked to build relationships with many of the musicians in other bands we played with, so we had a chance to spread the gospel with fellow metalheads.

We echoed the musical style of successful Christian metal bands of the day—Stryper, Bloodgood, Saint, Holy Soldier—and others that hit it big in the late 80s and early 90s. We played with more than a few of those bands as they toured Seattle. We slowly started developing a following. Our claim to fame was opening for Bloodgood in 1990 at the now-defunct Lake City Concert Hall. I'd taken Linda to see them a few years earlier, and little did I know that one day, we'd share the stage with these Christian metal legends.

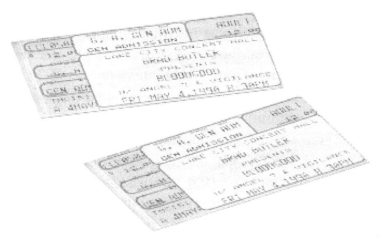

Eight hundred enthusiastic people caught our set when we opened for Bloodgood. This was the biggest audience we'd ever played for, and they loved our music. Our merch sold out about five minutes into our show, and we hoped to get other bookings after playing that concert. We all saw this event as our springboard to the top!

We drew our inspiration from Stryper, one of the day's most successful Christian metal bands. If they could make it with number-one hit songs and hugely popular videos airing regularly on MTV, as they unashamedly proclaimed their Christian faith, then so could we.

Things were going well with Angel 7, but sadly, our dreams

of becoming the next big Christian metal band were abruptly shattered. I got into a major disagreement with guitarist Steve— my close friend who had been instrumental in leading me to my true salvation experience. We began to argue over his acceptance of an IRS tax refund, which had been filed by the accountant where he worked. Rather than entering the correct sum of $1,000 for a refund due to Steve, the accountant had mistakenly added an extra zero, requesting a refund of $10,000. Steve interpreted this $9,000 windfall as a sign of God's blessing and the IRS's incompetence. Correcting the error was on *them*, not him, he argued. Another reason he felt no need to return the extra money was because he believed the US government had no right to collect income tax from Americans! The IRS's collection of taxes was illegal, as he saw it—yet another clear case of government overreach.

I argued that *he* was committing tax fraud and was in danger of legal trouble with the government. If he accepted the bogus refund, he was also in danger of violating the clear commands of Scripture on taxpaying. Countering my argument, Steve shot back that the IRS's mistake represented just one small win for the little guy, whom they'd been screwing over for decades. Stick it to the man!

We went round and round for several weeks, repeating the same arguments but getting nowhere. The situation worsened and started to get personal, with each of us accusing the other of not listening or caring. As time passed, the entire band—including wives and girlfriends—got involved in the dispute. Two factions began to form, reinforcing the growing sense of division. Some agreed with Steve and said they couldn't see a problem. Others sided with Tony and me since we both felt that Steve was not only clearly in the wrong, but he was also blatantly sinning. There seemed to be no peaceable way to settle this disagreement, and it was placing the band's future in jeopardy.

Chapter Thirty Five

The situation finally became so fractious that we all agreed to see Pastor Wayne at Calvary over the matter, as our friendship and the band itself were on the line. Tony and I talked privately before the meeting and felt we were in the clear because we had the Bible on our side in every respect. In addition to citing the commands for Christians to pay their taxes, we knew we'd done the right thing by adhering to the Matthew 18 conflict resolution model.[1] Following Jesus's teaching closely, first, we confronted Steve individually, then as a group. Unfortunately, he was still in denial, stubbornly clinging to his sin.

Jesus taught that if the conflict wasn't resolved after the first two steps and the sinning brother hadn't repented, the final phase of the process was to bring the issue to church leaders. This was why we sought out Pastor Wayne to help mediate the situation. Before the meeting, Steve and I agreed that whatever Wayne's decision might be, we would accept it as the final word and follow his guidance. We figured it was best to have an objective third party, a wise and godly pastor, who could oversee the conflict and help us resolve this contentious issue.

At the meeting, each side presented their argument. After hearing everyone out, Pastor Wayne deliberated for a few minutes and ended up siding with Tony and me. Relief washed over me, and I hoped we could finally move forward now that the matter was settled. Wasn't that the intended conclusion of Jesus's conflict resolution model from the Gospels? The outcome of church discipline should always be restoration. Hadn't I heard that in a sermon somewhere?

Turning to Steve, Pastor Wayne gently pointed out that, in this case, he was clearly in the wrong and was in danger of committing tax fraud. He advised that the best action would be to immediately pay the excess refund money back to the IRS. If there were fines and fees on top of the repayment, Steve would have to deal with the consequences of his actions. This would be the right thing to do legally and would have an added benefit: It would please God. Providing biblical precedent, Pastor Wayne cited Jesus's injunction in the Gospels for all believers to "pay to Caesar the things that are Caesar's."[2] "Nobody likes paying income taxes," Wayne admitted. "But we must obey when Jesus commands it."

Relieved, I sat back in my chair, thankful that the matter would be laid to rest. With the thorny situation firmly behind us, we could get back to rockin' for God and spreading the gospel in all those dark places. Unfortunately, that's not what happened. Despite what he'd said earlier about being willing to accept Pastor Wayne's decision, Steve dug in his heels. He vehemently disagreed with the minister's conclusion. Angrily citing the same line of argumentation he'd laid out before, he refused to pay the money back. Well, at least not immediately. Waffling, he claimed he *would* pay it back at some point in the future in small installments. If there was a charge or a fine leveled by the IRS, then so be it. He was content to let those government bean-counters figure it out later, so why worry about it? From his point of view, he'd done absolutely nothing wrong. We were all overreacting, even Pastor Wayne. All the blame lay clearly with government incompetence since they missed the oversight. The money, he asserted, was a much-needed windfall, a blessing from God that he sorely needed to pay his bills.

Of course, Tony and I disagreed entirely with Steve and were highly disappointed that he doubled down and failed to adhere to our advance agreement to follow Pastor Wayne's guidance. We felt we had done everything according to biblical guidelines, so we immediately decided to boot Steve out of the band. We figured it was time to treat him as a pagan or a tax collector, as Jesus commands believers to do in Matthew 18.

Chapter Thirty Five

We felt fully justified as we engaged in church discipline and shunning of our recalcitrant brother. Whatever Steve felt didn't matter because our actions were vindicated. From our point of view, we'd faithfully followed all three of Jesus's steps, but it still hadn't worked, so it was time for us to part ways. I felt fine about our decision, despite the many years of close friendship Steve and I had enjoyed, not to mention the crucial role he played in my salvation experience.

Our decision to kick Steve out of the band is an excellent example of Lifton's "doctrine over person."[3] One believer's interpretation of the biblical text takes precedence over personal relationships. We were right. The Bible and Pastor Wayne were on our side, so Tony and I were fully justified in tossing Steve aside and thinking nothing of it. If Steve was hurt, it was his fault for being in the wrong and committing a flagrant sin, despite our efforts to correct him. Besides, if he got into legal trouble, we reasoned that the scandal would reflect poorly on the band, damage our example as Christians, and ultimately destroy our efforts to evangelize the lost. It was better to treat him as an outsider and an infidel than to hurt the cause of Christ.

Regrettably, the decision to boot Steve out ended up splitting up the band since a couple of the other guys sided with him. Beyond shattering our dreams of becoming rock stars, the split instantly destroyed my long-term friendship with Steve. We did patch things up, but it was more than a decade later. And our relationship was never the same as before. Steve moved from Seattle to Spokane, Washington, and although we never saw each other again, we at least spoke a few times on the phone. Ironically, during the last few conversations, we argued vehemently about differing interpretations of end-times theology. Finally, we agreed to disagree and went our separate ways.

The breakup of our band after the meeting with Pastor Wayne

was the epitome of bad timing! After the Bloodgood gig, we'd had some offers to headline some local shows, and we'd been hopeful that this was our big break. It seemed a real shame that it was all over just as we'd begun to develop a following.

There was, however, some sunlight peeking through the dark clouds. The rock star dream wasn't completely dead. A few months after the demise of Angel 7 in the summer of 1991, Tony and I formed a new band with him on lead guitar and vocals, me on drums, and an entirely new lineup. Calling ourselves "Bad Faith," we quickly compiled a new set list, hooked back up with our former manager Brad, and started playing gigs around the Seattle area.

Things were looking up, but we were starting over, facing the hard slog of building up a following again. Before the Internet and social media, getting the word out about an upcoming show was difficult. We thought we'd caught our one big break when we opened up for Larry Norman, the legendary Christian rocker, at a concert in Portland, Oregon. Unfortunately, we got only a few gigs as a result. After that major disappointment, we had to start asking ourselves some hard questions about the band's future and the direction of our lives.

In November of 1991, after serving in the US Naval Reserves for six years, I completed my service requirements. No more playing sailor one weekend a month! Although I had two years of inactive service left, I was all but out. I could still get called to active duty if a war came along, but I wasn't too worried about it. My sentence was finished! I could finally start growing my hair long, which back in those days was indispensable if you wanted to play in any metal band, Christian or not. As we developed a following, I had paid a lot of money for hair extensions I could wear onstage, but I felt uncomfortable doing so. It was a contrived image, unlike what I looked like day-to-day.

Chapter Thirty Five

I was relieved when my service was done, and I could finally start growing my natural hair. No more faking it for me.

1   Matthew 18:15-17.
2   Matthew 22:21, NASB.
3   Freedom of Mind Resource Center, "BITE Model™ of Authoritarian Control."

Chapter Thirty Six

He Leadeth Me Oh Blessed Thought

We did the Bad Faith thing for another year or so, during which time I became more and more confident that God was calling me to go to Bible college. Two events occurred that convinced me it was time to make the move. First, we discovered that our manager Brad had never paid us for a single gig, as far back as our Angel 7 shows! It hadn't mattered that we never received our money since we were so eager to play anywhere that we hadn't minded or even questioned it. We were just dumb, fired-up kids ecstatic that we were out there on stage. Who cared about the money? We all had stars in our eyes, and Brad knew he could get away with it so long as he got us shows. As AC/DC put it, "Gettin' ripped off, underpaid...that's how it goes, playin' in a band. It's a long way to the top if you wanna rock n' roll!"[1]

Every time we asked about our payment after a concert, Brad would always blame it on the club owner: "Those dirty bastards ripped us off again! I'm sick and tired of this shit, man! I swear to God, you'll get paid next time." We always laughed it off as typical sleazy club owners screwing over the musical talent. How much more rock n' roll can you get? At least we were out there, playing concerts and building a faithful following. The good news of the gospel was going forth, so what did it matter if we got paid? We weren't in it for the money anyway, we told ourselves. This was our ministry! As long as the Lord got the credit and we were faithfully planting those gospel seeds, that was all that mattered.

In the end, Brad's unscrupulous ways finally caught up with him. When we started talking to *other* bands Brad represented, we discovered he'd laid the same lame story on them. None of us had been paid a dime for a single gig we'd played! The final straw happened one night at a rock club we'd performed at before. A friend of mine from another band we'd played with a few times angrily confronted the owner about why the hell he was constantly screwing the bands over. "The fuck is your problem, dude? Where's our fuckin' money you owe us for all our gigs, bitch? Fuck you, man!" The owner indignantly retorted, "Whaddya mean, fuck me? Fuck *you*! Guess what? I paid Brad every time you played here, so take it up with him. It's got nothin' to do with me, man. Now get the fuck outta my face!" Once that startling revelation occurred, Brad's days were numbered since he represented hundreds of rock and metal bands all over the Seattle area. God only knew how much of our money he'd pocketed over the years, but we never saw a single penny.

We were pissed off. Brad owed us thousands of dollars. When a bunch of us showed up at Brad's apartment to kick his ass and collect our money, we learned that he had skipped town. He'd heard the rumor that every rock and metal band in Seattle was wise to his shenanigans, so he caught a red-eye flight out of town the night before. His apartment sat deserted. He was long gone, and so was all our money.

Not only had our hard-earned cash vanished with Brad, but now that he'd bugged out, we'd also lost our connection with all the rock bars and clubs where we'd gotten gigs. It was getting harder and harder to find places to play. One thing you had to admit about Brad, despite being a con artist, a grifter, and a thief, he'd gotten us loads of shows. But now that connection was gone, and nobody was left to represent us.

The second development that convinced me it was time to start thinking seriously about Bible college involved the rapid changes in the Seattle music scene in the early 1990s. The massive explosion in grunge and alternative music put an end to almost all the old-school rock and metal bands. Up-and-coming Seattle-based outfits like Nirvana, Soundgarden, Pearl Jam, Alice in Chains, and many others were the new thing, and the Seattle rock scene died out virtually overnight.

Fighting against the tide, some metal bands refused to let the dream go and headed to Los Angeles, hoping to score a record deal before it all disappeared. Others packed it up and cut off their long hair hoping to land "real" jobs. Many musicians sold their instruments or put them away for good, giving up on the rock star dream altogether. Some of those who did keep playing are still around. "Dad rock bands" are still alive, performing cover tunes in bars all over the area to this day. The same is true of me. I have long since given up the dream of becoming a rock star, but I still love playing the drums. And I, too, play in a Dad rock band, performing classic rock and blues covers.

Our band observed that many clubs and rock bars where we'd played so many times were disappearing. The fact was, there just wasn't much of a metal crowd left. Seeking more profitable ventures, some transformed into sports bars or themed restaurants, while others shut their doors for good. Watching all those venues sell out or go under was highly disappointing. I interpreted all this as a sign that Bad Faith would never be the next big Christian metal band. Although giving up the dream of becoming a rock star was disappointing, perhaps this was an indication that God was working to make something better happen according to his providential plans and calling on my life.

Discussing our band's situation with a friend at church one Sunday, he gave me what seemed to be godly counsel. "In the book of Ecclesiastes," he sagely intoned, "King Solomon says that there are 'seasons of life.' Solomon was the wisest man who ever lived. He describes how there's a season for this and a season for that. Maybe Bad Faith's season is over, and it's time to start looking for the next opportunity in faith, as God leads you." I took that as wise advice and wondered what the Lord was up to in my life. I'd seen enough indisputable evidence over the last few years to believe that God played an active role in steering me safely along the righteous path. Who was I to doubt what he was doing? I needed to trust, obey, and believe in faith that God would make clear his plans for my life sooner or later.

Reading through the New Testament book of Romans one morning during my quiet time, I came across chapter 11, verse 29: "...for the gifts and the calling of God are irrevocable."[2] That seemed like a precise instance of God speaking to me through his infallible Word. Sitting at the table with my Bible open, I recalled those days riding around in my delivery truck, listening to Christian preachers on the radio. Clinging to the notion that I was supposed to become a preacher, I firmly trusted in the old spiritual-sounding Christianese statement, "When God closes a door, he opens a window." Bad Faith's door was closing, but that wasn't necessarily bad news.

It was clear to me that God's open window of opportunity beckoned. I had always held on to the dream that someday I would attend Bible college. I had no idea how I would pay for it. It seemed like an impossible aspiration, but I decided that if God calls you to do something, he will provide the means. I only needed to trust him and make the leap of faith into the unknown. But which Bible college should I attend? In America, there are hundreds of Christian colleges. No worries! Again, I felt God was providing me with clear direction and guidance.

One of the Christian radio programs I listened to while doing deliveries was called "The Multnomah Hour." It was produced by Multnomah Bible College in Portland, Oregon. This program showcased different preachers. I didn't remember any of them being particularly outstanding, but one feature of the program always stood out when the show's host interviewed current students around campus. In one episode, as I drove around doing my deliveries, I listened with interest to a young man describing a situation that was very similar to mine. God had called him to attend Multnomah, but he had no way to pay for it. The Lord had provided a way for him to attend through gifts, grants, and loans.

Even though I had listened to this young man's testimony years earlier, I felt that God was speaking to me through it at that very moment, and his message couldn't have been more explicit. His calling, after all, was irrevocable—and now it was time to pull the trigger. Like this guy, I had no money, but I felt it was clear that I should go ahead and apply to Multnomah Bible College. I needed to trust that the Lord would provide a way to make it happen if I stepped out in faith. I figured he would close the door and redirect me if he didn't want me to go.

Another sign that God was guiding and leading during this time involved my decision to marry. In early 1992, I had been dating Lisa for a few months, and it was clear to both of us that the Lord desired us to get married. Although it took some convincing, shortly after we'd gotten married in September of 1992, after several months of prayer and discussion, Lisa and I decided that I should apply to Multnomah. What's the worst that could happen? I would be out nothing if they rejected my application. If I didn't get accepted, that would be my answer from God, and I'd start praying and seeking his will all over again. If I got accepted, we would move to Portland to attend Multnomah.

All I knew for sure was that God loved me and had an excellent plan for my life. I was sure he was miraculously working behind the scenes to make something amazing happen, although I didn't know exactly what it was. I knew I needed to trust him and rely on his guidance in faith. A Christian friend at church approached me once during this period and declared boldly that God had given her a "word of knowledge" about our situation. She read Jeremiah 29:11 to me: "'For I know the plans that I have for you,' declares the Lord, 'plans for prosperity and not for disaster, to give you a future and a hope.'"[3] I was blown away, convinced that this virtual stranger had been sent to me by God to confirm that his plans for me were all for my good.

In the Spring of 1993, the long-anticipated letter from Multnomah finally arrived. It seemed that the prophetic word of knowledge the woman at church had been given was indeed correct. Not only did I get accepted, but other seemingly "supernatural" things happened to convince Lisa and me that we should move to Portland. Dave, the new pastor at the FourSquare church where we attended, had officiated our wedding. Dave was an alumnus of Multnomah. He reassured us that his experiences at Multnomah had been life-changing and that we wouldn't regret our time there. That seemed like yet another divine confirmation that we'd made the right choice and were safely operating within God's will.

In addition to these encouraging signs, we were able to move out of our rental house very quickly without paying any penalties, and from there, we temporarily went to live with Lisa's parents. The Lord provided a place for us to live in Portland with meager rent. The house belonged to a relative who had recently passed away. This seemed like one more confirmation that God was blessing the entire move, clearing any obstacles in our way.

In July 1993—we had been married less than a year and had our first baby on the way—we packed all our belongings and moved to Portland. I was incredibly excited that my long-cherished dream of attending Bible college was finally becoming a reality. It seemed that the Lord did have a calling on my life, and, as promised, he would reward us if we moved out in faith. God was providing, his Spirit was leading, and we were beginning a new, exciting chapter in our lives.

---

1   AC/DC, "It's a Long Way to the Top (If You Wanna Rock n' Roll)," *TNT*, Albert Studios, 1975.

2   Romans 11:29, NASB.

3   Jeremiah 29:11, NASB.

Chapter Thirty Seven

Third Time's a Charm

As I settled into my new student life at Multnomah, I could not escape a theological problem: Should I get baptized a third time? This question had been in the back of my mind since my conversion experience five years earlier at Steve's church. Whenever the issue came to mind, I would shove this unwanted and troubling thought back. However, as I studied the Bible and theology in my classes, I became convinced that a person should get baptized only *after* becoming a Christian. Baptism, I concluded, wasn't what theologians call a "salvific act," which is theological jargon for "something that leads a person to be saved." In other words, getting baptized doesn't cause salvation to occur. It's something you do to show that you've been saved.

I now believed that baptism is not a magical event. It is a simple matter of being immersed in or sprinkled with water. It's a symbolic act representing a spiritual reality in a person's life. Salvation, in my view, involved some mysterious, inner, spiritual interaction between an individual and God that should take place before baptism. I came to believe that baptism, although symbolic, somehow "seals" the believer's salvation and provides a public witness to that person's faith choice.

Because of the toxicity and traumas of my past and the utter failure of my first two baptisms, I didn't want to be baptized a third time.

"I'm just not good at this," I thought. For several years, I had viewed the experience at the service I attended with Steve as my genuine conversion, but I felt I had no obligation to get baptized a third time. I made a clear and valid decision to convert, which was the end of the discussion. "Baptism doesn't save anyone; I don't need to do it again!" I told myself repeatedly. That was my position, and nothing could dissuade me from it.

After all, the thief on the cross next to Christ didn't need to be baptized, and Jesus promised him, "...today you will be with me in Paradise."[1] Jesus's authoritative declaration was the end of the argument! Jesus was the sinless God-man, so his statement should be the final word. I told myself that baptism was merely a symbolic act and had no intrinsic magical power to save a new convert. Problem solved, or so I thought. Every time the subject of baptism came up, I would get triggered, agitated, and upset. I didn't want to talk about it. It is a small wonder, considering the craziness of my past life and the traumatic experiences following my first two baptisms. Why keep doing something that never seems to work?

In the fall of 1993, shortly after arriving at Multnomah, I landed a job as a youth pastor at Troutdale Community Church, a small Baptist church on the east side of Portland. We saw my getting this job as further confirmation that the Lord was providing our every need. The salary was five hundred dollars a month, which wasn't much. With funds from our other part-time jobs, we made just enough to cover our bills.

Now, as a member of a church staff, I had a nagging feeling that ate away at me constantly, a voice whispering in my head. "You're the youth pastor overseeing these kids. You're teaching them the Bible. But what kind of a leader and pastor are you? You haven't even been baptized yourself. What a complete hypocrite!" Just like all those times before, I was troubled with constant feelings of guilt and shame but felt that I couldn't talk to anybody about it. It was the impostor syndrome rearing its ugly head again.

I certainly couldn't admit that I'd never been baptized after my actual conversion to Jim, the head pastor who was also my boss. I was sure I'd be sacked for such a spiritual breach. I didn't know what to do, and the internal pressure mounted weekly as I taught the youth group Bible class. Something had to give, but I had no idea what to do.

Almost a year into my tenure as youth pastor at Troutdale Community Church, Lisa and I took a weekend trip to Seattle to visit friends and family. On Sunday, along with Lisa's parents, we happily attended the morning worship service at the FourSquare church we had gone to before moving to Portland. It was great to catch up with friends we hadn't seen in the months since we'd moved. I had nothing on my mind other than the thought of enjoying the service, greeting fellow believers, and looking forward to a great meal at Lisa's parents' home afterward. But that morning during the worship service, I felt God at work in my life, convicting my heart. I saw this as another example of a "divine appointment." Once again, the Lord was working mysteriously, guiding me forward in my spiritual life.

During his sermon, Pastor Dave talked about his own life experience. Now in his late thirties, he shared that he had been baptized as a teenager but hadn't truly understood what he was doing. Like me, he'd spent years struggling with various sins and other spiritual issues. Following this "spiritually dry time," as he called it, Dave finally realized he had never been saved and made a genuine commitment. I sat transfixed, amazed at the parallels with my spiritual journey.

As Dave continued to speak, he described how he had resisted being baptized a second time. But as time passed, he became convinced that his refusal to be baptized again was simply a result of his stubbornness and pride. He began to feel convicted that his prideful disobedience was causing a "spiritual blockage" to his Christian growth. I could relate to everything he was saying. Wasn't I experiencing that same sort of spiritual blockage in my life? I had to admit to myself that, indeed, I was.

Although I was a successful youth pastor and Bible college student, I felt like I was hitting a "glass ceiling" in terms of my spiritual growth. Could Pastor Dave be putting his finger precisely on my problem? Was this why I felt so fake and phony despite the fact that I was now a true Christian? Was this why I felt like an impostor? As a youth pastor, I hated hiding any secret from the young learners I taught. Members of my church looked up to me as a leader, but my embarrassing secret was eating away at me. I felt deeply ashamed for my unwillingness to swallow my pride, admit my need for a valid baptism, and re-enter the water.

As Pastor Dave continued his testimony, his story sounded more and more like my own experiences. He related how, for many years, he'd stubbornly resisted the conviction of God. One day, deep in prayer during his quiet time, Pastor Dave had a eureka moment, and the floodgates of spiritual perception opened wide. He realized that only his pride prevented him from being re-baptized, and this lack of obedience was hindering his spiritual growth! What happened next once he confessed his pride and was baptized a second time? Exuberantly punching his fist in the air, he declared, "Boom! Spiritual breakthrough!"

Supernatural growth and divine blessings were all mine for the taking, if only I would set aside my hubris and allow myself to be baptized, albeit for a third time. A tear rolled down my cheek as I decided, "Enough is enough!" I vowed not to resist the will of God any longer. Sitting in the church pew, my head bowed in resignation, I admitted defeat. I was through battling God. I decided to come clean and finally submit to his will. In short, I experienced a spiritual breakthrough that day. Pastor Dave had officiated my wedding, served as my mentor, and on this day, God used Pastor Dave to wake me up!

Things would not have seemed so clear and straightforward that day had I been able to see the future. One year later, Pastor Dave was found guilty of embezzling church funds, physically abusing his wife, and having an affair with the church secretary. After his firing, he left the ministry altogether, divorced his wife, and the last I heard was driving a taxi.

When I first heard about Pastor Dave's secret sins, I wondered: How exactly did the "spiritual breakthrough" he spoke confidently about that Sunday figure into his behavior? Wasn't true conversion supposed to make a significant difference, empowering him to live a victorious Christian life? But on the Sunday of *my* spiritual breakthrough, I knew nothing of the secrets my former pastor was hiding. All I knew, and all that mattered to me that day, was getting things right with God. And I knew exactly what I needed to do next.

Upon returning to our church in Portland, I steeled myself to have the conversation that was no longer optional. I told my boss, Pastor Jim, I wanted to speak with him after the Sunday service. Sitting in his office waiting for him, I studied the six-by-six-foot wall-to-wall chart behind his desk. Pastor Jim was halfway through a Doctor of Ministry seminary degree with a major in church growth. The wall chart displayed a baffling array of boxes, arrows, and lines that looked like a wiring schematic for a nuclear power plant. This was his master plan for growing our church—which was ironic, considering that our congregation had held steady at around thirty adults for the fifteen years since he had become the senior pastor. The wall chart was a recent development, configured two years earlier as part of his doctoral program. He had tried to explain the chart to me several times, but my only takeaway was that we were going to create what he called "fishing pools." These were seeker-friendly events that would bring in newcomers. Sadly, I never saw any evidence of growth by conversion in the two years I served as youth pastor there.

Pastor Jim's arrival to his office interrupted my silent questions about the perplexing church growth chart on the wall. Maneuvering his bulk through the door, he struggled to squeeze his rotund chassis behind his desk as he greeted me. I often wondered how he could repeatedly preach on the need for self-control—one of the biblical "fruits of the Spirit"—when it was so apparent that he was out of control with his poor diet and total lack of exercise. But I wasn't there to talk about his problems. I was there to talk about my own shortcomings.

Unburdening myself, I confessed to Pastor Jim that I had failed God and misrepresented myself to the church. I told him I was sure that I needed to be baptized, but I had resisted the Lord's will for a long time. I had not been willing to admit to the church the shameful truth that I, one of the pastoral staff, was not baptized. Well, technically, that wasn't true, I explained. I had been baptized twice but had not understood what I was doing either time. I told Jim about hearing Pastor Dave tell the story of what happened in his life after he had submitted to God's will. Based on what I had heard, I anticipated the same spiritual breakthrough once I was baptized again.

With bated breath, I waited for my pastor's response. I could tell he was surprised by what I shared. I wondered if I'd get sacked for withholding the potentially scandalous truth that I hadn't been baptized after getting saved. I felt nervous as Pastor Jim sat behind his desk with steepled hands, saying nothing. After a few moments of contemplation, he congratulated me for coming clean. I felt a massive surge of relief.

Pastor Jim then suggested we could turn a potential negative into a positive. "I've got a great idea," he said. "Why don't we make this a 'teaching moment' for the teens in the youth group? We'll hold a baptism at our upcoming church camp-out this weekend. You can explain the whole story to the church, and then I'll baptize you. Let's get this thing done!" I was relieved that I hadn't been fired. Once again, the Lord was there for me, providing guidance to turn a negative into a positive!

What had I been so worried about? A massive weight had just been lifted from my shoulders. Like all those times before, with both pastors Jerry and David, I walked out of Jim's office on cloud nine. Surely, this time would be my final baptism, and the third time would indeed be a charm.

A few weeks later, in August of 1994, Pastor Jim baptized me in a river at our weekend church camp-out. I was twenty-seven years old. The event was held at the Oxbow Regional Park just outside of Portland, and it really was a camp-out. Some pitched tents. Others brought their RVs, and we had a great time roasting hot dogs and marshmallows in front of a campfire on Saturday night. On Sunday morning, just before the ceremony, Pastor Jim seized the opportunity to give the assembled congregation standing alongside the banks of the river a mini-sermon related to my spiritual journey.

The entire youth group was there, alongside most of the rest of the church, watching and listening intently to Pastor Jim's words. I was glad that, unlike my second baptism, this was not done secretly but before the entire church. My pastor clarified why I felt the need to undergo a third baptism despite my two previous baptisms. He explained that according to the clear teachings of Jesus, this was the right thing for me to do. Speaking of Jesus, he said, "Hadn't the sinless God-man humbly allowed himself to be baptized by John the Baptist in the Jordan River? What better example could there be of true humility and obedience to the will of God!"

Pastor Jim stated that this day was the right time for my baptism now that I had set aside my pride and humbly admitted that I needed to get this done. Now that I was a genuine believer, he said, for the first time, I truly understood all the spiritual realities that baptism involved. Holding up his Bible, he declared, "Water baptism is nothing less than an outward manifestation of an inward spiritual reality." Yes, I was already a Christian, but in obedience to Scripture's clear teachings, with this act of baptism, I was confirming my spiritual status as a true believer. I was boldly proclaiming to the whole world that I was indeed a child of God.

I had the chance to say a few words before being dipped in the bitingly cold Sandy River. Even though we'd held our camp-out in late August, shortly before school started up again, the Sandy River water felt like it was January. I told them that I hoped my example would serve as a blessing to the church. Being a church leader didn't mean we were perfect or didn't make mistakes. I told my youth group, "Don't let your foolish pride stop you from obeying the will of God. He will certainly bless you if you submit to his will in obedience and humility."

Deep down, I still had a shred of doubt. I may have been saying words needed to convince myself as much as the assembled listeners. After all, each time I had been baptized before, somehow, things didn't turn out as I expected. I fervently hoped this third and final baptism would put an end to the problems I was experiencing and set me on a path of unprecedented blessing and spiritual growth.

Pastor Jim pronounced that same Trinitarian formula I'd been baptized with twice before: "I baptize you in the name of the Father, and of the Son, and of the Holy Spirit." Because he was so overweight and I was over six feet tall, I had a fleeting moment of concern as to whether he could lift me out of the water after immersing me. But for such a big man, he was surprisingly nimble, and I was quickly lifted out of the icy water, spluttering and shivering.

I was so relieved! This third baptism would be my last. I knew I was already a committed believer, but now I had put the seal on it and never needed to look back. I confidently expected the promised spiritual breakthrough that would soon be mine since I had set aside my stubborn pride and sinfulness and submitted humbly to the will of God.

Now, nothing would stop me from going from strength to strength as a dedicated and mature believer.

---

1   Luke 23:43, NASB.

Chapter Thirty Eight

Not So Shiny Not So Happy

I wish I could say that following my third baptism in that brutally cold Oregon river, I experienced a fantastic spiritual breakthrough like the one Pastor Dave had so confidently described. But I didn't.

Positively, the guilt and shame about *not* being baptized—which I had carried around since my conversion five years earlier—did go away. A huge weight was lifted off my shoulders when I stopped resisting the Bible's clear teaching about baptism, humbled myself, and re-entered the baptismal waters after my true conversion experience. Now, I didn't feel that I was actively disobeying God. Now, I felt markedly better about myself and my relationship with God. Now, I felt no shame teaching the youth group or preaching the occasional sermon. The impostor syndrome was over for me. But as much as I tried to think of this positive outcome as a spiritual breakthrough, it turned out to be so much less than what Pastor Dave had described.

In the months following my third baptism life went on pretty much as it had before. I still struggled with temptations, as did every other Christian I knew. I battled my demons as before. I had mistakenly thought that following my third baptism, my desire for porn would vanish, but it didn't. After my conversion I'd thrown away all my magazines, but the enticing allure of pornography was still there. R-rated movies with nude scenes, glancing through magazines featuring scantily clad women as I waited in line at the grocery store, and other unexpected triggers represented the temptation to backslide into sexual sin. To gain victory over these urges, I participated in accountability groups with other believers who struggled with porn. While it helped me gain some measure of self-control, the temptation was always lurking nearby in my brain. Getting up early before work for a quiet time of disciplined Bible study and prayer didn't get easier, and this lack of spiritual discipline was another source of shame and guilt. Significant spiritual growth was a carrot on a stick, constantly positioned just beyond my reach.

As the years unfolded, despite doing everything I thought the Lord wanted me to do in terms of academics, ministry training, and actual vocational ministry, it still seemed that God was not interested in helping me live a victorious Christian life. But I did have a sense that God was leading me. Just like years before, listening to Christian preachers on the radio while driving my delivery truck, I firmly believed that God had a plan for my life. Now as an obedient Christian walking in faith and trusting in the Lord, I was certain I was on the right path.

It was God who had led me to my position as youth pastor at Troutdale Community Church. Lisa and I developed close relationships with the young people we led as we mentored them, had fun with them, and walked with them through the challenges of adolescence. Halfway through Bible college in 1995, after serving the church for just under two years, Lisa and I made the difficult decision of saying goodbye to the youth group when I resigned my youth pastor position. God had led me to serve there, but I was burned out.

That same year, joining many of my Bible college buddies as well as several Multnomah professors, after leaving Troutdale Community Church, we began attending Northridge Community

Church. It was an up-and-coming church in the Portland suburb of Milwaukie. Thinking I would just lie low and recover from burnout, I enjoyed serving as a drummer on the worship team, preaching an occasional sermon, and teaching a few adult education classes while continuing my own education. After graduating from Multnomah Bible College in 1997, in September of that year I started a one-year Master of Arts Degree in theology at nearby Western Seminary.

Over the years, the people at Northridge Community Church noticed my ability to communicate and my leadership skills. In 2001 I became an elder in the church, serving with five other men. That same year, I began a Master of Theology Degree, also at Western Seminary.

Eight years after we first began attending Northridge, I became the Head Elder, and two years later, I was called as the senior pastor of the church.

I was serious about academics, and my ultimate objective was to become a professor in a Bible college or seminary—a goal that required a Ph.D. Sometimes it seemed like an impossible dream but following the completion of my Master of Theology in 2003, a doctoral studies program was my next step in the academic world.

In the years following my third baptism, that elusive spiritual breakthrough just never seemed to materialize. More and more, it appeared that any power to live a victorious Christian life came down to my efforts to make it happen. Despite all my academic work and all my efforts in ministry, I did not become one of the bright, shiny people who embodied the obedience, blessings, and victory of a supernaturally changed life. And I had trouble finding any believers in my day-to-day world who exemplified the kind of life I had thought to be readily attainable in one's walk with Jesus.

Pastor Dave

On the Sunday I visited his church back in 1994, as a first-year Bible college student, Pastor Dave spoke confidently about how he had experienced a significant spiritual breakthrough following his second baptism. But within a year of this event, the shocking news broke that he was leading a secret double life. As he stood in front of the congregation each week, dispensing seemingly wise counsel and godly advice, he was embezzling church funds, abusing his wife—physically and emotionally—and having an affair with his secretary. Where was the spiritual breakthrough for him? Wasn't he, as a pastor, supposed to be even more spiritual, wise, and godly than the laypeople in his congregation? Why couldn't he gain victory over sin and live a victorious life?

But I had to ask myself the same question. Why couldn't I gain that victory? As a layperson, I spent years in accountability groups, confessing my repeated sins and failures to other believers without gaining ultimate victory over my numerous transgressions. When I became an elder and pastor, I participated in pastoral accountability groups. Several of us church leaders met weekly for breakfast at a local diner. We'd confess our sins and failings to each other, as the Bible commands. Surprisingly, these men of God struggled with the same issues and problems that I did but could only disclose them to other pastors for fear of being fired. It seemed that they, too, "wore the mask" in front of their congregations, who had no idea about the secret sins and struggles of their ministers. Church wasn't a safe place for most of them to be real and vulnerable—they simply could not afford to be transparent.

I knew I was supposed to be experiencing sanctification— the lifelong process of becoming more and more like Jesus. Sanctification is a promise of God's word for true believers. But after years of dedicated effort and service—two and a half years as a youth pastor and twelve more as an elder and senior pastor—I couldn't see much evidence that I resembled the Lord at all. Wasn't God supposed to be invested in helping me improve my life?

Others I knew struggled too.

Valerie

For years following the birth of her daughter, my sister Valerie battled depression, guilt, and anxiety. She shared with me that when she moved in with her best friend's parents, not long after she gave up her baby for adoption, she would crawl under a bush in their backyard and sob inconsolably for hours until the tears no longer flowed. She would cry out over and over, *"I want my baby back!"* But no one was there to hear her cries to reunite with her daughter, who was now being raised by Christian parents and forever lost to Valerie. Was this just another lesson in faith and trust? Was God even listening? It took years of counseling for Valerie to be able to forgive our parents for their heartless and cruel behavior regarding her pregnancy.

Dad and Mom continued to shun Valerie for years, exactly as the Apostle Paul teaches believers to do in 1 Corinthians 4-5. Eventually, they grudgingly accepted her back into our family when it seemed she had finally gotten her life back on track. But a few years later, they passed judgment on her again when she moved in with her boyfriend, Mike. Valerie and Mike were "living in sin," and in my parents' view, Valerie had not learned her lesson when they had severely disciplined her for getting pregnant. They saw condemning her new living arrangement as a form of spiritual discipline that should lead her to acknowledge and confess her sin, opening the way for a restoration of fellowship. But in her case, their harsh judgment only pushed her away. Over the years, as they watched Valerie become estranged from both faith and family, I wondered if they consoled themselves by holding on to the belief that their harsh rejections had been "the right thing to do." Since it was how Scripture commanded believers to treat the wayward sinner, perhaps they held on to the hope that Valerie would one day repent and come crawling back, duly chastened.

My parents were happy when Valerie and Mike got married, since at least they were no longer actively sinning. They were delighted when Mike and Valerie rededicated their lives to Christ and began serving as youth pastors in the church where I had grown up and had experienced my first two baptisms. But several years later, it all fell apart. Both Valerie and Mike walked away from the church when ugly church politics forced them out as youth pastors. It seemed that my old home church hadn't learned its lessons after treating both pastors Jerry and David so badly years earlier. Ultimately, both Valerie and Mike abandoned their Christian faith. So why didn't sincere belief and spiritual commitment work for them? Where was their spiritual breakthrough?

My Parents

I mentioned earlier how unhappy my mom was and how she inappropriately unloaded her issues on me when I was a kid. This emotional incest did terrible damage to me personally and to my relationship with my dad. At twelve, Dad and I fell out over the lawn mowing incident. The damage had started long before, but that colossal argument ended our previously close relationship. Things were never the same after that, although we were able to patch things up to some extent and at least be civil toward each other. In my early twenties, my dad and I finally came to an uneasy truce, but we never once had any sort of deep and meaningful conversation about why our relationship had broken down, or what we could do to fix it. We could do "small talk" on safe topics, but my father was not the type of man to delve into his emotions too deeply. So, I reconciled myself to the fact that this was the best our relationship would ever be.

My parents' relationship was never great, thanks in large part to the patriarchal teachings of Bill Gothard and James Dobson. Patterning their marriage on the teachings of these two men, my parents should have experienced marital happiness and joy, but my mom was miserable in the Bible-imposed role of a submissive wife. When I was nineteen, their relationship deteriorated to the point that my dad rented an apartment and moved out for a year and a half. They appeared to be headed for a divorce, but after multiple sessions of marriage counseling, my dad agreed to move back home. They stayed together until my dad died in his late seventies after battling Parkinson's Disease for more than twenty years.

On the face of it, God had blessed their marriage, shepherding them over the rough patches and somehow making it all work. As good, faithful Christians, they had avoided a divorce—which the Bible teaches the Lord hates. And in the years just before my father died, my mom stood out as a shining example of a devoted wife, conscientiously caring for my father as his health declined.

Following the teachings of Gothard and Dobson was supposed to result in a family life blessed by God. But "a family life blessed by God" certainly did not describe our family. A few years before my dad passed away, I was working on my Ph.D. in the UK when we learned that my father had sexually abused two of my sisters. Following a police investigation, it was determined that he had child pornography downloaded on his laptop. By then, my parents lived in a retirement community in Palm Springs, California. The District Attorney decided not to prosecute my father due to his advanced age and health issues. The DA's statement made it clear that had my father been in good health, he would have been arrested, tried, and sent to prison.

Chapter Thirty Eight

Valerie and I confronted my father on numerous occasions, encouraging him to confess whatever else he had done in his life since we had no idea if he had abused other children in our family or church. But he stubbornly refused to divulge anything. He claimed that due to his early onset dementia from Parkinson's, he couldn't remember that far back. It was all a distant blur. To Valerie and me, this seemed like a convenient dodge—a way to avoid admitting whatever he had done—but much to my dismay, I couldn't prove it.

Rather than admitting he was a pedophile, he took refuge in the claim that he was a closeted gay man. The first time I spoke with him on the phone, just days after the news came out, my father spun an alternative explanation to the whole thing. He stated that several years earlier, just by pure chance, he had stumbled across a section of gay pornography in a local bookstore. Pausing for too long, he ruefully admitted that he had been strangely attracted to the images of naked men, and this awakened something deep within him. After leaving the bookstore, for the first time in his life, he claimed that he had begun to question whether he was gay. Of course, as a Christian, he knew this was horribly wrong, sinful, and evil in the eyes of God.

He went on to state authoritatively that there was a divine solution at hand. He was going to have his own spiritual breakthrough to conquer this sin! Having already spoken to the pastor at their local church about it, all the arrangements were made. He was going to get re-baptized within a week, get up early every morning to pray, and read his Bible faithfully like a diligent Christian. Magically, God would bless all that spiritual activity and somehow fix his misdirected sexuality. This would enable him to "go straight" and gain victory over his latent homosexuality—which he saw as a sinful lifestyle choice. Wonder of wonders, a second baptism might just help him too!

My response was to tell him that if he *was* indeed gay—which I doubted—that performing all those spiritual activities wouldn't help him to "go straight" and cure his supposedly sinful gay lifestyle. "It's not a one-for-one correlation, Dad," I responded. "This is magical thinking on your part—you can't expect God somehow to 'fix' you by your doing all those things. That's not how spiritual disciplines work, and trust me, I've done it all for years and found little success. If you truly *are* gay, why not just come out as a gay man? Be true to yourself. What's wrong with that?" But he stubbornly stuck to his guns, claiming that it would all work out when God miraculously intervened to solve all his sexual problems.

Reflecting on it now, I firmly believe that the entire storyline was nothing more than misdirection and lies on his part. As I checked with my other sisters, it turned out that he had spun each of them a completely different—and contradictory—set of alternative facts about the scandalous news. As I compared the competing stories, it was clear to me that he was merely telling each of us what he thought we wanted to hear, all in a devious attempt to throw us off the trail of the truth. After further research, I have discovered that this is a common pattern among sexual predators, who are adept at spinning lies and alternative storylines to explain away their actions. In this way, they hope to avoid accountability and prosecution.

The last time my dad and I talked on a Skype call, shortly after the scandalous news broke, I told him that since he claimed to be a Christian and since he knew he wasn't going to live much longer, he needed to set things right before it was too late. "One day soon," I warned him, "according to what you believe as a Christian, you'll be standing before the judgment throne of God. You and I both know you don't have many years left to live. God will ask you why you didn't confess your sins, as the Bible commands, and clear the record while you had the opportunity." Despite all my efforts at persuading him to come clean, he stubbornly took his secrets to the grave. We have no idea what he may have done to children to which he had access for years as he served as an elder, youth pastor, and worship leader in more than one church. Unfortunately, we will never know, and not having that sense of closure has proven incredibly difficult.

At first, my mom wholeheartedly supported forcing my father to confess and come clean. "If he's done anything wrong," she once told me early in the process, "Then let the police deal with it. If he ends up in prison, so be it." She also confessed to me once, as we discussed what to do about my dad, that she deeply regretted not divorcing him when he had moved out all those years before. She told me tearfully, "For more than fifty years, my relationship with your father has been nothing but a loveless sham of a marriage." After all the years of emotional incest, that statement wasn't much of a shock to me.

But as time went on, and it became clear that my father was in danger of being arrested, my mother's tune began to change. I believe she was afraid of losing out on his lucrative Boeing pension if he were indicted and sent to prison, but this is speculation on my part. Doing a complete 180, she began defending him and denying his actions. She pointed the finger of blame at my sisters and me for "framing an innocent man." If he had any compulsive behaviors, she claimed, like watching gay porn on his laptop as she sat mere feet away on the couch, then it was all due to his Parkinson's medication. Although this seemed to fit his explanation of being gay, at the same time, it didn't fit the established fact that he was also a molester of my two sisters. But I knew her words were born of denial and wishful thinking that flew in the face of the evidence stacked against him. Besides, much of what he was credibly accused of occurred decades before he had any symptoms of Parkinson's— and crucially, before he was on any sort of medication that might make him act out compulsively.

As the situation deteriorated, about six months after the story about my father surfaced, I finally had to decide to break off all communication with my mother. Living in the UK at the time made this decision even more difficult. My mother and I used to speak on the phone for hours each month. Even though I was a world away, we had stayed close. But I felt I had no choice in the matter as the situation became increasingly toxic and bitter. As circumstances escalated with my dad and he continued to refuse to confess, she sent me a series of increasingly vitriolic emails laden with false accusations. Speaking of my sisters and me, she charged, "You children have a sin-sickness that is causing you to accuse your dad—an innocent man—of horrible things." But when she stated later in the email, "I now know why I envy parents who never had children," that was my final straw. Even though her allegations were untrue, they were still hurtful and cut me to the core. This was my own mother, after all, whom I had been close to my entire life, now turning into an attacker venting her anger and bitterness on me and my sisters, some of whom were victims of my father.

My response was that, as a father, I could never say such a hurtful thing to my daughters, at that point in their early twenties. No matter what they might do, I will always love them and could never disown them or say that I wish they hadn't been born. In my final email to my mother, I wrote, "Don't say things you can never un-say. You can ask for forgiveness for what you said, but you still said it—and there's no going back from that."

I haven't spoken to my mother in nearly ten years. Her actions split my family down the middle. Some of my siblings sided with her, defended my dad, and accused the rest of us of making it all up out of sheer vindictiveness toward our father. After the dust settled, and the battle lines were drawn, Valerie is the only one of my five sisters with whom I am in regular contact. Fortunately, when she comes to visit me in the UK, we've been able to have many long conversations. On our sightseeing travels, sitting in the car for hours on long drives, we try and help each other process the legacy of our parents' actions and find a sense of closure. Although we always end the conversation with a helpless shrug, since we'll never know the truth about what our father did, at least we can help prop each other up emotionally and process through the difficult emotions.

Guy

My best friend Guy is another example of a Christian who tried diligently to live a victorious and godly life, only to fail repeatedly over the decades. What began as a seemingly harmless swap of porno magazines back when we were in high school turned out to be a destructive addiction that Guy struggled to overcome all his life. While my involvement with accountability groups helped me to achieve a level of victory over my old habit, the same could not be said of Guy. He battled with it far more deeply than I ever did.

Convicted that he was sinning against God by looking at porn magazines, watching X-rated movies, and delving into Internet porn when that became a thing, Guy tried everything he could think of to kick the habit—including, like me, begging and pleading the Lord thousands of times to take this cursed affliction from his life. But that never happened. Despite all his efforts, including Christian counseling and therapy, Guy could not kick the habit. One unhelpful Christian counselor advised him to "Imagine putting all your problems in a bottle and laying them at the feet of the cross, where Jesus died for your sins. That mental exercise will help you overcome your sinful desires for pornography." In his desperation, Guy actually tried doing that—but without any success.

A few years after our aborted plan to escape to Germany—Guy was going to leave civilian life to enlist in the Army, and I was going to join him by switching from the Navy to the Army—Guy and his wife Lisa got a divorce. She was the girlfriend he had gotten pregnant with years earlier, prompting him at eighteen to get a vasectomy because he felt so guilty. The following year, in 1987, they got married. But Guy's insatiable pornography addiction ended up taking a toll on their marriage. They divorced over it in 1988, and he lived as a lonely bachelor for the next few years, convinced that God was punishing him for his many misdeeds by not sending him a good and godly wife.

Everything changed when he met a young woman named Joy. Not long after meeting, they married and moved from Seattle to Miami, her hometown. Guy loved Miami, as it was such a marked change from the dismal Seattle weather. I spent a week with him in the summer of 2000, and we fulfilled one of my lifelong dreams: to make the epic drive from Miami to Key West. But even in his happy, newly married state, he confessed to me that this relationship, too, was breaking down due to his uncontrollable addiction to porn. Things had deteriorated to the point where he was sleeping in a separate bedroom, alone with a computer to satiate his unceasing porn addiction, which had completely taken over his life. He told me he had prayed thousands of times about it, begging and pleading God to take away the powerful addiction that was destroying a second marriage. But as before, no divine help was forthcoming, just as it had never materialized for me as I struggled with the same addiction. I left Miami at the end of the week vowing to pray for him, which I did every time I remembered, but my added fervent prayers did nothing to help.

Two years after my visit, in July of 2003, I received a frantic phone call from Joy. Could I drop everything and fly to Miami immediately? The day before, Guy had a terrible accident at work. He had fallen from a ledge while on a construction job and was in the hospital undergoing major surgery. I was able to make arrangements quickly, and within a week, I was on my way to visit my best friend, unsure if he would be alive when I got there. When

Chapter Thirty Eight

I arrived at the hospital in Miami, Guy had undergone several surgeries and by this point could sit up in bed and talk. He had broken his neck and was paralyzed from the waist down, but fully expected to live a long life, albeit in a wheelchair. The fact that he was alive certainly seemed like an answer to prayer!

But what Guy told me a few days after I arrived shook me to the core. I asked him how the accident happened, and he told me he had been working as a laborer on a construction site in downtown Miami. He was pulling some wires through a conduit, and to reach them, he clambered up onto a ledge about ten feet above the concrete floor. The cables he was pulling got stuck, and Guy—a big, strong man—put all his effort into pulling them through the narrow conduit. Suddenly, the wire snapped, and Guy felt himself hurtling backward off the ledge, falling straight toward the concrete floor.

"But here's the weird thing," he told me. "The second the wire broke my instinct was to twist in the air to try and land on my feet. I'm agile enough to have saved myself. At the very least, I could have avoided landing on my head like I did. I might have broken an arm or a leg, but certainly not my neck." He leaned in close and lowered his voice. "But that's not what I did." "What do you mean?" I asked incredulously. As one who has worked on many a construction site as a carpenter, I knew that I would do everything in my power to avoid serious injury.

Guy replied, "Although my initial instinct was to save myself, I heard a voice in my head as I fell backward. You might not believe this, but it's true, I swear. *God told me to let go and not fight it.* So, I let myself fall because I knew at that point that God had a plan. I landed on the floor, on the back of my head, and *heard* my neck snap." He leaned back on the bed, and I helped him adjust his pillow. He shook his head and said, "But you know what? It was okay. I have tremendous peace about it all." I sat there, open-mouthed, listening to him describe this unbelievable experience.

"Yeah, but hang on a second," I responded. My mind was racing with competing thoughts, and I couldn't believe what I was hearing. "You broke your neck, and you're paralyzed from the waist down. You're going to spend the rest of your life in a wheelchair. How exactly was God involved in *that?*"

"Ah," he replied confidently, wagging his finger at me. "Here's the thing. I've been in the hospital for two weeks now, and I've had multiple surgeries. This hasn't exactly been a walk in the park. It's been incredibly difficult and painful. But get this. Since the accident," he intoned, looking at me straight in the eye, "*I haven't had the slightest desire for pornography.* Not once, in more than two weeks." Stunned, I leaned back in my chair and thought about what he had said.

"Let me get this straight," I responded after a moment. "You're telling me that somehow, God *caused* this terrible accident, just so you'd be freed from your porn addiction?" Guy reflected for a minute. "Well, all I know is this. I've had a lot of time to think and pray since the accident. I can't explain all the theology behind it, or point to a specific Scripture verse, but I feel that this is the truth. I don't know if God caused it or allowed it when he could have saved me, but it doesn't matter. The bottom line is this: *I've finally been liberated from my lifelong addiction.* So, if that's what it took—God breaking me—then I'm okay with it. Praise the Lord, I've been set free!"

What could I say or do other than rejoice with my dear friend? As a Christian, I'd heard some bizarre explanations for why God allowed tremendous suffering into our lives, but this was right up at the top.

I flew home to Portland a few days later and stayed in touch with Guy and Joy over the next few weeks. It seemed as if he was on the road to recovery, undergoing physiotherapy at the hospital and transitioning into living an active life in a wheelchair. But when Lisa and I went on vacation, we returned to discover multiple frantic messages from Joy on our answering machine. She didn't say what it was about, but she kept repeating the request for me to call her back as soon as I could.

When I got through to Joy, she tearfully informed me that Guy had passed away two days before, on August 8th, 2003. An aneurysm in his leg had turned into a blood clot in his brain, and just like that, he was gone. I stood there with the phone in my hand in stunned shock. I was in total denial. Guy couldn't be dead! I'd been with him just a few weeks before. My best friend from high school, the brother I'd never had, was suddenly gone.

Was this God's perfect plan? To save Guy from his pornography addiction by causing the accident, only to "take him home" a few weeks later? I couldn't figure any of it out. Numbed by this unexpected loss, I prepared for the upcoming funeral to be held in Seattle, where Guy was born. A few days later, we made the three-hour trek from Portland to Seattle for the service. I was not looking forward to it in the slightest. Burying your best friend, especially when he was so young—just his mid-thirties—was one of the worst things I ever had to face.

A few years earlier, I'd been to the funerals of my cousins, Andy and Dan, which were made more difficult by the knowledge that both of them had died without coming to the Lord. As I believed at the time, they were consigned forever to the flames of hell—and it was all my fault for not doing a better job of warning them of their impending fate when I had the chance. Their blood was on my hands. But with Guy, it was different because I firmly believed he was in heaven, jumping and walking along the streets of gold. All his pain, suffering, and sorrow had vanished, but that didn't change the fact that my best friend was gone, just like that.

For the life of me, I couldn't work through what happened to Guy and how he responded. Despite the extremely difficult experience, why was Guy so weirdly *happy* that God had allowed him to break his neck to break him spiritually? Was it so he could finally overcome his porn addiction? And then, just when it looked like he would recover and live a full, happy life—mercifully free from his accursed porn addiction—the Lord took him and deprived us of Guy's presence. I needed answers. Was this the type of God that I could serve and obey wholeheartedly? Did the Lord take sin in our lives *that* seriously, to the point that he would literally crush us so we could overcome it? What did this say about how God allows suffering in our lives? How much is God willing to hurt us, to take away from us, to teach a lesson about faith and trust in him?

The funeral was incredibly difficult for me. I had written out a statement that I intended to read at the service, looking back on all the good times Guy and I had shared and the impact he had on my life. But on the day of the funeral, I was a basket case. I couldn't bear the thought of standing in front of mourners and breaking down repeatedly. I knew I would never be able to get through what I had written, so I asked the pastor officiating the funeral if he would share what I had written. When he read my recollections of Guy, all I could do was sit in the pew—head in hands—and sob inconsolably, the warm tears running through my fingers. My daughter Bree, who was nine years old at the time, later told me that it was the first time she had ever seen her dad cry.

After Guy's interment, I stood outside the funeral home to get a breath of fresh air as I attempted to get my emotions under control. It was then that I noticed Don—the stepdad who could feel the wind from angels' wings around his ears when he prayed—making his way toward me. I hadn't seen him in years, and I guess I hoped he had changed for the better. Perhaps he had some wisdom to impart to me about what had happened to Guy.

I shook his hand and started asking him how we might make some sense of Guy's tragic accident and death. Cutting me off in mid-sentence, Don interrupted with a jovial tone to his voice. "Hey Clint, long time no see! I hear you're a pastor now. Good for you! Glad to hear that you finally got your life straightened out. I remember when you and Guy were kids. Man, you two sure were a handful!"

"Thanks," I lamely said. "Yeah, I suppose we did go through a rough patch or two back then. Hey, listen, Don, I have a question about what happened to Guy. Do you think that maybe..." I couldn't get the words out before Don interrupted me again. "Nah, don't worry about Guy," he said, waving his hand dismissively. "I sure don't! I'm convinced he's in heaven now, singing and dancing with Jesus and the saints. He's resting in the arms of the Lord right now. Whatever troubles he had on this Earth—and believe me, he had plenty—are all a distant memory now." Sagely nodding his head, he said authoritatively, "Someday, we'll meet up with him again in heaven. That's all you need to concentrate on now. All the pain, suffering, and strife we undergo on this mortal coil are but a momentary burden in light of eternity, so the Apostle Paul says."

Don leaned in close and put a hand on my shoulder. "Of course, as a pastor, I'm sure that you already know this, but it's worth repeating. *God's ways are higher than our ways.* The Lord has a plan, and I admit—it's often mysterious and confusing. To be perfectly honest with you, most of the time we usually don't know what his plan is. But the Bible says that worry is a sin, and that's what faith in the Lord is all about, so I don't worry about the difficult circumstances God sends our way. For our part, we must 'trust and obey, for there's no other way to be happy in Jesus,' as the old hymn[1] says. One day, in eternity, we'll understand what God's plan was for Guy. All I know for a fact is this: The Lord accomplished everything he intended during Guy's lifetime."

I stood there open-mouthed, listening to Don's pious platitudes, stunned by their shallowness as well as the complete absence of grief and emotional empathy. No solutions to my vexing theological questions here, just Christianese answers like "trust and obey, for there's no other way." Here was a clear-cut case of Don using the "loaded language" of thought-terminating clichés. Apparently, Don didn't have to think too deeply about disturbing issues like Guy's accident and death, and how exactly the Lord was involved in it all, when he could instead take refuge in meaningless theological jargon.

I was about to ask Don to clarify some of his answers when he continued speaking. "I'm glad we got all that out of the way. So, this is what I really wanted to talk to you about," he said as he handed me his business card. "As you know, I've been a prison chaplain for years. I've developed a surefire way to evangelize nonbelievers. And here's the amazing thing: *It works every time.*" He stepped back and waved his hands excitedly as he went on. "I've led hundreds, if not thousands, of inmates to Christ at the prison where I work. These men might be the dregs of society, but God hasn't forgotten about them! Even these hardened career criminals need to hear the good news."

Don leaned in close once again and lowered his voice. "As a pastor, I bet you'd love to know my secret formula." Winking conspiratorially, he said, "Know this. *It works.* It really does. Think of the blessings you would receive at your church if you used my system. You will experience unprecedented conversion growth! You can't go wrong—and of course, new converts don't hurt the bottom line when it comes to tithing." Stepping back, he concluded, "Call me when you get a chance, and I'll be happy to come to Oregon and train your congregation free of charge. I'm not in it for the money. It's all about extending God's kingdom and saving souls. Praise the Lord, brother!" He glad-handed me and gave me a fatherly pat on the shoulder as he walked away.

Left holding his business card as he disappeared back into the funeral home, I stood there in stunned disbelief. Following his unexpected and traumatic accident, my best friend had just died tragically, and I needed to talk. I was confused about what Guy's death said about how God works. But rather than providing consolation or talking openly and honestly about how to view God in a moment like this, all Don could do was dish out Christian platitudes. And what he really wanted to do was give me the hard sell for his sure-fire evangelistic method! In disgust, I tossed his business card into the nearest trash can, herded my family into the car, and left the funeral home in my rearview mirror.

Leaving Faith

It was precisely those types of moments, when I experienced cognitive dissonance about my faith, that ultimately led me to abandon it. The God I had so faithfully served for almost my entire adult life seemed capable of doing awful things to his followers, sending terrible suffering and pain in their lives, apparently to teach them a lesson of faith and trust. Yet Sunday after Sunday, I and my fellow Christians sang praises to this same God, pledging to love and obey this apparently cruel and abusive deity. I spent decades trying to live a victorious Christian life, even to the point of getting baptized three times to try and "get it right," but never achieving that ultimate, promised supernatural spiritual breakthrough. Ten years ago, in my mid-forties, after decades of struggling and failing, I finally walked away from my Christian faith.

Someone described our times of doubt and uncertainty as "putting items on a mental shelf." Imagine a shelf that sits at the back of your mind. A serious problem occurs each time you doubt, question, or have uncertainties about your cherished beliefs. You might come across a situation like I did around Guy's accident and sudden death. I call these experiences "tension points" in our life of faith. As an evangelical Christian, I wrestled with a series of festering questions and doubts over the years. Making it more difficult, as a pastor, I had to provide solace for my congregants who struggled with the same doubts and questions I did. I couldn't very well tell them to abandon their faith, so I was put in the impossible situation of providing biblical answers to questions that I was also wrestling with.

There were multiple theological conundrums that came along during my years of faith that I could not resolve. There was always someone to "talk me off the ledge"—a fellow pastor, some wise mentor or guide who would quell the cognitive dissonance I felt at a particular time. Platitudes and Christianese explanations like Don's might ease the tension for the moment, but clear and convincing answers were absent. Each time I faced a new unanswerable question, I would metaphorically place that troublesome thought on my mental shelf and carry on as a faithful believer. That shelf can hold a lot of weight, but at some point, the years of questions, doubts, and concerns becomes too much, and the mental shelf collapses. It is at that breaking point that many believers make the difficult decision to abandon their Christian faith, or whatever religious belief system they have devoted their lives to serving.

That is exactly what happened to me. When we moved to the United Kingdom in 2005 so I could pursue my doctoral studies, after burning out as the senior pastor of Northridge Community Church in Portland, I was already on the path of questioning many of the beliefs I had inherited from childhood. It wasn't like there was *one* specific instance where I admitted to myself, "That's it. I'm no longer a Christian because of this experience, doubt, or question." *It was more like the death of a thousand cuts, a lifetime's worth of items placed on the mental shelf that finally collapsed.* But even after the shelf lay in a heap on the floor, I tried to repair it, nailing it back to the wall of my mind.

After completing my doctoral studies, even though I was already deconstructing my faith, I spent eight years teaching at a Bible college headquartered in Birmingham, England, with satellite locations around the country. On Wednesdays and Thursdays, I taught in the city of Leeds, a two-and-a-half-hour train ride— one way—from my home in Chester. On Fridays, I traveled to the Liverpool center, about a one-hour train ride. Later, I made the same trips from our new location in North Wales. I taught classes on theology, preaching, church growth, and Old and New Testament. My students came from all walks of life and multiple countries—all my Leeds students were from Africa. I struggled to teach my students the "truths" from the very Bible that I was struggling to believe in. Teaching through the book of Job one semester was challenging because by then, I had begun to reject the God of the Bible. As I saw it, he was a cruel and capricious deity that I could no longer, in good conscience, serve, worship, or seek to obey as I'd done almost all my life.

Toward the end of my time at the Bible college, one student in Leeds confronted me after class and asked me point-blank: "Are you even a Christian?" I had the audacity during that session to question whether the Bible was inspired or inerrant, which led many of the students to become angry and defensive. "If I wasn't a Christian," I responded to her, "Then I wouldn't be teaching at a Bible College, would I?" But reflecting later on her prescient question, I had to wonder if, in fact, she had hit the nail on the head. Perhaps she was right. I wasn't a Christian any longer. I just didn't want to admit it.

---

1   John H. Sammis, "Trust and Obey," 1887.

Epilogue

Why We Left

I ronically, it was my time in ministry that led to the abandonment of my lifelong Christian faith. My good friend, David Hayward, also known as "The Naked Pastor," says there are two "parallel tracks" that most Christians discover during their journey out of faith. One track is their relationship to the church, while the other includes their relationship to God, their theological beliefs, and their view of the Bible. Most evangelicals who deconstruct their faith start on one of these two tracks. Hayward states that *whichever track you begin your deconstruction journey on will ultimately intersect and cause problems with the other track.*

On the one hand, various issues with ministers, lay leaders, or church members may lead a believer to question how God could sanction an organization in which so many toxic, harmful, and abusive actions can occur. On the other hand, doubts, questions, and concerns about God, the Bible, and one's theological worldview may be the starting point, resulting in conflicts with the church and its leadership.

I had one foot on each track while on staff at Northridge Community Church in Portland. As an elder and then later as senior pastor—although I didn't realize it at the time—I was starting to take small, quiet steps away from my faith. I began reading progressive Christian writers like Rob Bell, Donald Miller, Brian McLaren, and Father Richard Rohr. These authors radically challenged my inherited fundamentalist convictions in a way that eventually led to my jettisoning a number of beliefs which I had cherished all my life. Entering this progressive Christian phase marked the beginning of my deconstruction journey. I was no longer a fundamentalist or an evangelical Christian. I was in the process of becoming, as McLaren puts it, "a new kind of Christian."

As The Naked Pastor predicts, these new progressive theological and biblical perspectives I began sharing with other elders and with the church in my sermons led to conflict. I was labeled a "liberal" and accused of heresy by the more conservative members. One elder pulled me aside after a weekly Elder Board meeting and warned me to be careful about spreading my new perspectives. If I continued to push liberal theology, he gravely informed me, I might be in danger of losing my job at the church. I found this confusing. Why wasn't everyone in our church as excited about these incredible new theological horizons as I was? Rather than embracing new points of view, most were threatened by what I was discovering. Their response was to double down, dig in, and staunchly defend their long-held, traditional beliefs. I wasn't worried about being left behind in the Rapture like that liberal preacher from *A Thief in the Night*—I was concerned that I might lose my job!

At the same time, I was also on the other deconstruction track, questioning my relationship with the church and the God behind it. Serving as youth minister at Troutdale Community Church was my first taste of paid ministry. I was surprised that after only two years, I was beyond exhausted—burned out—simply due to hard work serving God and the church faithfully. After leaving Troutdale, I served twelve years at Northridge. First, I transitioned from drummer on the worship team to elder. Then I worked part-time as a staff member while completing my Master's in Theology Degree. Ultimately, I became the Head Elder, then later, the senior pastor. When I first started as a part-time elder, it was not unusual for me to work more than seventy hours a week when I was only paid for thirty. Consequently, I found myself on the edge of burnout once again. I knew the symptoms now. But I had pledged to serve God and his church faithfully, so I kept putting in the long hours. I sacrificed quality marriage and family time for God and his church. I wanted to make it a success, so I kept my nose to the grindstone.

A few years later as senior pastor—finally being paid a full-time wage—I tried everything I could think of to help the church be internally healthy and grow numerically. This included launching an intensive churchwide prayer movement, opening an after-school youth program, evangelistic outreach into the community, and attempting to get the congregants involved in various ministries I started. Although sharing some of my newfound, progressive theological insights created some tension, much bigger issues began to surface. In the fall of 2004, we took the radical decision to suspend all normal Sunday services for six months. Each Sunday we spent time as a church praying together and discussing the issues and problems plaguing the church. At first, those of us in leadership hoped and prayed that this would be a season of help and healing for the congregation. If we could deal with the problems plaguing the church, I reasoned, we could finally move forward in health and unity, and the church would start to grow.

But as time went on, and the experiment continued, it became clear that the congregation had deep-seated trauma that went back to a period long before I became a leader there. Although I tried valiantly to deal with the issues head-on, this proved to be extremely difficult, if not impossible. Over the years the church had evolved into an extremely dysfunctional and unhealthy place. One startling revelation that came out of our Sunday discussion groups was the fact that a number of emotionally abusive members had been hurting other congregants. They had battered them mercilessly with their "Truth" from the Bible—a classic case of Lifton's "doctrine over person." Unfortunately, none of those instances had ever been confronted or dealt with by former church leaders.

After several months of suspending services, things finally came to a head. Factions were forming, and resistance to our church re-launch increased on the side of those who had opposed the whole thing from the start. One longtime member angrily confronted me one Sunday. "It's like this," he said belligerently, shoving his finger in my face. "I'll make it as clear as I can for you. We just want our church to go back to the way it was before we started all this nonsense!" "What? You want this church to go back to being dysfunctional and unhealthy, and not growing, like it was before?" I responded incredulously. "I don't know what you are talking about," he retorted. "It used to be great. I'll take it up with the Elder Board, since clearly, you're not listening to anything I say!" He then stormed off in a huff. Although some lives were indeed changed due to our radical experiment, it was clear that some were not ready to abandon their toxic ways.

In April 2005, to avoid an ugly church split, the elders and I agreed to make the difficult decision to close the church. Predictably, the old guard—their self-designation—blamed me as the "evil puppet master behind the whole thing." They accused me of "pulling the strings for my own gain." These longtime attendees did not want to see their beloved church shut its doors, but they refused to deal with their own significant contributions to our problems. This was a challenging and trying time for me and my family. The very people I had selflessly served for twelve years lied about me, spread vicious rumors, and believed the worst things they heard about me—despite my never giving them any cause to doubt my integrity.

As incredibly painful as that transition was, there were two silver linings. First, less than a month after Northridge closed, we planted a new church in the same building. We named it "Imagine" because the remaining members from Northridge were excited to imagine what God could do in their lives. I was happy to hand over the leadership of Imagine to Mike, my associate pastor, who had been through the wars with me for the last few years. The second silver lining was that the church's closing allowed me to leave pastoral ministry. It was time to pursue my earlier dream of earning a Ph.D. and becoming a Bible college or seminary professor. I firmly believed that God was calling me and my family to make a major life change. Lisa and I had spent many hours in prayer and studying the Bible to discern God's will for our lives.

Our journey began when we left Portland in September 2005 for Boston, Massachusetts. I served for three months as a preaching intern for Dr Haddon Robinson at Gordon-Conwell Theological Seminary. In December 2005, our family flew from Boston to the United Kingdom so I could pursue my doctoral studies. I enrolled at the University of Chester in the Northwest of England in January 2006. I focused on researching and writing on the intersection of Old Testament biblical studies and homiletics (preaching). I completed my doctorate in 2010.

When we arrived in England, I was completely burned out from my time in ministry. The last two years at Northridge had been bruising, and I needed time to recover—spiritually, physically, and emotionally. Due to how poorly I'd been treated as a pastor, I wanted to have nothing to do with church or other Christians. It was my intent to never attend church again. However, as a progressive Christian, I still considered myself a believer. Despite my desire to avoid church, we met some great people who invited us to attend Northgate Church, a charismatic congregation in the city of Chester. We liked what we experienced there and faithfully attended for four years. Leaders of this church became aware of my previous work as a pastor and began to call on me for various ministry roles. My wife and I led a home study "life group" for several years, and I preached in the church a few times. After completing my Ph.D., I taught at Springdale College–a Bible college that later changed its name to "ForMission"–for eight years. I still saw myself as a dedicated servant of God, doing my best to teach, mentor, and help others prepare for ministry.

During this period, both tracks described by David Hayward finally intersected, and I decided to abandon the lifetime of beliefs I had clung to so devotedly. I'm writing another book explaining in more detail the period beginning with my time at Northridge and how I went from being a full-time minister and academic to an ex-evangelical. That is a long story and deserves its own book!

Since making this decision, I've heard Christians tell me and other ex-Christians different reasons as to why we left the faith.

You Left Because You Got Your Feelings Hurt

In 2023, I listened to a John MacArthur sermon on *YouTube* entitled "Deconstructing Christians, Part 1."[1] My friend David Johnson and I did an episode breaking down his points in the sermon on the *Skeptics and Seekers Sunday Sermon* podcast. My history with MacArthur all those years ago, when I worked at the bottling plant and switched off his radio show, made this episode more poignant. I was genuinely interested to hear what MacArthur had to say about people like me who had left their Christian faith behind.

Listening to his sermon yielded no surprises. MacArthur advances the same tired old arguments most of us who have left the Christian faith have heard far too many times. Perhaps, he muses, we left the church because we experienced abuse, homophobia, or racism. It could be that one of our fellow Christians hurt us. Or maybe, he surmises, we "had one bad experience with a pastor or leader." Unfortunately, rather than admitting that these types of experiences are common in churches, MacArthur downplays such issues. In the process, he accepts them as normal events that shouldn't bother a "healthy Christian."

For the record, I am in total disagreement with MacArthur's argument. Being a victim of a church, experiencing racism or homophobia, or being abused by someone in leadership are all good reasons to walk out the door. Questioning the Bible, the church's doctrines, or the pastor's teachings can brand you as a divisive troublemaker. Whatever the issue may be, raising troublesome questions on matters like these makes it difficult to stay without sacrificing your personal integrity. My decision all those years ago, working at the water bottling plant, to question MacArthur's theology on the "gift of tongues" would have gotten me into serious trouble had I been a member of his church.

Women suffer the most in such systems. Girls who are sexually abused by a clergy member are typically blamed for leading him astray, and the abuse often continues. All too often, she isn't believed when she tries to speak out, and the abuser is either protected or quickly restored to ministry after "repenting." Married women are accused of being a "Jezebel" if they don't joyfully submit to their husbands "as unto the Lord." They can get into trouble with church leadership if they refuse to knuckle under and accept the patriarchal structures so commonly found in churches. One may end up in trouble for any number of alleged infractions of the rules laid down by those in charge. Oftentimes this falls under the label of "church discipline," which gives those in charge biblical sanction to remove the offending person. Simply removing your mask and admitting that you have one or more serious problems or are struggling with some sin could also get you booted out. Given these realities, it appears that churches can be far from safe places.

Ironically, MacArthur himself has exhibited abusive, harmful, and highly controlling behavior toward his congregants. These instances have been extensively researched and reported on by *The Roys Report* site, among others.[2] MacArthur fails to acknowledge that he's part of the problem and instead shifts the blame to the victims. It's abusive and controlling pastors like him that explain why so many of us are fleeing the church in droves, never to return. Countless ex-evangelicals exactly like me continue to suffer from Religious Trauma Syndrome, which is part of the damaging legacy of our former religious lives.

Behind the issue of church and spiritual abuse lies a larger question: What about the God these evangelicals claim to serve? If he exists, why isn't he doing more to protect his flock and drive out the bad shepherds who are controlling, manipulating, exploiting, and abusing their followers? I wonder what their God would make of the televangelists flying around the world in their private jets, living a flamboyant lifestyle in their mega-mansions, all paid for by gullible people they've suckered into giving their hard-earned dollars.

You Left Because You Wanted to Sin

In his sermon, MacArthur violated his own Calvinist theology by also stating that ex-Christians leave the faith because "They just wanted to go out and sin." He labels ex-believers as "defectors" and "apostates" who consciously rejected the truth about God, turned their backs on him willingly, and embraced a lie. But in his theological system, one of "the elect" cannot lose their salvation—it's a case of "once saved, always saved."

His argument reminds me of the famous line spoken by Cypher in *The Matrix*.[3] As he contemplates turning his back on "the real world" and selling out Neo, Cypher makes the following observation to Agent Smith as he sits in a restaurant about to enjoy a delicious steak. He says, "You know, I know this steak doesn't exist. I know that when I put it in my mouth, the Matrix is telling my brain that it is juicy and delicious. After nine years, you know what I realize?" After taking a large bite and sighing contentedly, Cypher proclaims happily, "Ignorance is bliss."

According to MacArthur's theology, then, former evangelicals are like the traitorous Cypher. Knowing that reality is found in the truth about God, Jesus, and the Bible, they turned their backs on this "reality" and chose a make-believe world. In his view, their new and chosen godless existence is nothing more than an illusion, the blissful oblivion of a life of sinning with assumed impunity. In MacArthur's view, ex-believers would rather live a life of ignorance to enjoy sin's temporal, fleeting pleasures.

But quite simply, that is not the case. As my story makes abundantly clear, the exact opposite is true. I did not turn my back on what I knew to be the truth to embrace a blissful ignorance. Cypher knew that the matrix was an illusion, but instead of holding fast to the truth, he denied reality—and embraced the lie. But that was not how it was for me. In my case, I tried the system of faith and found it wanting. I attempted everything I could to make it work for most of my life—including letting go and letting God—but ultimately, I had to admit it was a lost cause. *I discovered reality when I left the pretend world of faith.*

You Left Because You Were a Victim of Bad Theology

Hearing my story, some Christians assert that my problem all along was being a victim of inaccurate biblical teaching and bad pastoral guidance. It certainly wasn't God's fault. As a ten-year old, sitting in Pastor Jerry's office seeking salvation, what if I had heard the "right" answers flowing out of the "right" theology? Clearly, all my problems would have been avoided.

I will admit that, to some extent, I was the victim of bad theology and poor pastoral guidance. At nine, the first time I watched *A Thief in the Night*, it deeply traumatized me. After the third viewing, the fear it engendered drove me to seek salvation to avoid missing out on the Rapture. "Aha!" Other Christians would triumphantly say. "Don't you see? That type of traumatic experience shouldn't be why a person wants to become a Christian. Sadly, you were misled by your church's aberrant theology." But that wasn't Pastor Jerry's response when I sought him out for salvation. For his part, he was more than happy that I'd been "scared straight" by the movie. It was the same response I received from my mom when I'd come home from VBS at five years old, fearful of going to hell.

If that's what it took to "wake me up"—open my spiritually blinded eyes and get me saved—then it was all to the good by his reckoning. Pastor Jerry's solution to my existential fear of missing the Rapture and going to hell was straightforward: All I had to do was get baptized. That one simple act would solve all my problems, save me, and remove my rapture anxiety. But it didn't work. As I see it now, all my baptisms were nothing more than magical thinking.

If I was in fact the victim of bad theology and poor pastoral guidance, the pressing question is: *Where was God in all of it?* Why didn't God play a more active role in helping me out as he watched me receive bad advice from my uninformed pastor? Since salvation is so incredibly important, how could God sit back and simply let it all happen without intervening?

And where was God all those years when I struggled so badly and failed to live the victorious Christian life? How come Jesus and the Holy Spirit didn't come to my aid all those thousands of times I begged God for help? What about all those sinner's prayers I prayed? Where was that elusive spiritual breakthrough I so desperately desired?

If Christianity is the one true religion, then why do so many people just like me yearn for an assurance of their faith that they cannot find? I always struggled with the fear that I might lose my faith, becoming one of those blackened coals Pastor Jerry pulled out of the fire at summer camp.

Others can blame poor pastoral leadership, bad theology, misinterpreted Bible verses, and so on, but ultimately, these are all excuses for a silent, hidden God.

I conclude that God should have been more invested in helping me *succeed*. That is, of course, if Christianity is true and if God does, in fact, exist. In reality, the *entire enterprise* was nothing more than magical thinking on my part, combined with decades of indoctrination and social conditioning.

You Left Because You Never Were a True Christian

One of MacArthur's claims—one that is hard to reconcile with his other arguments—is that those who leave were never real Christians.

This is highly confusing. As I mentioned earlier, MacArthur's hardline Calvinist theology takes the position that if someone is truly one of "the elect," they can't lose their salvation. But MacArthur didn't address this glaring inconsistency in his sermon.

Apparently, based on his logic, I and so many other ex-evangelicals were never part of "the elect" chosen by God for salvation. MacArthur is not alone in making this assertion that real Christians don't leave. "You left. This proves conclusively that you were never a true believer!" This is a claim that apparently makes some Christians feel reassured about their faith. They seem to fear we ex-believers represent some intellectual or spiritual contagion: "If it happened to you, maybe it could happen to me. What you have might be catching!"

But I must ask, "What about all my years of dedicated service to God?" If I and others like me could spend decades seeking to trust and obey without ever realizing we were outside of God's kingdom, then surely the blame must lie on God. Why didn't he make it clearer that we were never saved in the first place?

One of the reasons I wrote this book was to disprove this baseless accusation. I hope that as you've gone through my story, you can clearly see that I sincerely wanted to love and obey God with all my heart for most of my life. I was baptized not once, not twice, but *three times*—each time convinced I was doing the right thing. Ultimately, I gave faith my all to make it work.

On my podcast, I've interviewed many ex-pastors, ex-missionaries, ex-priests, and ex-vicars who are now atheists or agnostics. We all agree on this: *We were 100% Christians, all-in, dedicating decades of our lives to the cause of Christ, the church, and the gospel. We did everything we could to try and make it work.*

Let me give you a brief rundown of our lives as genuine believers, just in case you mistakenly think we weren't fully committed to Christ's cause and were somehow not "true believers."

As Christian laypersons, many of us spent countless hours, year after year, attempting to set aside a daily "quiet time." For me, this always proved to be a difficult habit to build into my life, and I always felt guilty about my lack of effort. When we did manage to snatch a few minutes for this spiritual discipline, we diligently studied and marked up our Bibles with pens and highlighters. Some of us tried to stick with a "Bible reading plan" to work through the entire book each year. We spent innumerable hours in prayer for our lost family members, friends, and co-workers, beseeching God to save them from hell. We begged God to heal sick loved ones and organized church-wide "prayer chains" to involve numerous Christians in the hoped-for healing.

Why We Left

Dedicating decades of service to the church, we were heavily involved in multiple ministries. We participated in church activities such as VBS, Children's Church, Sunday School, youth groups, foreign mission trips, church choirs, worship teams, building maintenance, groundskeeping, and more. We joined accountability groups so that we'd have someone to report to regularly about our spiritual progress and the failures we experienced as we desperately struggled to live the victorious Christian life we had been promised.

Those of us intent on becoming church leaders took it a step further. Pursuing ministry training, we often went into debt to attend Bible college and seminary. It took me decades to pay off my student loans, and it was long after I'd left the ministry when I made the last payment. We stayed up late into the night studying. We sacrificed weekends to prepare for grueling exams. We learned Greek, Hebrew, and sometimes French or German, studied massive theology books and attended conferences. We wrote academic papers and scholarly dissertations. We earned Bachelor's, Master's, and Doctorate degrees in theology and ministry.

When we finally became church leaders, we selflessly served others in our congregations. We often worked an exhausting schedule of sixty to eighty hours a week with pay not commensurate with our educational level. Frequently, our families and marriages suffered because we were hardly ever home. Instead, we were at the church working and serving until late at night or giving up our valuable weekends. Money was typically tight because many churches are stingy in paying their leaders, so our families often struggled with added financial stress.

To prepare lessons or sermons, we diligently studied the Bible, translating Greek and Hebrew and reading commentaries late into the night. I, for one, took the job of preaching seriously. During the week, for example, after hours of studying the text, I wrote out my sermons in full, and then memorized them. I'd spend hours practicing them numerous times before Sunday mornings to maintain eye contact and engage without relying on sermon notes. All this massive effort was made so that we could preach the Word of God faithfully each Sunday and often on Wednesday nights, too. We tried to apply the Bible to our congregants' lives in meaningful and practical ways. The result of all this effort would hopefully result in them growing spiritually, becoming more like Jesus, and loving and obeying God even more.

We wore ourselves out, discharging our responsibilities to ensure the various church ministries continued. We taught youth groups and preached at youth outings and outreach events. We led home Bible studies, organized and spoke at men's and women's retreats, and ran church camps. We oversaw and played on worship teams, put on Vacation Bible Schools, taught at Sunday School, led adult education Bible classes, and much more.

We shared our faith whenever and wherever the opportunity presented itself, taught our fellow believers how to do it, and put on revivals and crusades to win the lost. To set an example of successful evangelism, many of us went out in our neighborhoods knocking on doors to reach the community for Christ. The aim was to help our churches grow numerically by conversion rather than relying on "transfer growth"—people who were already Christians moving from one church to another.

Our outreach wasn't limited to our home neighborhood, state, or country. Many of us took groups from our church on international mission trips to spread the gospel worldwide. When I was a youth pastor, we raised the money and took our youth group to Tecate, Mexico, to build houses for the poor. A few years later I participated in an evangelistic trip to Nairobi, Kenya, where we preached the gospel in slums, shopping malls, and schools. Our group also spent a week building a church in the city of Eldoret, north of Nairobi.

Our phones would ring late at night, on weekends, or on our day off. Despite the inconvenience, we would always answer the call because we were in the ministry to serve others selflessly. If someone was sick or in the hospital, we'd drop everything and rush to their bedside, no matter what time of night or day. Families who lost a loved one merited even more time and attention, regardless of what it took out of us. We performed weddings and funerals, often for a small fee or no pay. Such services were viewed as part of our jobs, in addition to all the other responsibilities we shouldered.

What did we get from our congregations for our troubles, exhausting hard work, and long hours? Were we thanked, appreciated, and valued? Sometimes we were. There were always some individuals who conveyed their appreciation. But like Pastor Jerry, many of us wouldn't be allowed even a short sabbatical to recharge our batteries when we were in danger of burning out. Often, elders or deacons who worked "real" jobs were unsympathetic to our plight and wouldn't allow us to take time off for even a much-needed vacation.

Many of us in church leadership were also mistreated by our parishioners. We put up with abusive, cruel, gossipy Christians, enduring lies, slander, and any number of slights we didn't deserve. People questioned our motives, and for some of our congregants, virtually every decision we made did not seem right. They talked about us behind our backs, often spreading lies, divisiveness, and discord through the congregation like cancer. Despite his or her years of faithful service, people in the church always seemed willing to believe the worst about their minister, often with little or no evidence to back any of it up.

Epilogue

Despite all this, we kept on serving. We acted as mediators between angry congregants and attempted to settle petty disputes that constantly seemed to arise. I became an expert at resolving conflicts between churchgoers who had fallen out over some trivial matter.

As a result of this relentless and demanding schedule, many of us burned out in ministry. The lucky ones were able to take some time off to rest and recover before they went back into the fray.

Unfortunately, some of us did not recover from the constant rigors of church leadership. Due to vicious church politics, like what happened to Pastor David, some of us were railroaded out of our jobs by our fellow Christians. Some just simply had enough and packed it all in, never returning. For whatever reason, many of us quit the ministry altogether, and in most cases, we didn't blame God. Instead, we pointed a finger at ourselves, stating that the burnout we experienced was our fault because we had failed to establish healthy boundaries. Somewhere, we had learned to blame ourselves for not establishing the correct priorities and balance in our ministries, personal lives, families, and marriages. We minimized the factor of the unrelenting, exhausting schedules we kept week in and week out for years.

When we left, we discovered that all our theological degrees weren't worth the paper they were printed on. One can't get a job flipping hamburgers at McDonald's with a Ph.D. in biblical studies! I was one of the lucky ones who, thanks to the G.I. Bill and my Community College degree in carpentry, was able to land a secular job after I left the ministry. Unfortunately for many, their pastoral expertise and qualifications are meaningless in the secular world of work. Thus, they often struggle to find gainful employment after leaving the ministry. Being a pastor or missionary for decades isn't typically a marketable skill set!

Why We Left

So, were we ever genuine believers? Surely, it's impossible to read through the description of what I've just laid out and cynically conclude that we weren't fully invested in both God and his church. We were all-in, giving everything to the Lord and to our fellow believers, sacrificing valuable family and marriage time so we could work countless hours. Some of us were paid better than others, but no level of financial compensation would be worth the intensity and long hours of our work schedules decade after decade. We did it all for the sake of the gospel. Why else would we do all that difficult and often thankless work if we didn't believe with all our hearts that everything we taught and stood for was true?

No one can accurately accuse us of being quitters, defectors, or apostates who left because we had "one bad experience." Our decades of selfless service to ministry, God, and the church give the lie to that groundless assertion. Such an accusation makes a hollow mockery of our years of faithfulness.

For many reasons, we walked away from both the church and the faith, never to return. No, it wasn't so we could have a "license to sin," as John MacArthur baselessly charges. In retrospect, in my case, I would say today that my journey out of Christianity can be more accurately described as a years-long process of my authentic self finally and fully breaking through the thin shell of my religious self.

I've mentioned a few times how I believe Lifton's concept of "doubling" best characterizes how I lived most of my adult life within the faith. My true identity had been suppressed for virtually my entire time as a religious person. My "religious self" damaged me psychologically on numerous levels. However, through the process of deconstruction and reconstruction, I have been able to reclaim my authentic self, thereby jettisoning the religious veneer. This religious self was the mask I wore most of my evangelical life—but it wasn't who I truly am.

It's more than fair to say, however, that my journey out of Christianity in no way is normative. Every one of us exvangelicals has their own story, and our experiences within the faith have similarities and differences. In the final analysis, we left it all behind because, for whatever reason, Christianity and God stopped working for us. *But it certainly wasn't due to a lack of effort on our part.*

I Left Because God Is Inert, Invisible, and Silent

One of the questions I wrestled with on my way out of faith was: "Why isn't God as overtly active in the world as he appears to be in the narratives of Scripture?" People don't see the unbelievable miracles we read about in biblical stories. A skeptic once observed, "Why aren't the faith healers all clearing out their local hospitals of all the sick and dying, rather than holding moneymaking crusades?" Of course, when a miracle fails to materialize, the blame is always placed on the person who needs the miracle. They must have unconfessed sins or not enough faith. It's always something, but it's never God's fault.

With the exception of Pentecostal and charismatic churches, most evangelicals aren't even claiming to hear from God directly and audibly, as the ancient prophets claimed to do. That is unless you count the so-called "prophets and apostles" who so confidently proclaimed that God had told them there would be a Trump re-election landslide in 2020. If you take the Bible as true, you must designate those voices as false prophets.

In the face of God's silence, I must ask: Where is God's active presence today? Why is he so mysterious and hidden from view? Why does he make it so difficult to believe in him, especially when the risks of not believing are incredibly high?

Christian apologists are quick and confident in their answers. "First of all, as Jesus taught, the path to heaven is exceedingly narrow, and as a result, few ever find it. Moreover, God's mysteriousness and hiddenness help develop and deepen our faith in him! By faith, we need to trust that he's there, still taking a hand in the running of the world and our daily lives." It seems that no matter what your challenge to faith might be, there's always an answer to quell that pesky cognitive dissonance. And if all the logical answers fail to render comfort for the questioning Christian, he or she is likely to be reminded that questioning one's entire belief system is emotionally threatening and personally destabilizing. Why in the world would you do it?

Christian apologists also argue: *"God still speaks to humanity today, not necessarily verbally like he did with the prophets, but through the infallible pages of Scripture.* The Bible is God's inspired, infallible, and inerrant Word to humanity, so it's up to us to decipher its meaning. In that way, we do indeed 'hear from God today,' but he communicates to us through the words of the Bible. That's why finding a healthy church with a good pastor who can explain and apply it to our lives is so important!" But these answers fail to address the immense subjectivity involved in interpreting an ancient text with dead languages. They also overlook the pastor's own presuppositions and theological biases that color his or her interpretation of the Bible.

There are far too many people who believe the "wrong" things that will land them in hell if we believe what Christians say on the matter. That liberal preacher from *A Thief in the Night* missed the Rapture because he believed the wrong things. Although he thought he knew the truth, his watered-down gospel was fatally flawed. As a result, he was left behind and failed to make it to heaven. But if that's the case, and so many are going to end up in hell for their erroneous but sincerely held beliefs, then why isn't God doing more to clarify the *true* message?

Epilogue

Surely, an omniscient God could do more to demonstrate the truth of the belief system that allows humanity to get to heaven and avoid hell. Why exactly are so many billions of people consigned to the flames of hell for eternity? What about those poor unfortunates who only discover when it's too late to make the right decision that Jesus will turn on them and send them to an eternity in hell? None of this seems loving and certainly not fair by any standard, but especially for such an allegedly wise, merciful, and benevolent deity as the Christian God.

The final escape hatch can be found in liberal or progressive Christianity, where the belief is that no hell exists, and everyone will go to heaven. But I chose to go one step further. *The God of Christianity is invisible and silent because he isn't there.*

***** The End *****

1   John MacArthur, "Christian Deconstruction, Part 1." *Grace to You*, May 28, 2023, https://www.youtube.com/watch?v=kQdvtayYDr8.

2   See, for example, investigations of MacArthur carried out by *The Roys Report* here: https://julieroys.com/?s=john+macarthur.

3   Lana Wachowski and Lilly Wachowski, 1999. *The Matrix*. United States: Warner Brothers.

Feedback Invited

If you can relate to my story on any level, then I'd like to hear from you. We all face human struggles—working on our failings, dealing with loss, and struggling with anxiety from not getting it right all the time. I hope what you read has made you feel a little bit less alone. Your comments would be extremely helpful.

To add your rating and optional comments, go to www.Amazon. com, type "Clint Heacock" in the search box, and press Enter. Find *Not So Shiny Not So Happy People* in the list, then click on the image of the book. On the *Not So Shiny Not So Happy People* page, find and click on the customer reviews link, which is beside the star rating for the book. When the customer reviews page opens, click the "Write a Customer Review" button. A new page will open. Click on the number of stars you want to give the book. You can stop there, or you can add some comments, even one short sentence could be helpful to prospective readers.

Thank you in advance for your response.

Clint Heacock

Staying In Touch

I began the *MindShift Podcast* in 2017 to share not just my story but also with the intent of interviewing others who escaped and survived controlling religions or cults. In May 2024, I changed the name to *The Dismantling Doctrine Podcast*, but the program still has the same emphasis as under the previous name. When I started the podcast, I was still in my "progressive Christian" phase and hoped to help those questioning their faith find ways to hang on to it. Since then, as a listener said, "You have deconstructed your faith live, on-air." I certainly don't believe what I used to when I started the show, which is an interesting development. It proves that the deconstruction journey is not a single stop but a lifelong growth and change process.

The show had still another name that preceded *MindShift Podcast*. I first called it *The Preacher's Forum* since I'd studied homiletics for my Ph.D. During this time—the tail end of my progressive Christian phase—I was passionate about trying to help up-and-coming preachers and ministers avoid some of the same pitfalls I'd experienced in ministry. Since then, I have had a definite "mind shift" and ended up packing all of it in, but that's all part of the journey, as I've come to see now.

In years of doing the show, I've been surprised to discover that I have much in common with ex-cult members. In the preceding chapters, I've described instances in my life where I was a victim of some cult-like techniques. As I interview ex-cultists, we note that our experiences involved the same sets of destructive psychology and tactics used on us in our respective high-control groups. Reclaiming our authentic selves involves reconstructing our lives. If you're interested in listening to these interviews, find out more by subscribing to *The Dismantling Doctrine Podcast* on Apple Podcasts, PodBean, Spotify, or other major podcasting platforms.

You can follow me on X (formerly Twitter) at MindShift2018 or on Instagram at MindShiftPodcast. You can also subscribe to my *The Dismantling Doctrine Podcast* You Tube channel: https://www.youtube.com/channel/UC43ozAm7iK0LpCb9p3TCdvw. Finally, please like and follow the Facebook page for *The Dismantling Doctrine Podcast.*

I'd also welcome your thoughts, comments, and questions about this book. If you want to contact me, you can message me through the Facebook page and keep in touch with the latest episodes and content that drops regularly. You can also financially support the show on Patreon and receive great content that is unavailable to the public at this link: https://patreon.com/dismantlingdoctrine.

Clint Heacock

More Books from Insighting Growth Publications

David Madison

Ten Things Christians Wish Jesus Hadn't Taught: And Other Reasons to Question His Words
English and Spanish Versions

Guessing About God

Chris Highland

Broken Bridges: Building Community in a World Divided by Beliefs

Tim Sledge

Goodbye Jesus: An Evangelical Preacher's Journey Beyond Faith

Four Disturbing Questions with One Simple Answer: Breaking the Spell of Christian Belief

Leaving Faith: Holding On Letting Go Looking Back Moving Forward

How to Live a Meaningful Life: Focusing on Things that Matter

Printed in Great Britain
by Amazon